BUD

Beliefs a

The Sussex Library of Religious Beliefs and Practices

This series is intended for students of religion, social sciences and history, and for the interested layperson. It is concerned with the beliefs and practices of religions in their social, cultural and historical setting. These books will be of particular interest to Religious Studies teachers and students at universities, colleges, and high schools. Inspection copies available upon request.

<u>Published</u>

The Ancient Egyptians   Rosalie David

Buddhism   Merv Fowler

Gnosticism   John Glyndwr Harris

Hinduism   Jeaneane Fowler

Humanism   Jeaneane Fowler

Islam   David Norcliffe

The Jews   Alan Unterman

Sikhism   W. Owen Cole and Piara Singh Sambhi

Zoroastrianism   Peter Clark

<u>In preparation</u>
The Diversity of Christianity Today   Diane Watkins
The Doctrine of the Trinity: God in Three Persons   Martin Downes
Death and Afterlife: An Introduction to Christian Eschatology
Tony Gray
You Reap What You Sow: Causality in the Religions of the World
Jeaneane Fowler
Christian Theology: The Spiritual Tradition   John Glyndwr Harris
Jainism   Lynn Foulston
Taoism   Jeaneane Fowler

<u>Forthcoming</u>   *Bhagavad Gita (a student commentary)*
*Confucianism   The Protestant Reformation: Tradition and
Practice Zen*

Buddhism

Beliefs and Practices

Merv Fowler

sussex
ACADEMIC
PRESS

BRIGHTON • PORTLAND

2 4 6 8 10 9 7 5 3 1

Published 1999 in Great Britain by
SUSSEX ACADEMIC PRESS
Box 2950
Brighton BN2 5SP

and in the United States of America by
SUSSEX ACADEMIC PRESS
5804 N.E. Hassalo St.
Portland, Oregon 97213–3644

British Library Cataloguing in Publication Data
A CIP catalogue record for this book is available from the British Library.

Library of Congress Cataloging-in-Publication Data
Fowler, Merv.
Buddhism : beliefs and practices / Merv Fowler.
p.   cm.
Includes bibliographical references and index.
ISBN 1–898723–66–4 (pbk. : alk. paper)
1. Buddhism.   I. Title.
BQ4012.F69   1999
294.3—dc21   99–20721
CIP

Printed by Biddles Ltd, Guildford and King's Lynn
This book is printed on acid-free paper

Contents

___

Preface and Acknowledgements   ix
Abbreviations   xi

Introduction   1

1   Towards Enlightenment   4
The legacy of India   4
The life of the Buddha   8
The account of the Buddha's life in the *Buddhacarita*
   and other sources   10
Asceticism and enlightenment   14
The First Sermon of the Buddha   20
A note on the search for the historical Buddha   22

2   The Development of Community   24
The *Sangha*   24
The emergence of the Theravada and Mahayana schools   27
The First Council, 483 BCE   30
The Second Council, *c.* 383 BCE   32
The Third Council, 250 BCE   33
The Fourth Council   34
The decline of Buddhism   35
Divergences between Hinduism and Buddhism   36
The *dharma* of the Buddha   38
The First Noble Truth: *dukkha*   39
The five aggregates   42
The Second Noble Truth: *samudaya*, the origin of *dukkha*   44
Dependent Origination   46
The Third Noble Truth: the cessation of *dukkha* – *nirodha*   48
The Fourth Noble Truth: the Path or the Way – *magga*   48
The *Pancha Sila*   54

Sila, Samadhi, Panna   58
Sila   58
Samadhi   59
Panna   62

3 The Theravadin Doctrine   **63**
Monastic life   63
Puja   69
Meditation (*bhavana*)   70
Theravadin festivals   74

4 The Mahayana Doctrine   **78**
The rise of the Mahayana   78
The *Madhyamika* school   83
Sunyata   86
Dharmas   87
Bodhisattvas   88
The concept of reality   90
Nirvana   91
The Absolute   92
Upaya: skilful means   92
The *Yogacarin* school: *Cittamatra*   93
Reality   94
Cittamatra: mind only   96
Seed consciousness   96
Yoga   97
The Doctrine of the *Trikaya*   97
The *Dharmakaya*   98
The *Sambhogakaya*   99
The *Nirmanakaya*   99
Thathagatagarbha   99
Buddha-nature   100
The spread of Buddhism   102

5 Nichiren   **105**
The life of Nichiren   105
The *Lotus Sutra*, or *Lotus of the True Law*
    (*Saddharma-pundarika Sutra*)   113
Nam-myoho-renge-kyo   116
Nam   117
Myoho   117

Renge   118
Kyo   118
The true object of worship – the *Gohonzon*   119
The nine consciousnesses   120
The ten worlds   121
Ichinen sanzen   122
Soka Gakkai International   124

6   **Tibet: The Land of Snow**   **127**
Rather late beginnings   128
Tibetan monks and *lamas*   133
Buddhas and *bodhisattvas*   135
Tibetan scriptures   136
Tibetan ritual   137
Tibetan ceremonies and life-cycle rites   140
Tantra   142
Tantric symbols   144
The Tantric practitioner   147
Shingon   151

7   **Zen**   **154**
Zazen   161
The master–pupil relationship   163
Monks and monasteries   164
Lay Buddhists   166
Origins of Zen   167
The koan   168
Satori   170

8   **Pure Land**   **171**
Amida   173
Scriptures   174
Pure Land   177
External influences   179
Amidism in Japan   179
Shinjin   181
Shinjin and *Nembutsu*   183
Jodoshu and Shinshu doctrine   184
Japanese festivals   184

9 The State of the Art 187
  Soka Gakkai 192
  Tibetan 193
  Pure Land 194
  Friends of the Western Buddhist Order 194
  Soto Zen 195
  Theravada 196

The Cover Pictures 198
Notes 199
Glossary 211
Further Reading 217
Index 221

Preface and Acknowledgements

In a recent article entitled *What is Buddhism?*[1] the author highlights the difficulties westerners have in coming to terms with Buddhism. For before we can begin to assess the cultural-religious background upon which assumptions about Buddhism are based, we need to "get clear" about our own. Regardless of our personal religious convictions, we remain bound by western culture, a culture which is obsessed with "doing" things, and constantly asks of us, "What did you *do* last evening/on the weekend/in the holidays/at Christmas?" This obsession with *doing things* is part of the western baggage which we carry into our eastern studies, not only obscuring our vision of Buddhism, but encouraging the concoction of so-called "Buddhist" aphorisms and stories by western writers with an incomplete understanding of the eastern mind.

This book has resisted the temptation to *do things* with Buddhism and, difficult though this task may be at times, attempts to present the beliefs and practices of some of the various schools of Buddhism as they really are. The work is the culmination of years of teaching, study, and conversations with many Buddhist friends and scholars; their contribution is immense, though any errors and misunderstandings remain my own. Inevitably, not everyone will agree with what is said here, and readers have every right to disagree, for criticism is the fuel of scholarship.

I am particularly grateful to Anthony Grahame, Editorial Director at Sussex Academic Press, whose patience and understanding bear full testimony to the publisher's claim to be "author-friendly". My thanks to Jim Pym, editor of *Pure Land Notes* (the Journal of Pure Land Buddhism) for reading and correcting the first draft of my chapter on Pure Land Buddhism, and for much helpful advice, particularly in referring me to the most apposite primary and secondary source material. I am equally grateful to Jamie Cresswell and Kasuo Fujii for acting in a similar capacity with regard to the chapter on the Buddhism of Nichiren Daishonin, for allowing me access to the extensive library at Taplow

Court, and for the generous provision of reading materials to undertake this study. I am also indebted to Yvonne Chindoo-Roy, a former student at the University of Wales College, Newport, where I teach, for her knowledge of Buddhism in Burma, and for her study of Theravada Buddhism in England.

Finally, I wish to acknowledge the immeasurable contribution of my wife, Jeaneane, who has given purpose and meaning to my own life and to the lives of countless others, and without whom this book would never have been written. It is to you, Jeaneane, and to your two new-found and much-loved sisters, Nancie and Cherie, that this book is dedicated in love and respect.

Merv Fowler
February 1999
Newport

Abbreviations

Diacritical marks for transliterated text have been omitted from this student edition. The following abbreviations may not be familiar to every reader:

BCE   before common (or Christian) era
CE   common (or Christian) era
Skt.   Sanskrit
Jap.   Japanese
Chin.   Chinese
Dhp   the *Dhammapada*, one of the books of the *Khaddaka Nikaya*, the fifth major division of the *Sutta Pitaka* in the Pali Canon

The Pali word *nikaya* means "collection" and the following letters refer to the appropriate *nikaya* or collection from the Pali Canon:

D   *Digha Nikaya*
M   *Majjhima Nikaya*
A   *Anguttara Nikaya*
S   *Samyutta Nikaya*

This shall ye think of
all this fleeting world:
a star at dawn,
a bubble in a stream,
a flash of lightning in a summer cloud,
a phantom of a dream.
Diamond Sutra

Introduction

Often called "the religion without a God", or "not so much a religion as a philosophy", Buddhism is really a mind-culture. To view Buddhism as a unitary belief system, either philosophical or religious, is folly: Buddhism is not one system of belief but a matrix of systems. In the western world, scholastic convention accepts nine systems of Indian philosophy, and Buddhism as one of them. Hinduism is accorded no less than six of these, which rejoice in the names of Samkhya, Yoga, Purva Mimamsa, Vedanta and Nyaya-Vaisesika. Yet a plethora of Buddhist beliefs is conventionally grouped under the one rubric – Buddhism; this is an oversimplification. Religions tend to reflect the culture in which they grow up, but, although a child of India, Buddhism owes no necessary allegiance to any one culture; India, Tibet, China and Japan share no common land, language, people nor heritage.

It has been said many times of other religions that there is no such thing as Christianity or Sikhism . . . there are only Christians and Sikhs. But is the same true of Buddhism? All the schools of Buddhism are not mutually exclusive entities which can only be studied independently; without exception, all are concerned, ultimately, with the realization of Enlightenment, or Buddhahood; this is their common ground. Although all Buddhists share this common ground, their approach varies enormously; commonality of beliefs and practices is not a feature of Buddhist schools. Walking meditation, as found in Tibetan and Soto Zen Buddhism, is not practised by all schools, any more than silent meditation. The rich and awe-inspiring iconography that is a hallmark of Tibetan Buddhism shrine rooms is not a common feature of Buddhism, anymore than the often beautifully carved *butsudans* of Japanese Buddhism. Musical instruments, especially drums, are used in Tantric Buddhism as well as certain sects or traditions (a term usually confined to Tibetan terminology) of Nichiren, but are not favoured by all Buddhists.

Some Buddhists make use of *mantras* as a meditational aid, while others use *mandalas* for the same purpose; some use both, some neither. There is no common chant or scripture and no common language which unites Buddhist practice and practitioners across all schools, and this feature will vary even amongst different sects within one school. Not all schools observe the five Buddhist Precepts to abstain from taking life, taking what is not given, sensuous misconduct, false speech, and partaking of intoxicants. Indeed, Tantric Buddhists go so far as to encourage violation of the Precepts when it is deemed necessary, and will make a vow to consume large quantities of meat daily when an aversion to meat-eating is admitted. Some schools believe that, far from being the root cause of suffering, as the Buddha proposed in the second of The Four Noble Truths, "desire" is a necessary condition of life and should be recognized as such.

Some Buddhists believe that enlightenment is gradual, others instantaneous; some believe it to be permanent, others momentary. Buddhist schools, such as Tibetan, are ritual conscious, and fastidiously observe Buddhist festivals; others, such as the Nichiren schools, observe none. The Buddha's teaching of "no soul" is absent from Pure Land teaching as is his teaching on self-reliance . . . and so it goes on. A distinguished Mahayana scholar told me recently that the one thing all Buddhists have in common is the need to overcome the three defilements – greed, anger and delusion. But again, this is not so. The Nichiren schools believe that anger is one of the ten life-conditions to which we are all subject, a vital and dynamic life-force which, channelled correctly against man's inhumanity to man, social injustice, environmental pollution and the like, ultimately can only bring benefit to mankind.

When a school is seen not to conform where other schools have commonality of belief, it is sometimes said that the school in question cannot be truly representative of Buddhism. Over the years I have heard this said of Tantra, Pure Land and Nichiren, while Zen was once thought to have no necessary associations with any form of Buddhism. Fortunately, this sentiment, which comes close to sectarian exclusiveness, finds little support in responsible circles today, and it is hoped that this book will be considered to be equally responsible. Accordingly, this book does not set out to impose a thematic framework upon the Buddhist schools; creating categories into which constantly changing constituents fit, while at the same time ignoring or evading those which do not happen to belong in a particular theme, justifying their exclusion at any given point by labelling each in turn as being "unrepresentative of Buddhism", at least in the particular aspect under discussion. Rather, the approach here is to examine the beliefs and practices of some of the main Buddhist schools discretely, and not superimpose those of other schools where they do not belong. Bearing in mind at all times that *all the schools of Buddhism are not mutually exclusive entities*, it is hoped that the spirit of Buddhism will be best served in this way.

The book opens with an examination of the legacy of India, followed by the life of the Buddha using primary and secondary source material, and includes a note on the search for the Buddha of history. The development of Buddhism includes the four Buddhist councils, and the emergence of Northern and Southern Buddhism. There follows a section on what the Buddha taught and another on Theravada Buddhism. An introduction to Mahayana Buddhism is followed by an examination of the beliefs and practices of four of the main Mahayana schools – Nichiren, Tibetan, Zen and Pure Land – with shorter sections on Shingon and Tantra. The book ends with a look at the state of Buddhism in the world today. After reading this book the reader will recognize the rich diversity in the matrix of belief systems commonly known as Buddhism. It is precisely the enormity of this richness which makes the study of Buddhism such a fascinating and enthralling journey.

1

Towards Enlightenment

The legacy of India

Neither the Buddha nor Buddhism appeared *one fine day* in a cultural vacuum, having no roots and no substance. Both are the offspring of India. That country is without equal as a nation whose spirit of acceptance of all that is new, and reluctance to discard that which is old, have typified the very heart of its people in their search for the highest spirituality, their quest for the Ultimate Reality. This is the essence of the Indian mind.

Some fifteen hundred years BCE, this same Indian mind, when confronted by nomadic Aryan tribes, long since departed from the central Asian steppe, applied the same philosophy that it had employed since time immemorial, by absorbing the new into the old. The Aryan wanderer did not come alone nor, for that matter, on one occasion. In waves of settlement sometime in the middle of the second millennium BCE he began to enter the Indian subcontinent along a valley which later gave its name to the highly sophisticated civilization which was already in decline at the time of the Aryan invasions, the Indus Valley. With the Aryan came his herds of horses and cattle, his weavers, tanners, potters, carpenters and metal workers; with the Aryan also came his social structure, and his religious belief systems.

An all too familiar picture at the end of the Late Bronze Age in the ancient East is one of settlement by a pastoral people who, by dint of conquest, deemed themselves to be intellectually and culturally superior to those they had vanquished, but in fact were directly responsible for reducing what was formerly a high level of civilization to a village culture. The Aryans were but one of numerous groups of Indo-European migrants who, over many centuries since the beginning of the second millennium BCE, had left their homeland for pastures new in both Europe and Asia; the group which entered India in the middle of the second millennium BCE may well have done so from Iran. This group was blind to the high degree of cultural sophistication enjoyed by the indigenous population, whom they called "barbarians". For their part, they rejoiced in the name *Arya*, emphasizing the "cultivated" or "noble" nuance of this term, rather than its true meaning, "agriculturalist".

The superiority they glowingly bestowed upon themselves did not manifest itself in literary achievements, however, for they were illiterate. As formulated as their religious belief systems may or may not have been, beliefs were handed down orally. The western mind has always regarded oral tradition as suspect, and very much the poor relation of the written word as far as accuracy of transmission is concerned; the eastern mind has no such delusions. Nevertheless, we have to look for a record of what Aryan/*Vedic* religion was like in the second millennium BCE to the *Rg Veda*, the earliest of the four *Vedas*. This text not only survived a long period of oral transmission, but contains material which was long out of date by the time of the Aryan incursions, as well as material which postdated the settlement; consequently, the record is not without its problems.

Throughout the ancient East, settled communities have always had one eye on their crops and one on their gods, looking to the latter to propitiate the former. Although the discovery of a terracotta female figurine may have no necessary connection with religion,[1] it seems likely that a profusion of these artefacts excavated from pre-Aryan times in the Indus Valley attests to the presence of a fertility cult centred around the Mother Goddess. Nomadic or semi-nomadic tribes, however, were less concerned with fertility than the elements which affected their herds and controlled their wanderings. Their social structures were normally patriarchal, their gods similarly male-oriented.

Unsurprisingly, the early concerns of the *Rg Veda* are not directed towards the fertility of the soil with its attendant Mother Goddess worship, but with nature. Although female deities are not without mention in the *Vedas*, none enjoys independent status and each is dependent upon her consort for her position. The male gods, on the other hand, are gods in their own right. These *Vedic* gods were looked to for the controlling influence they have on human existence. Hence Agni, the god of fire, is mentioned in almost a third of the hymns of the *Rg Veda*. Not only was Agni functional in providing heat and food, but Agni alone had the capacity to consume the sacrificial offering, thereby transforming it from its gross state into a form (smoke) which was acceptable to the gods. Similarly, the natural elements of rain and thunder, wind and storm, each has its attendant deity which can be discerned at both the microcosmic (as the breeze which fans the flames in the domestic hearth) and the macrocosmic (as the raging whirlwind) levels.

There were also different levels at which the sacrificial ritual known as *yajna* could be perceived. Sacrifice could only be offered by the hereditary brahmin priesthood and tensions developed over the monopoly it held over *yajna*. The need for a multiplicity of gods also began to be called to question, and in later *Vedas* this is apparent. In *Rg Veda* 2:1 vv. 3–5, for instance, Agni is identified with all the gods:

> Hero of Heroes, Agni! thou art Indra, thou art Visnu
> of the Mighty Stride, adorable . . .
> Agni, thou art King Varuna whose laws stand fast;
> as Mitra, Wonder-Worker, thou must be implored.[2]

If Agni, in one of his manifestations, takes the form of a thunderbolt, it is small wonder that he is identified with Indra, the greatest of the Aryan gods, and lord of war and weather. Basham raises the interesting question, "Was there only one Agni, or were there many Agnis? How could Agni be one and many at the same time?"[3] It was questions like these which perplexed the Aryan mind and led to the development of monism, so prominent in *Upanisadic* teaching.

The vast multiplicity of gods which epitomized *Vedic* thought were not autonomous, however; each was reponsible to the cosmic norm, *rta*, the regulating force which was at the heart of the cosmos, the custodian of which was Varuna. *Rta* was the regulating pulse which governed manifest existence, both on the microcosmic and the macrocosmic levels. *Rta* it was which gave the planets their orbits, caused the sun to rise and set, the seasons to come and go, and nature to survive. It was also *rta* which set the norms for social and moral behaviour. Those who did not conform to these norms were answerable to Varuna, as were the gods. The concept of *dharma* ("what is right"), which later became a fundamental principle of Hinduism, had its birth pangs in *rta*.

The doubts which had begun to arise in the Aryan mind regarding the individuality of the gods gained momentum, and by the time of *Rg Veda* 2:1 Agni, long associated with Indra, was being identified with all the gods. Also gaining momentum was the move towards monotheism. If the identity of the gods was becoming indistinct, then there must be a force behind the gods, but this force could not be *rta*! *Rta* was certainly a force *par excellence*: equally certainly it was more fundamental than any deity, but it was an impersonal force, a universal Law which had to be upheld, rather than acting of its own volition.

In late *Vedic* literature, such as the *Brahmanas* and the *Aranyakas*, the so-called forest writings, there are clear indications of the move towards a more speculative and mystical approach to religion which became crystallized at the end of the *Vedic* period known as *Vedanta*. The literature of this period is known as the *Upanisads*, which means "to sit down near", a reference to the close proximity to the *guru* of the pupils or *chelas* who seated themselves at his feet. The teaching, however, did not centre on the imparting of a corpus of knowledge, for this was not the way of the *Upanisadic* sages; their thrust of thought directed itself to evoking from their pupils the intuitive knowledge which is best described as "wisdom" which we all have, but exhibit all too infrequently.

Upanisadic literature represents the high watermark of the Indian mind, a mind which was forever searching for the Truth, the nature of the self, and of Ultimate Reality. Given this resolve, it is small wonder that these truths were not considered to be ones which could be taught or learned; they had to be *realized* at the deepest intuitive level of under-standing. This level of understanding was entirely commensurate with the level of consciousness of the pupil at each stage of his development, and the thought-provoking questions of the *gurus* would be measured accordingly.

Upanisadic thought is anything but consistent; nevertheless, there is a common focus on the acceptance of a totally transcendent Absolute, a trend which arose in the *Vedic* period. This indescribable Absolute is called Brahman, which is incomprehensible to the human mind, but which nevertheless is the *Ground of all Being*, from which everything else emanates. The inevitable question to this theory is that anything which is incomprehensible to the human mind must, by definition, remain beyond humankind's understanding, so how can it be known? The *Upanisads* address this question by affirming that the Absolute, though Unmanifest, is directly linked to manifest existence through the innermost essence of each manifest entity – a permanent, unchanging essence called the *atman*.

On this view, realization of the deepest intuitive knowledge or wisdom, which the *chelas* sought, meant realization of Brahman, an experience which could only take place when the experience is without subject and object, when the egoistic self has been overcome and the realization dawns that the true Self is Brahman. Known as the Brahman:*atman* synthesis, this theory, which is central to *Upanisadic* thought, is the cornerstone of Indian philosophy; it was also as a reaction to this theory of a permanent, unchanging self that Buddhism first drew breath.

Certain orientalists in the West have regarded the Pali Canon as a systematized account of the Buddha's teaching, from which the development of Buddhist philosophy justifiably may be traced. Yet these discourses were never intended to be systematized; they are no more systematic than the thought-provoking dialogues of the *Upanisadic* sages of India, who worked patiently yet tirelessly to evoke the intuitive wisdom they knew lay sleeping within each and every one of their students. The development of Buddhist philosophy is to be found not in the Pali Canon, but in the tensions which grew up between *Upanisadic* and Buddhist thought as well as Buddhism's own internal differences.

The life of the Buddha

The Buddha was born into an age of considerable social and political unrest, in the northern India of the sixth century BCE. It was a time when smaller tribes were being absorbed into larger monarchies and this brought about a period of insecurity which promoted a quest for personal identity, the purpose of life, and the meaning of ultimate truth and reality. Questions were being asked such as "What is the nature of eternity?", "What is real in a world of change?", "Why does humankind suffer?", and "What should we pursue as the spiritual goal of life?"

We have no one direct historical account of the Buddha's life. Instead we have various narratives which highlight different aspects of his life and teaching. The earliest accounts were not written until three or four hundred years after he lived, although some Buddhist scriptures were transmitted orally for several centuries from a time shortly after his *parinirvana*. The disciples and followers of the Buddha handed down their accounts of the Buddha's life and teaching, but often added their own thoughts and opinions; it is therefore difficult to abstract the historical events from the hagiographic nature of the material. These additions range from simple, brief descriptions to highly elaborated accounts occupying several volumes. Some accounts of the Buddha recount his descent from heaven, his miraculous deeds, his remarkable physical appearance and the like; other accounts refer to more metaphysical aspects, seeing the Buddha as a cosmic Buddha who comes to earth at a needy moment, being manifested in a series of existences in the world.

Like other Indian religions, Buddhism accepts the doctrines of *karma* and *samsara* and the Buddha, too, is believed to have been reborn over an incalculable period of aeons, each aeon being an unthinkably long period of time. When the Buddha achieved Enlightenment he became omniscient and was thus able to view his past lives through all this vast period of time; he told his followers about his past life experiences. Many of these stories are recounted in what are called the *Jatakas*, one group of which relates, in particular, the lives of the Buddha in animal form.[4] Other sources describe his previous lives in human form and so we hear of his meeting, in one life, with a great enlightened sage, Dipankara; we read of his sacrifice of his own body to a weak and hungry tigress in another; and his loss of life as a Preacher of Patience in yet another. All these stories from past lives are said to have occurred in *cosmic* time, so called because they occurred in lives beyond the present *historical* time in which we live. The Buddha of *this* aeon, Siddhattha Gotama (Skt. Siddhartha Gautama), is thus the historical Buddha and is distinguished so by being called *Sakyamuni*, "the sage from the tribe of Sakyas".

Disentangling the hagiographical material from all these accounts, in an attempt to establish the true historical background, is a task undertaken not only by scholars in the West, but by eastern scholars within Buddhism also. Japanese scholars in particular have done thorough work in this field, but also notable for their efforts are the monks of Sri Lanka. The earliest sources have been scrutinized carefully in an attempt to disentangle fact from legend. There are four major accounts of the life of the Buddha. Three of these are written in Sanskrit: the *Mahavastu*, the *Lalitavistara* and the *Buddhacarita*. Another work, the *Nidanakatha*, is a Pali work – Pali being the language of the canonical scriptures of Theravada Buddhism,[5] the branch of Buddhism found in Sri Lanka, Burma, Thailand and Cambodia. The first complete biography of the Buddha is presented in the *Buddhacarita*, "The Acts of the Buddha", which was written in the first century CE by the poet, Asvaghosa. The first thirteen cantos are extant in Sanskrit, the rest in the Tibetan translation.

It is a valuable account in that it is a complete one of the Buddha's life, and it is the one which I shall be relying on in particular for the events of his life. Dates for the life of the Buddha are uncertain and chronology for this period is accurate only within a decade. The conventionally accepted dates for the Buddha's life are 566–486 BCE, though Professor Gombrich has recently assigned the Buddha's death to the last decade of the fifth century BCE.[6]

The account of the Buddha's life in the *Buddhacarita* and other sources

The *Buddhacarita* tells us that Siddhartha was born into a family of the Sakya clan in the kingdom of Sakya (modern Nepal). Sakya was in north-east India in the foothills of the Himalayas, on the northern edge of the Ganges basin. He was born, so the account goes, into the *ksatriya* class, and the family's name was Gautama. His father was a *raja*, ruler of the Sakya kingdom, so Siddhartha Gautama, as he was called, was a prince living in a luxurious palace. Siddhartha is said to have been the personal name given to the prince by his father. It means "Aim-accomplished", but it occurs only in late texts and is unlikely to have been his original name. Indeed, Michael Pye makes the apt point that if we are "historically sober" we would have to say that we do not know what he would have been called by either family or friends.[7] Michael Carrithers observes that the Sakyas were one of a number of peoples domiciled in the then developing north Indian civilization whose systems of government are best described as "tribal republics", since they were ruled over by councils of elders or oligarchies. Certainly, some may have had leaders elected for a fixed term; equally certainly, these leaders were not kings, "and therefore the later tradition that the Buddha was a king's son must be dismissed".[8] However, to exclude all the traditions which are late, hagiographical and dubious would be to leave little left to discuss in the life of the Buddha and would do a disservice to Buddhist belief. We therefore need to examine the hagiographical accounts of the Buddha's life as much as the truly historical, if they are discernible.

Buddhist tradition relates that miraculous, portentous events are associated with his birth; for example, he was born out of his mother's side. It seems that all Buddhas are characterized by unusual births. The purpose of such a birth story is to portray the birth of an exceptional being and, indeed, the *Buddhacarita* certainly does this, for Siddhartha was born in full awareness, and was already in a high state of consciousness from the cumulative states of all his past lives. So, we are told, he walked immediately and is reputed to have said:

> "I am born for supreme knowledge, for the welfare of the world, – thus this is my last birth," – thus did he of lion gait, gazing at the four quarters, utter a voice full of auspicious meaning.[9]

His mother died seven days after giving birth, for the womb which had borne a Buddha could not then carry another ordinary mortal. She was reborn in a celestial realm.

Traditionally, the people of the Sakya kingdom were somewhat independent and unorthodox in their thinking and nature, and were less likely to accept established traditions such as the rigid brahminism of Hinduism or the four-fold class system. The kingdom was an area which would produce other unorthodox thinkers besides the Buddha. The capital city of the area was Kapilavasta, and this would have been the place where Siddhartha was born. There is an inscription there today from ancient times stating "The Blessed One was born here". It would have been here in this capital that, according to the *Buddhacarita*, a forecast of the future enlightened life of Siddhartha was given to his father the *raja* by the sage Asita:

> He will proclaim the way of deliverance to those afflicted with sorrow, entangled in objects of sense, and lost in the forest paths of worldly existence, as to travellers who have lost their way.   Book 1: 77

Alarmed by the sage's remarks, we are told that the *raja* imprisoned the growing boy within the boundaries of three palaces; one for the cold season, one for the rainy season and one for the hot season. He wanted his son to have a view of reality which was divorced from any concept of suffering or unhappiness. Without knowing of the natural state of humankind, he would not need to proclaim any path to something beyond it.

It was in these luxurious circumstances that Siddhartha grew up in a life of pure pleasure and indulgence, in which he married and had a son. This is an important aspect of the Buddhist tradition, perhaps important enough to have been embellished in the early sources to enhance its meaning. Characteristic of Hindu religion is the belief in *asramadharma*, the idea that each individual must pass through the four stages of life – celibate student, married householder, recluse and wandering mendicant. To achieve *moksa* and end the cycle of *samsara* it was believed to be necessary to experience all the *asramas*, though it was sometimes accepted that some could be born straight into the last *asrama*. Siddhartha's life reflects this pattern of *asramadharma* and his life in the palace is clearly the second *asrama*.[10] Moreover, the Buddha's eventual denial of the extremes of luxury and asceticism, which promoted a *Middle Way*, made this early period of luxurious and sensuous enjoyment an important one.

We can call Siddhartha at this stage a *bodhisattva*. This word is used in Buddhism in two senses. In Theravada Buddhism it means one who is on the way to enlightenment, but since Theravada Buddhism believes there can be only one Buddha in each aeon, there can be only one *bodhisattva* in this aeon, this historical time, and this would be Siddhartha when he was a Buddha-to-be. In Mahayana Buddhism the term *bodhisattva* was used, as it still is, to depict someone who has attained enlightenment (*bodhi*) but who has delayed final enlightenment, full *nirvana*, in order to stay in existence and help others to reach enlightenment too.

Despite his sheltered and luxurious life, we are told that Siddhartha heard about life outside the confines of the palaces and wished to experience the wider world. The *Buddhacarita* tells us:

> Having heard of the delightful appearance of the city groves beloved by the women, he resolved to go out of doors, like an elephant long shut up in a house.   Book III: 3

Siddhartha pleaded with his father to be allowed outside his confined existence, and the *raja* agreed to allow his son beyond the palace up to a certain radius. All unpleasant sights, cripples, beggars and old people were hidden away, but it was to be Siddhartha's fate to experience what are now called the four signs. It is likely that these were illusions, some sources suggesting that they were engineered by the gods. Whatever Siddhartha's experiences were it seems they were shared only by his chariot driver and it is likely that they were supernatural experiences. On his first journey from the palace, Siddhartha saw, for the first time in his life, an old man. The *Buddhacarita* tells of the immense and violent shock that this caused the *bodhisattva*:

> Then he, the great-souled one, who had his mind purified by the impressions of former good actions, who possessed a store of merits accumulated through many preceding aeons, was deeply agitated when he heard of old age, like a bull who has heard the crash of a thunderbolt close by.   Book III: 34

His following excursion brought the experience of a sick man, and we are told that his reaction was one of despair. It is a depair filled also with amazement and sadness that the world is surrounded with old age and sickness and yet each individual seemed not to face it at all, but closed his or her eyes to it. The *Buddhacarita* tells us:

Having heard this account, his mind deeply distressed, he trembled like the moon reflected in the waves of water; and full of sorrow he uttered these words in a low voice: "Even while they see all this calamity of diseases mankind can yet feel tranquillity; alas for the scattered intelligence of men who can smile when still not free from the terror of disease!" Book III: 45–46

It is the third vision of a corpse which brings the strongest reactions and which adds the final and very poignant experience of the nature of reality and life. Again, Siddhartha is amazed that humankind closes its eyes to this fact of death:

Is this end appointed to all creatures, and yet the world throws off all fear and is infatuated! Hard indeed, I think, must the hearts of men be, who can be self-composed in such a road.   Book III: 61

After these experiences, Siddhartha was a changed man. No longer could he view palace life as the norm of existence. All the things which normally attract the senses were no longer attractive to him; he saw them all as illusory:

I do not despise worldly objects, I know that all mankind are bound up therein; but remembering that the world is transitory, my mind cannot find pleasure in them.   Book IV: 85

This concept of the impermanence of all life and all the world was to be a very important one in Buddhism; because of the existence of old age, sickness and death, happiness, beauty and the many things which humankind clings to in life were seen by Siddhartha to be illusory, and therefore should not be part of the life of the high-minded. He said:

Real greatness is not to be found there, where there is universally destruction, or where there is attachment to earthly objects, or a want of self-control.   Book IV: 91

A final excursion is depicted as a visit to the forest in search of peace. Here, again, Siddhartha was filled with pity and remorse. He saw the plough overturning the soil, the ploughmen suffering in the dust and the wind, the weary oxen, and the insects and tiny creatures that the plough had killed. This is the sense in which he sees all life as *dukkha*, unsatisfactory, suffering in the sense of the disharmony of all existence. As he reflected on his experiences, he is reputed to have said:

It is a miserable thing that mankind, though themselves powerless and

subject to sickness, old age, and death, yet blinded by passion and ignorant, look with disgust on another who is afflicted by old age or diseased
or dead.   Book V: 12

Seeking solitude, Siddhartha gained his first insight into the three signs
he had received:

> As he thus considered thoroughly these faults of sickness, old age, and
> death which belong to all living beings, all the joy which he had felt in the
> activity of his vigour, his youth and his life, vanished in a moment.
> He did not rejoice, he did not feel remorse; he suffered no hesitation,
> indolence, nor sleep; he felt no drawing towards the qualities of desire; he
> hated nor scorned another.
> Thus did this pure passionless meditation grow within the great souled-
> one . . .   Book V: 14–16

While reflecting in this way, Siddhartha experienced his fourth illusion.
This took the form of a mendicant, a homeless, wandering ascetic,
someone on the fourth of the Hindu *asramas*. This marked the final
turning point from his former life and he saw clearly, at that time, the
dharma which he had to pursue. Accordingly, he decided to escape the
palace in order to seek the state of deathlessness, to find the answers to
the problems of old age, sickness and death in life. Siddhartha had experienced the disillusioning aspects of life, and he wished to seek liberation
from them. What he had experienced was the predicament of
humankind, the fact that (wo)man, placed in a temporal, materialistic
existence, intoxicates him or herself with diversions, and ignores the
materialistic realities of ageing, suffering and death. Siddhartha saw this
ignorance, and the ensuing indifference to the suffering of sentient
beings in life, as immoral.

Asceticism and enlightenment

Bidding farewell to a stunned father, who, upon receiving the news,
"shook like a tree struck by an elephant", pleaded with his son not to
go, "in a voice choked with tears", Siddhartha summoned his faithful
steed, Kamthaka, and prepared to forsake the palace. He had spent his
youth and early manhood in extreme luxury; now he was to experience
their very opposites in a life of total asceticism as a wandering recluse.
He had come to realize the transience of all life and the necessity of tran-

scending its suffering. In the *Buddhacarita* he is reported as telling Chandaka, his grieving groom:

> Do not think of mourning for me who am thus gone forth from my home; union, however long it may last, in time will come to an end.
> Since separation is certain, therefore is my mind fixed on liberation; how shall there not be repeated severings from one's kindred?
> Do not think of mourning for me who am gone forth to leave sorrow behind; it is the thralls of passion, who are attached to desires, the causes of sorrow, for whom thou shouldst mourn.   Book VI: 16–18

For Siddhartha, the world became an illusion in which people chased happiness in things which were impermanent. Material existence could not possibly be Reality, for Reality must be deathless. And so he tried to find the deathless state through extreme asceticism. For six years he became the most devoted of ascetics, eventually reducing his daily intake of food to a handful. His wasted body is vividly described in the canonical discources:

> my spine stood out like a corded rope, my ribs projected like the jutting rafters of an old roofless cowshed, and the light of my eyes sunk down in their sockets looked like the gleam of water sunk in a deep well.   M I 245

The *Buddhacarita* tells us:

> Having only skin and bone remaining, with his fat, flesh and blood entirely wasted, yet, though diminished, he shone with undiminished grandeur like the ocean.   Book XII: 96

Although he is admired by five companion Hindu monks who accompany him at the time, Siddhartha comes to realize that he is nowhere near finding the answers he seeks in life through the yoga of the ascetic. He thus reflects:

> "This is not the way to passionlessness, nor to perfect knowledge, nor to liberation; that was certainly the true way which I found at the root of the Gambu tree."
> "But that cannot be attained by one who has lost his strength," – so resuming his care for his body, he next pondered thus, how best to increase his bodily vigour.   Book XII: 98–99

And so Siddhartha came to reject the ascetic path to enlightenment.

Having regained his physical strength, he left his companions and journeyed to the holy town of Gaya, situated on a tributary of the Ganges.
There, Siddhartha sat down under the shade of a great pipal tree and
made a vow:

> I will not rise from this position on the earth until I have obtained my
> utmost aim.   Book XII: 97

So he vowed to stay in that spot until he achieved Enlightenment. He
sat very quietly, very still, in the lotus *asana*, and began to go through
the traditional *dhyanas* of meditation, gradually allowing his thoughts
to subside until no new thoughts arose, and a feeling of joyful elation,
coherence and tranquillity remained. At the final stages, a state of perfect
balance, perfect equanimity was achieved. It was an equanimity which
allowed him to reach back through all time and thus through previous
lives; it was the point at which *karma* is nullified. Although completely
aware of his surroundings, Siddhartha was unaffected by them. His
mind was free to travel in any direction and to any part of human experience past, present and future but without any conditioned emotion.

But the path to Enlightenment was not completely smooth. The
Buddhacarita tells us that Siddhartha experienced the temptation of
Mara, the foe of all *dharma*. The foe of *dharma* is desire and aversion.
Mara began his attack on Siddhartha by sending all his forces against the
bodhisattva. But Siddhartha pointed his right hand down to the earth to
ask the earth to witness his meritorious acts of past existences and his
right to pursue the goal of Enlightenment at this point. The earth
responded with such an earthquake that the demons of Mara fled in
haste from the scene. So Mara tried more subtle tactics and sent his
daughters Discontent, Delight and Thirst, and his three sons Flurry,
Gaiety and Sullen Pride to deter the *bodhisattva's* quest. But they were
defeated by the equanimity of the mind of Siddhartha. The tempting of
Siddhartha here represents allegorically the subtle enemies of the mind
and the ego, which prevent the individual from gaining freedom from
samsara.

And so Siddhartha proceeded through the stages of meditation to the
point of Enlightenment. He perceived all his former births and his
previous lives. He is said to have recalled a hundred thousand of his lives
and all the pleasures and pains of each of them. He saw clearly the long
thread which had brought him through countless generations to the
present moment, and came to the conclusion that all that we view as real
in the world is totally insubstantial. He now had *deva*-vision and could

see and understand all the inhabitants of the cosmos and all the *karmic* forces which made up their happiness and sadness, evil and good, beauty and ugliness, and so on. But he himself was neither this nor that, beyond all such dualities. He was free: he had a knowledge of all that was to be known, free of the sense-pleasures, free of becoming and free of the ignorance which causes the individual to be reborn. As Michael Pye says:

> the great journey which he had pursued through so many existences had reached its end, all that was to be done had been done.[11]

Siddhartha had reached the state of *anatman* or "no self", "non-ego", and had realized *nirvana*. The *Buddhacarita* tells us that:

> From the summit of the world downwards he could detect no self anywhere. Like the fire, when its fuel is burnt up, he became tranquil. He had reached perfection, and he thought to himself: "This is the authentic Way on which in the past so many great seers, who also knew all higher and lower things, have travelled on to ultimate and real truth. And now I have obtained it".[12]

It is worth remembering that neither the *Buddhacarita* here, nor any other text for that matter, equates the extinguishing of a flame with *nirvana*, a point missed by many, but drawn to our attention by Walpola Rahula:

> An Arahant after his death is often compared to a fire gone out when the supply of wood is over, or to the flame of a lamp gone out when the wick and oil are finished. Here it should be clearly and distinctly understood, without any confusion, that what is compared to a flame or a fire gone out is *not* Nirvana, but the "being" composed of the Five Aggregates who realized Nirvana. This point has to be emphasized because many people, even some great scholars, have misunderstood and misinterpreted this simili as referring to Nirvana. Nirvana is never compared to a fire or a lamp gone out.[13]

As the dawn broke, Siddhartha became the Buddha, the Awakened One:

> Thus he, the holy one, sitting there on his seat of grass at the root of the tree, pondering by his own efforts attained at last perfect knowledge. Then bursting the shell of ignorance, having gained all the various kinds

of perfect intuition, he attained all the partial knowledge of alternatives which is included in perfect knowledge.

He became the perfectly wise, the Bhagavat, the Arhat, the king of the Law, the Tathagata, He who has attained the knowledge of all forms, the Lord of all science.   Book XIV: 66–68

At that moment, sources tell us that the blind could see, the deaf could hear, and the lame could walk; there was beauty and peace in all the world:

Pleasant breezes blew softly, rain fell from a cloudless sky, flowers and fruits dropped from trees out of season – in an effort as it were, to show reverence for him. Mandarava flowers and lotus blossoms, and also water lilies made of gold and beryl, fell from the sky on the ground near the Shakya sage, so that it looked like a place in the world of the gods. At that moment no one anywhere was angry, ill or sad; no one did evil, none was proud; the world became quite quiet, as though it had reached full perfection.[14]

Clearly, Siddhartha had transcended the apparent limits of human perception, a point recognized by the Buddha when he later affirmed that to speculate over the frame of mind of an enlightened being is to invite confusion and madness.[15] Nevertheless, human curiosity, being what it is, will forever ask, "But what happened precisely?", a concern addressed rather well by Andrew Powell:

The Buddha's Enlightenment is the central fact of the Buddhist religion. It is as fundamental as the Crucifixion is to Christianity. The great edifice of Buddhist philosophy and ethics which developed in succeeding centuries could never have been constructed without this one crucial occurrence. So what exactly happened? What is Enlightenment? Unfortunately it is rather difficult to say because it is an experience, one which cannot readily be reduced to the conventional formulas of language. If it could be easily explained, then it would no longer be Enlightenment.[16]

Coming out of his long seven-day trance into the realization of full Enlightenment, the sources inform us that Mara again tempted the Buddha to reject the world and achieve final *nirvana*, *parinirvana*. But it is at the request of the two Hindu gods, Indra and Brahma, that the Buddha decides to remain in the world to guide others on the path and teach them the true *dharma*. The story is a strange one, perhaps reflecting allegorically some uncertainty in the Buddha as to how, practically, he could put humankind on this true *dharmic* path. Perhaps this is what the conflicting ideas of the appearance of Mara and the deities represent.

So the Buddha did not attain final *parinirvana* but completed the remainder of his life in his physical body without producing any more *karma* which would cause him to be reborn. His purpose now would be to teach the *dharma*, and in making this decision there was evident a radical shift from the individualistic and elitist striving for *moksa* of brahmanical Hinduism; it was a turning towards humankind (with the possible exception of women!), regardless of class.

When once again the Buddha was reunited with his father, the latter was able to recognize the new role of his son, and accept also that Siddhartha's decisions had been the right ones. He said:

> If you had chosen to remain bound up with the things of this world, you could as a universal monarch have protected mankind. Instead you have conquered the great ills of the Samsaric world, you have become a Sage who proclaims the Dharma for the weal of all.[17]

Importantly, there is no indication of any involvement with a transcendent Absolute or theistic concept of the divine during the process in which the Buddha achieved Enlightenment. Similarly, when the Buddha reached his goal there was no sense of unity with, either partially or wholly, a transcendent Absolute. The gods seem to have helped Siddhartha towards Enlightenment, and he is depicted as visiting them in their heaven to give them spiritual calm and teaching. The gods of Buddhism are *karmic*; they are only there because they have accumulated immense amounts of good *karma*. But because they have *karma* they are inferior to the Buddha, and are still fellow travellers with all humanity on the *samsaric* path. So Enlightenment for the Buddha brought him superiority to these gods and not knowledge of an Absolute. When asked who taught him Enlightenment, the Buddha replied:

> No teacher have I. None need I venerate, and none must I despise. Nirvana have I now obtained, and I am not the same as others are. Quite by myself, you see, have I the Dharma won. Completely have I understood what must be understood, though others failed to understand it. That is the reason why I am a Buddha.[18]

The First Sermon of the Buddha

Leaving the said pipal tree, which later became known as the *bodhi* tree, the Buddha travelled towards the great Hindu centre of Kashi, which is modern Benares. Approaching the city, the Buddha met the five companions of his ascetic years who, according to Asvaghosa, were totally overpowered by his charismatic person, despite their original plan to ignore him as he approached; other sources, probably more accurately, suggest that the Buddha failed immediately to convince his former friends of his Enlightenment. Reaching Isipatana, the Deer Park in the city, the Buddha sat down with his companions and taught them what has become known as *The First Sermon of the Buddha*. This sermon set out the *dharma* for humankind, and the Buddha taught what became known as *The Four Noble Truths*. He used the symbol of the wheel and its eight spokes to teach (though not in one sitting!) what came to be known as *The Noble Eightfold Path*. These and related teachings became the Buddha's *Middle Way*, the path to *nirvana* which was neither sense indulgent nor ascetic. It is a way, he said, which would lead to the appeasing of all ill and yet was one which was free from happiness and joy.

We can gather from the different sources that, for the next forty or forty-five years of his life, the Buddha travelled in the middle Ganges region as a religious wandering monk, teaching and gathering disciples. He would have been considered a *sannyasin*, a holy man, and would have been treated with respect and reverence, as all such holy men in the Indian tradition. Gradually, his communities of monks, the *Sangha*, expanded. The hagiographical aspects of Asvaghosa's account of the life of the Buddha claim that the Buddha's ministry was characterized by the performance of many miracles. He had, for example, to ward off the jealousy and attempted murder by his cousin Devadatta, so on one occasion he calmed a stampeding elephant and on another disintegrated a huge rock which Devadatta had contrived to fall on him. Opposition such as Devadatta's was unusual, for support for the Buddha was considerable, even coming from local rulers such as King Bimbisara of Magadha. As a result of this latter support, Magadha became a centre of Buddhism for some centuries.

Finally, some time towards the end of the fifth century BCE, the Buddha felt his death approaching, and he passed away as a result of food poisoning,[19] though the *Discourse of the Great Decease* attests that he recovered from this and died from natural causes. As a *tathagata*, one who has fully arrived and is in a state of "thusness" or "suchness", the

Buddha could have continued living until the end of the present aeon, the accounts inform us, but he relinquished this right to live longer. The realization that the Buddha was about to die was too much for his devoted disciple, Ananda, and the old man was reduced to tears. The Buddha told him:

> do not mourn, do not weep. Haven't I told you that we are separated, parted, cut off from everything dear and beloved? . . . You have served me long with love, helpfully, gladly, sincerely and without reserve, in body, word, and thought. You have done well by yourself, Ananda. Keep trying and you will soon be liberated.[20]

Tradition states that one morning, the Buddha gathered alms at Vaisali, gave the town one last "elephant look" and then set his face towards Kusinagasa, quite near to his birthplace. There, surrounded by his disciples and local inhabitants, he entered into the stages of meditation and finally relinquished his body. The Buddha was dead. No residue of *karmic* forces – negative or positive – remained which could bring about another birth. Walpola Rahula warned that popular descriptions of the Buddha's demise which speak of his "passing into the state of *Parinirvana*", inferring a state of eternal peace and liberation, have no warrant:

> This popular expression "entered into Nirvana" has no equivalent in the original texts. There is no such thing as "entering into Nirvana after death". There is a word *parinibbuto* used to denote the death of the Buddha or an Arahant who has realized Nirvana, but it does not mean "entering into Nirvana". *Parinibbuto* simply means "fully passed away", "fully blown out" or "fully extinct", because the Buddha or an Arahant has no re-existence after his death.[21]

A very detailed account of the Buddha's death is given in the Pali scripture, the *Mahaparinirvanasutra*, "Sutra of the Great Final Nirvana", and Asvaghosa recounts most poetically the preparations for the cremation of the Buddha. True to Hindu custom,[22] the Buddha was honoured with ornamentation and garlands and his body taken to the Mukuta shrine where it was burned. According to tradition, the bones of the Buddha, which did not burn, became relics, and were venerated by the monks until they were shared amongst seven monarchs, the monks retaining only a few. The relics were placed in specially erected *stupas* which later became Buddhist temples. Many lay people visited them alongside the monks, offering garlands and bowing in reverence to the memory of the Buddha in the hope of acquiring good *karma*. It was this kind of veneration which paved the way for the subsequent beliefs and practices of Mahayana Buddhism.

A note on the search for the historical Buddha

The search for the Buddha of history has proved as frustrating as the quest for the historical Jesus, so much so that the late nineteenth century saw the historicity of the former called to question. However, since the ancient authors who recorded the deeds of the Buddha were not chroniclers but poets, this should cause no great surprise. Happily, this wave of scepticism has passed and it is now generally accepted that there was indeed a Buddha of history. As we have noted, recent scholarship has assigned his demise to the closing years of the fifth century BCE, having attained the recent status of an octogenarian.

If it is the poet Asvaghosa of the first century CE whom we have to thank for preserving the earliest complete biography of the Buddha, we should also note that this is a biography which elevates the historical Siddhartha Gautama to the realm of the epic hero, at the same time preserving the trials and tribulations of the mere mortal:

> The hero is a mortal experiencing conflicts; undergoing genuine temptations; trying, and ultimately rejecting, false courses; excercising choice at every point; and prevailing, not through fate or divine intervention, but through his own action. He is motivated by compassion for suffering humanity and exhibits the martial virtues of courage, steadfastness, initiative, and self-discipline.Throughout his ordeals he sustains a delicate sensitivity and an unshakable dignity.[23]

The narratives which depict the life of the Buddha, both before and after his Enlightenment, were never intended to be taken as literal interpretations. It is important to remember that the purely biographical narratives which added a dimension of dramatic tension, were also intended as inspiration to later disciples. In this light, they belong to the world of allegory, and the palace narratives illustrate how, with maturity, we have the perspicacity to reject material possessions and, with immaturity, ignore the unpleasant facts of existence.

Professor Gombrich reminds us that this story is not associated with Siddhartha in the Pali Canon, literature which nowhere so much as mentions this name. It is also ironic that on the very day Prince Siddhartha recognizes and rejects the futility of the life of plenty, he fathers a son and leaves him to a material fate:

> In the Canon this story is not told of Siddhattha, and the birth of the son is omitted. The story of the four encounters is told of Vipassi, six Buddhas back (DN II, 21–9). According to this text, the *Mahapadana Sutta*, the early lives (and to some extent the later lives) of all Buddhas follow a very similar pattern, and the five Buddhas between Vipassi and Gotama will have experienced the same encounters.[24]

The Development of Community

The *Sangha*

Once the Buddha had achieved Enlightenment, he began to attract a number of followers. This was the beginning of the *Sangha*, the community of monks,[1] though it is doubtful if the Buddha had any idea how it would develop when he discharged his disciples with the words:

> Go monks and travel for the welfare and happiness of the people, out of compassion for the world . . .   Vin 1:21

We should not consider that everyone who met the Buddha either agreed with his teaching or accepted his Enlightenment. Tradition recounts that he met a wandering ascetic, Upaka, just after his Enlightenment. Upaka listened carefully to what the Buddha had to say about his Enlightenment and about *nirvana* but went on his way shaking his head and remaining unconvinced. Similarly, the five companions to whom the Buddha taught his First Sermon in the Deer Park did not simultaneously nor immediately recognize and accept the teaching of the Buddha. Only one of these ascetics understood sufficiently to become the first monk ordained by the Buddha. As yet, of course, there were no regulations or official kind of ordination; according to tradition, the Buddha merely summoned the monk, praised the *dharma* (Skt.), *dhamma* (Pali) and asked the initiate to follow it. But once one monk had been ordained, two others followed suit and, while the Buddha taught the remaining two, the other three ordained monks went out to beg for their food and for food for the others. Here, then, we see the beginning of the corporate brotherhood of the monks, the *Sangha*, being supported by the collection of alms from the lay people.

To become ordained it was normally accepted that a man (not a woman at first) should become an *arahant*, a perfected one who had reached the egoless state of *nirvana*. Having reached this state of perfection, the shaving of the head and beard followed, as did the wearing of yellow rags and abandonment of the home. Once ordained, these *arahants* were sent out by the Buddha to teach the *dharma* and, as the *Sangha* grew in size, it became necessary for these ordained monks to ordain others rather than have everyone travel long distances for ordination by the Buddha himself. Soon, the process of ordination became fixed with the pattern of the candidate shaving hair and beard, putting on the yellow robe, squatting down before the monks with palms together in salutation, and reciting the Three Refuges three times:

> I go to the Buddha for refuge
> I go to the *Dharma* for refuge
> I go to the *Sangha* for refuge

Much of the success of early Buddhism was due to the attraction it had amongst the higher political and social levels of society. The King of Magadha, Bimbisara, became a lay disciple of the Buddha. The King invited the Buddha to a meal and gave him a secluded bamboo grove where he and his disciples could stay. This shows the extent to which the new teaching found acceptance and social recognition. Although Buddhism appealed to the highest levels of society, it also addressed the lowest levels. The extent to which this happened is evidenced by the amount of support given to the monks by the ordinary lay people. The monks depended on lay disciples, both rich and poor, for alms, an important point we must not underestimate. It became the pattern in these early days that those who became monks left their homes and were given food and basic necessities by those sympathetic to the teaching. The act of giving to the monks was considered to be doubly meritorious, since in addition to accruing merit through compassion and generosity, this would foster a wholesome state of mind in a laity pursuing the Buddha's *dharma*.[2] In effect, a rare relationship and co-existence developed between king, people and *Sangha*. The king patronized the *Sangha*, which taught the people to obey the king; conversely, the *Sangha* instructed and advised the king who ruled the people and who thus encouraged their support for the *Sangha*. It was a mutually successful relationship.

It is uncertain just how much the Buddha laid down rules of discipline for the growing order of Buddhist monks. Some of the basic precepts of Buddhism probably existed at this early time, but after his death the discipline texts added many others. Some rules were added through experiences of the Buddha himself. For example, it is customary for a candidate to monkhood to gain consent of parents before ordination. The custom originated because of the ordination of the Buddha's own son without both parents' consent. It was pointed out to the Buddha by his father that a parent's love for his or her son is a very deep one and that ordinations, therefore, should always be with parental consent. The Buddha agreed.[3] From this we can see how rules for the new teaching were being added so that relations between monks and lay people were harmonious.

Women were only reluctantly admitted as nuns. At first, women could only be lay disciples, but later the Buddha allowed a female order to be set up. There is, however, much evidence to suggest that at first he did not accept that a woman could attain *nirvana* in this life. He did accept that women could be reborn in a heavenly realm and from *there* could attain *nirvana*, but the idea of a woman achieving *nirvana* in human life seems to have been difficult for him to accept. His mother, we should remember, had to be reborn on a celestial plane, and did not reach enlightenment in earthly existence despite being the mother of a Buddha! But there is also evidence that the Buddha was, if reluctantly, willing to accept that a woman could become an *arahant*. When his aunt and stepmother pleaded to be ordained, he is known to have voiced this to his disciple Ananda, but he did not accept her ordination or the setting up of an order of nuns without reluctance:

> Five years after the Buddha's Enlightenment, his aunt Maha Prajapati Gautami accompanied by five hundred Sakyan women went to the Lord in Vaisali and requested permission for women to leave home for the homeless life of the Doctrine and Discipline so well expounded by the Tathagata. The Buddha refused three times. Gautami and her companions cut off their hair, dressed in the yellow robes and went to the Buddha. Ananda, the Buddha's cousin and attendant monk, interceded for them, but three more times the Buddha refused his permission. Later on he conceded that if a woman were to accept eight strict rules (*gurudharma*) this would replace ordination (upasampad) for her, and she could obtain the four fruits of the religious life. Gautami and the five hundred Sakyan women joyfully accepted this proposition and were thus ordained (*Vin.* II, 253–6; A IV, 274–7).[4]

Usually he warned his disciples to take no notice of women. He told his disciple Ananda to act as if he did not see women. When Ananda asked "What if we do see them?" the Buddha answered "Don't speak to them", and when Ananda asked what the monks should do if the women spoke to them, the Buddha replied "Keep wide awake!" All in all, the Buddha believed that women were an obstacle to a man's attainment of *nirvana*.

As the Buddha's life came towards its end, there was no thought of appointing a successor. Different Buddhist orders had begun to establish themselves independently, but were always united by the *dharma*, the teaching of the Buddha and the *Vinaya*, the rules for discipline of the monks, which had developed during the lifetime of the Buddha. Although the Buddha denoted no one to succeed him, one name stands out through successive generations following the death of the Buddha. That name is Sariputra, whose understanding and teaching of the Buddha's *dharma* influenced Buddhism for several hundred years. As an ordained *arahant*, he had attained full enlightenment in the time of the Buddha and after the Buddha died he presented the Buddha's knowledge in a way which could be easily assimilated and remembered. Although accepted by the orthodox Buddhists, the later more liberal schools were critical of Sariputra. A distinction can be drawn between the two. Orthodox Buddhists who accepted Sariputra's teaching became known as the *Wisdom School* because Sariputra held that Wisdom alone out of the five cardinal virtues of Faith, Vigour, Mindfulness, Concentration and Wisdom, could bring about salvation. Much later, when the Mahayana school flourished, it referred to those who followed Sariputra's teachings as the *Old Wisdom School* and considered itself as the *New Wisdom School*.

The emergence of the Theravada and Mahayana schools

Approximately within five hundred years of the Buddha's death, Buddhism developed its characteristic features as we now know them; the major division being between Theravada and Mahayana. The Theravada School, or School of the Elders, is the sole surviving school of some eighteen original lines which spread throughout southeast Asia; unsurprisingly, it is often referred to as Southern Buddhism. Theravada followed the more conservative, original teachings which came to be recorded in Pali, though many of the scriptures of Southern schools which are no longer extant are preserved in Sanskrit. The Northern Mahayana developed as a more liberal branch which also recorded its scriptures in Sanskrit. The developments included the realization that within us all there is a potentiality inherent in the heart known as the

Buddha-nature; and the concept of the *bodhisattva* who, out of deep compassion for others, postpones *nirvana*. Buddhism in its early years was mainly concentrated within the *Sangha*, the religious community but, according to the traditional account, the first sixty monks whom the Buddha had converted and ordained were despatched to teach the *dharma*:

> Go monks and travel for the welfare and happiness of the people, out of compassion for the world, for the benefit, welfare and happiness of gods and men. No two of you go the same way. Teach the Doctrine, monks, which is fine in its beginning, middle and end, with its meaning and letter, sheer and whole, and proclaim the pure holy life. There are beings, naturally of little passion, who are languishing for lack of hearing the Doctrine; they will understand it.[5]

The *dharma* was the guiding light of this community and linked the ever-growing *Sangha* as it spread throughout the Ganges region, the area of the greatly increasing Magadhan empire. As this empire grew, swallowing the smaller tribal territories, so the Buddhist *Sangha* increased. Obviously, the rapidly expanding *Sangha* needed some sort of cohesive focus, and after the death of the Buddha the tradition tells us that four major Councils were held which aimed at authorizing the Buddha's teaching by establishing an orthodox canon of scripture. This was to be the focus of all the communities which made up the widely-spread *Sangha*.

We may be certain that the Buddha wrote nothing. Indeed, recent scholarship has shown that writing did not obtain in India until a century and a half after the Buddha's demise, during the reign of Asoka.[6] The Buddha's teaching was imparted entirely in the form of conversations and discourses, which were preserved in oral tradition for more than four centuries: "This accounts for certain stylistic devices – repetitions, poetic flourishes, etc. – which made for easier memorization."[7] The integrity of the oral tradition was maintained through *communal* chantings known as *samgiti,* which enabled the *dharma* to be held in the collective memory and thus preserved.

The Theravadin scriptures are often said to be the only original canon, an understandable assumption since Pali was, presumably, the language of the Buddha. While it is true to say that the Pali Canon is the only *surviving* canon of early Buddhism, it is quite incorrect to say that Pali was the only original: there was no standard single form. Indeed Pali terms are not used in Tibetan centres even today. Furthermore, the

Buddha did not speak Pali, but Magadhi, at least while he was in the region of Magadha, as presumably he would have spoken Kosalese in neighbouring Kosala. India is a huge continent with thousands of languages and dialects and, being Enlightened, the Buddha held no delusions of the superiority of one language over another. Rather, he enjoined the monks to teach in the local language, as the *sakkaya niruttiya* shows:

> Two monks [it is related] of fine cultivated language and fine eloquent speech, came to the Buddha and said: "Lord, here monks of various names, clan-names, races [or castes], and families are corrupting the Buddha's words by repeating them in their own dialects. Let us put them into Vedic (*chandaso aropema*)." The Lord rebuked them: "Deluded men! How can you say this? This will not lead to the conversion of the unconverted" . . . And he delivered a sermon and commanded all the monks: "You are not to put the Buddha's words into Vedic. Whosoever does so shall be guilty of an offence. I authorise you, monks, to learn the Buddha's words each in his own dialect (*sakkaya niruttiya*)".[8]

As the vast majority of early Buddhist schools vanished into the mist of time, taking their scriptures with them, the literature of early Buddhism's sole surviving school, the Theravada, endured. Most of the body of Theravada literature still extant (which is preserved almost in its entirety) was compiled on the island of Sri Lanka several centuries after the Buddha's death.

The original disciples of the Buddha would have passed on his teaching orally to those who, in turn, would have become disciples and taught in the local language. Thus an established line of teaching and interpretation came about. The integrity of the oral tradition was preserved through oral chanting, and the monks at the four Buddhist Councils prefaced their chanting with the words "Thus have I heard ...", words which are still extant in the written scriptures today. The Theravadin scriptures, which later became known as the Pali Canon, were eventually committed to writing; written scriptures are a secondary phenomenon but an important one. Though read by layman and monk alike, it is the latter who is expected to study the scriptures in depth, recite major portions and teach from them. The older a text is, the more importance it is given; it may even become a relic.

The canonical literature which has survived is known as the *Tipitaka* "Three Baskets" (Skt. *Tripitaka*) of the *dharma*; in early Buddhism the manuscripts were probably kept in baskets before being handed on to the next generation of monks, hence the name. The *Tipitaka* comprises the *Vinaya Pitaka* (the basket of discipline), the *Sutta Pitaka* (the basket of sermons) and the *Abhidhamma Pitaka* (the basket of higher teaching). Both the *Vinaya Pitaka* and the *Sutta Pitaka* were accepted by early Buddhism and the Mahayana, but the "basket of higher teaching" became the ground for contention between the two schools.

The First Council, 483 BCE

The First Council is said to have been held at Rajagaha immediately after the Buddha's death. The Council met in order to recollect the Word of the Buddha, to make the Buddha's doctrines formal, and to lay down the rules of discipline for the *Sangha*. It was attended by five hundred senior monks reputed to be *arahants*. The Buddha's doctrines composed the *dharma* and were carefully preserved in oral tradition by the monks:

> Upali recited the monastic code of conduct or Vinaya as he remembered the Buddha expounding it; and Ananda recited the teachings themselves, the *Sutta*. These renderings were debated and a definitive version agreed (though not unanimously).[9]

At this Council, three sections of the Buddhist *dharma* were formalized as authoritative teaching:

The *Vinaya Pitaka* consists of the rules and regulations for the monks (*bhikkhus*) and nuns (*bhikkhunis*) to follow, as the word *vinaya'* (discipline) suggests. The original monastic rules are known as the *Patimokkha*, the "Book of Discipline", and contain 227 rules or precepts which were recited at gatherings of the monks held at the new moon and the full moon. As well as setting out a detailed code of conduct for the monastics' daily lives, the *Vinaya Pitaka* deals with the settling of disputes and the disciplining of offenders. A surprising feature of this "basket of discipline" is diversity; despite sharing a common basis, the texts are anything but uniform.

The *Sutta Pitaka* or "basket of sermons", which is easily the longest and most important element of the *Tipitaka*, is also the one most popular with lay Buddhists. Recited at the First Council by the Buddha's faithful disciple, Ananda, these recollections of the Buddha's discourses fall into five sections. The Buddha's teachings in the form of dialogues are linked by a common "thread" (Pali *sutta*, Skt. *sutra*).

The *Sutta Pitaka* consists of five sections of dialogues, long ones first, the

Digha Nikaya, then medium-length discourses, the *Majjhima Nikaya*, the *Samyutta Nikaya* which are thematically grouped discourses, the *Anguttara Nikaya* or "Gradual Sayings", and the small texts of the *Khuddaka Nikaya*, which include the *Dhammapada* and the *Jatakas*.[10]

A notable feature of the *Jataka* stories is an apparent willingness to accept the Hindu teaching on reincarnation with its very strong links between one life and the next, rather than the Buddhist idea of rebirth, with its belief in *anatta*. The *Jatakas* (literally "birth stories") are immensely popular amongst the laity.

Also popular with lay Buddhists is the *Dhammapada*, which is said to be to Buddhist scripture what the Sermon on the Mount is to the New Testament. *Dhammapada* means "the path of truth", a reference to the collection of 423 vivid verses which give practical advice on how to follow Buddhism as a way of action, and the laity would know much of the *Dhammapada* by heart and recite from it in times of need. Indeed, the *Dhammapada* in particular and the *Sutta Pitaka* as a whole are a great source of comfort to the lay Buddhist who will turn to them for advice on matters of daily living and the developing and sustaining of all manner of personal relationships.

The *Abhidamma Pitaka*, on the other hand, is a later addition which became the subject of dispute between the Northern and Southern schools. The "basket of higher teaching" is not a favourite reading of the lay Buddhist; this esoteric literature is studied by scholarly monks who scrutinize the many interpretations of this "Higher *Dharma*", which is basically a philosophical and metaphysical analysis of the Buddha's teaching.

These three formalized teachings of the Buddha became so venerated that it was considered heretical to challenge them, particularly the *Vinaya*, and when, a century later, a breach of discipline by a group of monks occurred, the situation was serious enough to summon a Second Council. However, let us not make the mistake of assuming that there was unaminity of opinion at Rajagaha:

Not everyone who attended the First Council at Rajagaha agreed that what had been recited there was the authentic Word of the Buddha; other members of the Sangha had been absent and, declining to adopt the authorized version, preserved and handed on their own versions of what the Buddha had taught. All this, added to the long oral phase when changes must inevitably have crept in, means that we cannot say with certainty of anything that, "These are the precise words of the Buddha ... " Buddhism cannot therefore be a "book" religion in the same sense that, say, Islam or Judaism claim to be. It possesses no divinely revealed and hence "infallible" and ultimately authoritative canons.[11]

The Second Council c.383 BCE

The Second Council was attended by a much larger gathering of seven hundred monks. A certain group of monks, those of the Vajji territory, were disobeying the rules. They were reprimanded and defeated but decided to hold their own Council, a decision that was to bring about a split in the *Sangha* which was to become crucial in the development of later Buddhism, for it is at this point that we find the origins of present-day Theravada and Mahayana.

The breakaway group called themselves the *Mahasanghika*, "The great *Sangha* party", and were characterized by a more relaxed attitude to the *Vinaya*. Their approach was more progressive and less exclusive and was very much favoured by the laity. Placing less importance on discipline, they tended to stress meditation, something which the layman and woman could practise in their own homes. They did not exclude householders from the *Sangha* so that it would not be necessary for an individual to leave home and enter a monastery if he or she wished to join. They were also more disposed to consider the inclusion of women, and more readily accepted the less-gifted monk as well as the greatly-gifted. However, the most far-reaching expressions of the *Mahasanghikas* lay in their attitude to scriptures and their concept of the Buddha. With regard to the former, they were prepared to accept scriptures which were composed at a later date than the Buddha, and this paved the way for the full flowering of the literature of Mahayana Buddhism. Concerning the concept of the Buddha, there was a general tendency to see the influence, power and essence of the Buddha as being ever-alive and ongoing. This made the Buddha supernatural and supramundane. There developed, too, the idea that since the Buddha was always present, existing past, present and future, his teaching was also ongoing and would be expounded continually. It was ideas such as these which led to the concept of *bodhisattvas* in Buddhism, beings who had realized *nirvana* like the Buddha, who shared his same essence and who delayed their final *nirvana* to remain in the world and help all others realize *nirvana* too.

The orthodox group, being less flexible, believed in strict adherence to the letter of the tradition and were known as the *Sthaviras* or "Elders". They stressed rules of conduct – the moral approach – on the path to *nirvana*. It is these *Sthaviras* who were the forbears of Hinayana Buddhism, the only surviving branch of which is Theravada Buddhism. *Hinayana* was a derogatory term given to the older tradition by the descendants of the *Mahasanghikas*, the Mahayana party. It means "Inferior Vehicle" (to salvation) as opposed to the name *Mahayana* which means "Great Vehicle". Modern Theravadins still find the word *Hinayanists* offensive, and many modern scholars prefer the term "early Buddhism". As a result of this division, the common core foundations of the Buddha's teachings were developed distinctively and are preserved on the one hand in the sole surviving (Pali) canon, which still represents the orthodox scriptures of Southern Buddhism (Theravada), and on the other in classical Sanskrit scriptures which became the canon of Northern Buddhism (Mahayana).

> Several times in Buddhist history, hundreds of learned monks have assembled to rehearse the Canon (and its commentaries). Though these assemblies are referred to in English as Councils, they are really Communal Recitations . . . Buddhist schools differ in the Councils they recognize. Only the first two are recognized by all schools.[12]

The Third Council, 250 BCE

The third Buddhist Council met during the reign of the great Indian Emperor Asoka. He reigned over the Magadhan Empire from 270–232 BCE and it was a reign which was most significant for Buddhism. During the intervening years, the influence of Buddhism had been considerable: the *Sangha* had become firmly established, and the Magadhan society preserved the moral teachings of the Buddha's *dharma*. This was because the Buddha's teachings were something of a social philosophy, as well as a metaphysical system, binding citizens and state in mutual obligations.

Since the conquest of the Punjab region by Alexander the Great in 326 BCE, the Indian dynasty led by the Mauryan kings had been gradually regaining power. When the news of Alexander's death was known in India, an army officer, Chandragupta, defeated the Greek forces and founded the Indian Empire. Asoka was Chandragupta's grandson and the most celebrated of the Mauryan kings. His reign was the most significant one for Buddhism for, after an eight-year period of extending his territories, he turned totally to Buddhism and became an *upesaka*, a layman of the *Sangha*. It is from his reign that we are able to date some of the events in Buddhist history, since Asoka developed the custom of having Buddhist ideals and commemorative events in the Buddha's life engraved on stone slabs and pillars, many of which survive to this day. In this way, the renowned humanitarian social policies of Asoka are evidenced and illustrate the extent to which Buddhist ethics had influenced the Mauryan Empire. Asoka left his mark on Buddhism, too, with the legacy of the many *stupas* which he had built and his encouragement of Buddhist art.

The Third Council met to discuss another dispute within the *Sangha*. Buddhism had spread throughout the Empire, but Hinduism existed alongside it and there was much mutual exchange of ideas. It was inevitable that the non-theistic philosophy of orthodox Buddhism should court the older Hindu practices and, in particular, infuse into its philosophy the belief in a totally transcendent Absolute of the nature of Brahman. This, indeed, was the basis of the dispute which the Third Council faced. A group of monks who were called the *Sarvastivadins* had come to accept a very pantheistic religious philosophy, and are important because of the impetus they gave to the development of Mahayana Buddhism. Against the *Sarvastivadins* were the orthodox *Sthaviras* whom Asoka supported. However, the dispute could not be solved and the *Sarvastivadins* became a separate group and established themselves in the western regions of Kashmir and Ghandara.

The Third Council also endorsed the major part of the Pali Canon, the *Tipitaka*, and was responsible for much missionary activity. This missionary activity was encouraged by Asoka and he even sent his son (or younger brother) to Sri Lanka where Buddhism was firmly established. Missionaries were also sent to the Himalayan regions, possibly to Burma, Sumatra and Malaya and to the Greek kingdom of north west India from which the well-known Theravadin text, the *Milindapanha* derives, the record of philosophical debate between the second-century BCE Greek ruler there, King Milinda and a Theravadin monk, Nagasena.[13]

The Fourth Council

A Fourth Council was subsequently held during the reign of the north west Indian King, Kanishka (73–103 CE). By this time, Mahayana Buddhism had spread considerably and had become firmly established in many countries. The Fourth Council met to try to reconcile the differences between the two schools of thought: the orthodox old wisdom school and the new wisdom schools of Mahayana. But the Mahayana response was a great surge of literature: the work of Asvaghosa, for example, came from this time. The period from 100 CE to 400 CE is one which could be called the golden age of Buddhist literature. From this period came the different scriptural philosophies of the two major branches of Theravada and Mahayana Buddhism, but while they were different, they were not necessarily separate. The analogy of the wheel is often used to describe the relationship between the two, the hub of the wheel being Theravada and the spokes Mahayana. Core beliefs are inevitably derived from orthodox doctrines, but Mahayana has given these beliefs different and extended interpretations.

The decline of Buddhism

It is interesting that Buddhism foretold its own demise, then as now. In the Pali Canon the Buddha is reputed to have recognized its decline in his own lifetime and anticipated its disappearance in the future so that, in keeping with the Indian concept of cyclical existence, the Buddha's *dharma* is constantly being forgotten and rediscovered.

Some *sutras* depict a gradual decline in periods of about five hundred years, others speak of a period of true *dharma* and counterfeit *dharma*, but there is a general agreement in most schools of thought that this decline would come about. There are, however, a number of more empirical reasons why Buddhism declined, in India in particular. To begin with, Buddhism lost most of its distinctive character when Mahayana in India intermingled with popular beliefs and cults. Existing virtually side by side with Hinduism, there was always the inevitablity that the two religions would influence each other at the local level. Professor Gombrich draws our attention to the lamentable fact that today the official government position in Nepal (above all places!) is that Buddhism is considered to be simply a sect of Hinduism:

> This means that it need not figure in the school syllabus: Hinduism is taught, but there is no requirement to teach the "Buddhist" part of it, and if Buddhists complain, they can be told that their religion, Hinduism, is indeed taught.[14]

Buddhism, too, was a monastic religion and a non-violent one. Buddhists, therefore, were not able to resist incursions, in particular the Muslim invasions of the eleventh century. Buddhism, consequently, virtually disappeared from India as a separate religion, although some areas remained distinctly Buddhist. Religiously and culturally, however, the effect of Buddhism was always evident.

The dawn of the common era saw the rise of Mahayana Buddhism in lands far from India, when the profound religious insights of the Northern School, with its concept of Buddha-nature as well as the *bodhisattva* ideal, made their appearance in the Far East. Of the great Mahayana schools, Kegon, Tendai and Shingon, only the first-named is not extant in Japan today, and Nichiren, Pure Land and Zen are still thriving. Another branch of Mahayana found its way into Tibet, where it made considerable impact; today, however, although this influence is still evident outside Tibet, and in Tibetan monasteries in the form of religious ritual and ceremony, Tibetan monks still practising in their homeland are not permitted to study, nor to disseminate their knowledge.

Divergences between Hinduism and Buddhism

The vast majority of teaching about Buddhism worldwide goes to one of two extremes. Either Buddhism is considered to be a form of Hinduism, or its Indian background is ignored. Both extremes are equally wide of the mark. To ignore the Buddha's Indian background is as damaging to a study of Buddhism as the acceptance of Buddhism as a branch of Hinduism. The critical study which accepts the Buddha as a child of India and undertakes an evaluation of his opposition to the *Upanisadic* theory of the self, however, is at the very least a responsible one.

One significant difference between early Buddhism and Hinduism lay in the rejection of ritual in Buddhism. The Buddha saw ritual as a hindrance to the journey of the individual to *nirvana*. Ritual is therefore still kept to a minimum in Theravada Buddhism. *Rupas*, the statues of the Buddha, are honoured rather than worshipped, but in Mahayana Buddhism the incorporation of ritual has become considerable. Buddhism also rejected the excessive physical asceticism which is often found in Hinduism. The Buddha emphasized a "Middle Way" of a healthy body and a calm mind, so that extremes were avoided. Some aspects of later Mahayana, however, have leaned towards the more ascetic practices. Early Buddhism also rejected theism in any form and was not dependent for its belief system on the existence of one or more deities. Gods which are featured in the Buddhist scriptures were part of the cosmic backcloth but played no part on the path of the individual to *nirvana.* It was Mahayana Buddhism which brought the more overt theistic practices and beliefs, characterized by the presence of the many Buddhas and *bodhisattvas* to whom religious, theistic practices could be devoted. Theravada Buddhism, however, maintains the belief that the Buddha himself did not achieve *nirvana* through the aid or intervention of any supranatural divine force, therefore human beings also can become perfected without such superhuman aid.

The Buddha encouraged individuals to work out their own salvation. In early Buddhism, the Buddha was a saviour only in as much as he taught the way to salvation. There is therefore an emphasis on *individual* effort and not on the idea that there need be any intermediary or inter-cessionary figure, human or divine, to assist one on his or her path. Thus early Buddhism did not believe that the effects of *karma* (Skt.) *kamma* (Pali) could be eradicated by some divine being. It was Mahayana Buddhism which developed the concept of such intermediaries, with its doctrine of *bodhisattvas,* a concept which in some schools of thought led to the acceptance of salvation through faith alone – a lessening of the rigidity of the law of *karma.*

As we shall see, Buddhism has a distinct belief in *anatman* (Skt.) or *anatta* (Pali); this is the doctrine of no-self, which does violence to the teaching of the *Upanisadic* sages. It stresses the belief that all life is impermanent and ever-changing, an ever-moving process of becoming and dying. There is no permanent inner essence such as the Hindu *atman* in Theravada Buddhism. Later Mahayana came to accept the presence of Buddha-nature in all things: this is an unchanging and permanent essence in the deepest part of the self. This doctrine of impermanence leads to a belief more in rebirth rather than reincarnation; rebirth suggesting a rebirth of the *karmic* energies of one life in the next, but without the stronger identification of personality and physical links which reincarnation suggests.

The Buddha rejected the class and caste systems, a policy which was perhaps typical of the Sakya tribe from which he came. The Buddha, we should remember, chose to reject his own class for the life of the wandering ascetic. Although he came to reject the ascetic path, too, preferring the Middle Way between asceticism and indulgence, a return to the privileges of his class was out of the question. For the Buddha, there was no place for class, caste or the superiority of the brahmin priesthood. He never accepted that discipleship in Buddhism was dependent on class, caste or occupation; rather, his emphasis was on mastering the mind to find the peace within. Nevertheless, although the early *Sangha* was open to everyone, its initial appeal was not to the less fortunate, as a sample of over three hundred monks and nuns shows:

> More than two-thirds of them came from large towns, and of these two-thirds 86 per cent from just four cities: Savatthi, Rajagaha, Kapilavatthu and Vesali. As for *varna*, of 328 religious 134 (about 40 per cent) were brahmin, 75 *ksatriya*, 98 *vaisya* and 11 *sudras*; 10 were outcastes. From various terms applied to their families we can further deduce that nearly half of them came from wealthy or powerful houses. Thus the brahmin recruits were not the traditional village priest but rather upper-class urbanities. If these figures have any foundation, they show that Buddhism, though it admitted anyone to the Sangha, was not primarily a religion of the downtrodden.[15]

The *dharma* of the Buddha

The word *dhamma* (Pali) *dharma* (Skt.) has different meanings in Indian thought: here it is used in the sense of "right" as opposed to "wrong". The basic teachings of the Buddha are the *dharmas*, the right ways or teachings about life. Indeed, Buddhists in Asia do not use the term "Buddhism", preferring to speak of the *dharma* of the Buddha. Before the Buddha's first teaching and after his Enlightenment, he drew a wheel on the ground. This symbolized the starting of the wheel of order, law or *dharma*, the wheel being an ancient Indian symbol. After drawing attention to the wheel of *dharma*, the Buddha expounded the importance of realizing the need for *dharma*. He taught the Four Noble Truths.

The Indian mind has long been tormented by the problem of *dukkha*, the realization that mankind will have to endure the suffering experienced not just in one lifetime, but in virtually countless lifetimes, some eighty-three thousand million lifetimes according to Hindu thought. This treadmill was seen by Indian philosophers as an "aimless wandering" through eternity, a continuous cycle of death and rebirth, repeated *ad infinitum*, appropriately termed *samsara*, "that which turns around forever". It was to the problem of suffering that the Buddha turned his attention. He urged his monks not to waste their time and energy speculating over metaphysical and philosophical problems such as how the world began, and how it would end; instead, they should direct their attention to the arising and cessation of suffering within their own being.

Because the Buddha recognized the problem, identified the cause of the problem, affirmed that there is a cure, and prescribed a remedy, it comes as no great surprise to find that his *dharma* is often compared to that of a medical practitioner, who writes a prescription for treating the human condition. This is why the Buddha is known as "the Great Physician". In his very first sermon in the Deer Park at Isipatana the Buddha set out the kernel of his *dharma*, as found in the Four Noble Truths. In the original texts these Four Truths are prescribed, appropriately, in capsule form, though there are many other early texts which expound the teachings thoroughly and frequently in a variety of ways. The Four Noble Truths are:

1 *Dukkha*
2 *Samudaya*, the root cause of *dukkha*
3 *Nirodha*, the end of *dukkha*
4 *Magga*, the way to end *dukkha*

The First Noble Truth: *dukkha*

Although tensions exist between *Upanisadic* and Buddhist thought, the problem of suffering *(dukkha)* is a common concern, the running sore of Indian philosophy. In both philosophical belief systems, release from suffering is accompanied by release from bondage and hence escape from the *samsaric* cycle, the attainment of *moksa* (Hinduism) or *nirvana* (Buddhism). Of the two, the *Upanisads* depict this ideal state in the more positive terms, describing it as "consciousness" or "bliss". For the Buddhist, however, realization of *nirvana* is described in negative terms, to be achieved by the annihilation of sorrow, the blowing out of the three defilements of desire/greed, hatred/anger, and delusion.

Both philosophical systems agree that this ultimate state is beyond description, for this would reduce it to the level of human understanding. The ultimate, however, is beyond comprehension, beyond experience, beyond language. But it is not beyond belief, any more than the person who has never experienced, and is quite incapable of describing, perfect health would deny that such a state exists. Both systems are also of one accord regarding the attainment of the ultimate:

> Both have to speak of the ultimate as devoid of empirical determinations, as incomparable to anything we know; silence is their most proper language. They also agree that no empirical means, organisational device, sacrifice or penance, can bring us to the goal. Only insight into the nature of the real can avail.[16]

It is here that the tensions between the two systems become manifest, however, to such an extent that they part company, for what is real to one is anathema to the other. For the *Upanisadic* sages, the real is the Self, is *atman*, is Brahman. It is the attachments to and associations with the Self's appurtenances in manifest existence which spin a web of deceit, delusion and unreality, placing limits upon that which is real and beyond limitation. In this light, it is clear that the Ultimate Reality, the Self/Brahman/*atman*, call it what you will, is beyond description, *neti neti* "not this, not that", beyond the senses and beyond human perception.

Accordingly, the reality of the *Upanisads* is not one of empirical knowledge, wherein the seers expound all they know of Brahman before a receptive audience. On the contrary, their starting point is an intuitive knowledge, over which they do not hold the exclusive rights. Theirs was the way not of expounding upon, but of drawing out, provoking the student into drawing on the wisdom which is inherent, though dormant, within us all. The *Upanisads* are unequivocal that bondage to the *samsaric* cycle is due entirely to ignorance *(avidya)*, the ignorance of knowledge of the Self. Realization of the Self *(atmakama)* in *Upanisadic* thought is the fulfilment of *(aptakama)* and hence the transcendence of *(akama)*, all desires; this is the sole means of overcoming the ignorance which binds mankind to the *samsaric* wheel of bondage.

To the Buddhist, however, any talk of an *atman* or permanent, unchanging Self, the very kernel of *Upanisadic* thought, is anathema, a false notion of manifest proportion. For the Buddha, what masquerades as a person is in fact no more than a bundle of five dynamic constituents. Notwithstanding the fact that the Buddha's *dharma* centred upon the problem of suffering, to give *dukkha* such a limited interpretation and conclude that the First Noble Truth's affirmation is "all life is suffering", is to misrepresent the Buddha's *dharma*.

Let it be said that the prominent feature of Buddhism is neither pessimism nor, for that matter, optimism, but realism. It is realistic in the sense that it sees the world for what it is and mankind for what it is, with no promises of rewards and threats of punishments from a Creator God who is all-knowing and all-seeing, an omnipotent God who resides "somewhere up there"; who created us imperfectly, yet for reasons best known to himself punishes us for our imperfections (or at very least does nothing to alleviate them). The reality of the situation, according to the Buddha's *dharma*, is that man is the author of his own destiny.

The Pali word *dukkha* is used as the direct opposite of *sukha*, which means being at "ease" in the sense of being happy or comfortable. It is therefore tempting to translate *dukkha* as "dis-ease" or "unsatisfactory", a comment on the ills of the world, the disharmony manifest in human existence. Although in common parlance, *dukkha* is undoubtedly used to convey the meaning of "suffering" in the sense of being in "pain" or "misery", it also has the nuance of "imperfection", "impermanence" or "emptiness". Rather than baldly translate *dukkha* as "suffering", and thereby misrepresent its many nuances in the First Noble Truth, following Rahula, I will leave the Pali word untranslated.[17]

The acceptance that *dukkha* permeates the whole of existence is not to affirm that there can be no place for happiness. Indeed, the many different forms happiness can take are clearly set out in the *Anguttara Nikaya*, while in the *Majjhima Nikaya* (both these early Pali texts contain original collections of the Buddha's discourses) the Buddha praises the blissful equanimity experienced in the high spiritual state of *dhyana*. However, all these states of happiness, which include physical and mental happiness, as well as the joy experienced in family life, sense pleasures and even *dhyana*, have one thing in common – impermanence. It is this common factor, especially the failure to recognize this commonality, which makes all things *dukkha*.

Buddhism is a belief system which regards reality as a process, a state of flux; unsurprisingly, this is known as Process Philosophy. For Buddhists, there is no such thing as a state of unchanging permanence: the real is never being, but forever in the process of coming to be, or becoming:

> According to Buddhism, whatever exists is a stream of becoming; nothing that exists is permanent. A beautiful but fragile blossom best exemplifies the Buddhist view of existence, for beautiful as it may be, it is clearly a passing phenomenon, as all who have seen the wind and rain driving newly opened cherry blossoms to the ground know very well. For one who thinks that these blossoms should be permanent this may seem tragic, but for someone who understands that change – the continuous rising and falling of existence – is the very nature of existence, the joy of seeing the beautiful blossoms is not destroyed by their falling. Only when this vast stream of becoming is mistaken for a conglomeration of *permanent things*, subject to various modifications, but nonetheless unchanging at their very core, does change threaten to destroy existence.[18]

It has been said already that Buddhism is neither pessimistic nor optimistic but realistic. The realism of the Buddha's *dharma* is conspicuous in his advice on happiness. Liberation from *dukkha* may be achieved only by the acceptance that all happiness is impermanent. Even within a loving family enriched with caring parents and happy children this happiness is not meant to be permanent; efforts to artificially enforce this supposed permanence will produce only unhappiness. In any event, even to talk of a permanent relationship is linguistic nonsense; since, according to the Buddha's teaching, no person can be considered to be a permanent entity, there can be no such thing as a permanent relationship. Whilst it is perfectly acceptable to enjoy any relationship while it lasts, to regard this relationship as immutable and thereby form permanent attachment is folly. Failure to recognize this basic fact can only induce heartache and suffering, yet day after day we continue to live our lives as if we will walk this planet at least for a couple of centuries, if not for all eternity![19] The *dukkha* produced with the realization that our happiest moments are precisely that – moments and no more – as well as the everyday suffering we encounter from unpleasant persons, conditions, or the like, are well known to us, and require no explanation. But there is another form of *dukkha*, known as *samkhara-dukkha*, which requires our attention. What in common language is spoken of as a "person", an "individual", or simply "I" or "me", was never viewed by the Buddha in the same light as non-Buddhists see it. For the Buddha, any being is not a permanent, unchanging self, but simply a combination of five aggregates or *khandhas* (Skt. *skandhas*); it is these five aggregates which *are dukkha*.

The five aggregates

It's not that I'm afraid of death, I just don't want to be there when it happens.   Woody Allen

The Buddha's statement that, contrary to popular belief, an individual has no permanent self or soul, but is really no more than a combination of five factors which are in a state of constant flux, is, by definition, an affirmation that the five factors of so-called individuality *are* suffering. Since these constituents which comprise what we normally call a "being" are constantly shifting, inevitably suffering will permeate every being's life at some time or other. The five aggregates are:

The Aggregate of Matter: The whole of matter is included here, including our five sense organs and the identifiable features recognized by our sense organs, such as those things which may be identified through being visible or audible. Also included are some of those thoughts and ideas which are about matter. *The Aggregate of Feelings or Sensations* which may be pleasant, unpleasant or neutral. The hair standing on the back of one's neck together with a cold chill down one's spine would be examples of the second aggregate. *The Aggregate of Perceptions* which recognize, identify and interpret the sensations experienced by our senses. In the above example it is this aggregate which would recognize the sensations in question as symptoms of fear. *The Aggregate of Mental Formations*: Time and again the Buddha stressed that *karma* can be produced only through volition. In other words the action must be intentional. In this *karma*-producing aggregate fifty-two volitional activities including hate and desire, wisdom and ignorance are to be found; also included is the fallacious idea of a self or *atman*. *The Aggregate of Consciousness*: This last aggregate is entirely dependent upon the previous four aggregates and does not constitute the equivalent of a self or soul.

Central to an understanding of the First Noble Truth is the realization that there is no more to (wo)man than the five attachment groups known as the five *skandhas*, and that these five groups are in a state of constant flux. In the course of this flux suffering must inevitably arise; therefore the five attachment groups *are dukkha*. This is really a doctrine of no *soul* rather than a doctrine of no *self*. As Michael Pye states:

> there is no central organising principle apart from these, which could be thought of as independent of them and which might have some spiritual destiny of its own. Thus the Buddha taught that there is no such thing as a disembodied soul, or for that matter a soul beyond our ordinarily constituted consciousness.[20]

The self is totally impermanent and in attempting to make things permanent it suffers. The five constituents are always changing and are never the same from one moment to the next. They continually create *karmic* forces which will re-group after the person has died; having created the forces the person must be reborn to experience the results. The Buddhist, therefore, has to put aside the concept of "I" and "mine" in order to be free from suffering. Edward Conze puts it very simply:

> Here is the idea of "I", a mere figment of the imagination, with nothing real to correspond to it. There are all sorts of processes going on in the world. Now I conjure up another figment of the imagination, the idea of "belonging", and come to the conclusion that some, not particularly well

defined portion of this world "belongs" to that "I" or to "me".[21]

So individuality has to be eliminated by ridding oneself of the belief in it. Conze further states:

> The insertion of a fictitious self into the actuality of our experience can be recognised wherever I assume that anything is mine, or that I am anything, or that anything is myself.[22]

Only through wisdom can we eliminate individuality. Wisdom involves the knowledge of impermanence – that everything is in a state of change, nothing ever becomes for everything is always becoming; of no-self in that there is no permanent unchanging "I" apart from the *skandhas*; and the knowledge that all life is *dukkha*, and the reason for this.

The Second Noble Truth: *samudaya*, the origin of *dukkha*

Recognition that suffering is caused, rather than just happening, is one of the hallmarks of the Buddha's greatness. For him, this was beyond question, indeed, it is the second of the Four Noble Truths. Having made this diagnosis, the Great Physician set about writing the prescription. The Buddha was unequivocal that once the factors upon which suffering is dependent are removed, suffering will cease.

To this end, and in keeping with the Indian concept of life as cyclical, Buddhists have designed what is generally known as the Wheel of Becoming *(bhavacakra)*. This is really a pictorial representation of the theory of dependent origination when applied to those processes which are said to make up what is normally described as the self. As the name implies, it represents the notion that *there are no beings, only becomings* in diagrammatic form. The three driving forces of ignorance, greed, and aversion are depicted at the hub of the wheel and are represented by a pig, a cockerel and a snake, each linked together, each biting the other's tail. The hub is surrounded by a circle with a black and a white half, depicting the *karmic* movement of beings ascending to a higher state and descending to a lower existence. Notwithstanding their denial that there are any clear-cut divisions between the processes which constitute a person, Buddhists have isolated an arbitrary twelve factors, in their efforts to demonstrate the causes of suffering.

If we start with *ignorance*, which is generally taken as the root cause of suffering (still bearing in mind that we are viewing a continuous process with no beginning and no end), the twelve factors may be listed as:

1 Ignorance	7 Perception
2 Impulses to action	8 Desire
3 Consciousness	9 Grasping
4 Body and Mind	10 Becoming
5 Six senses	11 Birth
6 Sense impressions	12 Old age and Death

Each of the twelve factors on the *bhavacakra* is generated by the preceeding factor,

> the arising and the falling of the various factors of existence constitutes the unending continuum of process that makes up reality. Human beings are caught up in this cycle, being born, suffering and dying; being born, suffering and dying, time after time. Life brings death and death brings life, as these are no more than phases in the eternal process.[23]

For the Buddhist, removal of the factors which cause suffering will bring about the elimination of suffering, but it is important to realise that the Buddha did not advocate nihilism. In other words, he did not teach that the elimination of suffering could only be achieved by the annihilation of life.

In order to appreciate what the Buddha did mean, we have to return to his teaching on the five *skandhas*, the dynamic bundle of constituents which make up a person, what most people would call the "self". The Buddha did not teach that there is no such thing as the self, but that there is no permanent, unchanging self; in other words there is nothing which could be said to constitute a self beyond the five *skandhas* – this is the theory of *anatta*. The "ignorance" referred to on the Wheel of Becoming is the delusion that as well as the five *skandhas* which constitute a person, within each person there also exists a self.

In this light, it is clear why ignorance is said to be the root cause of suffering. The delusion that a self exists beyond the five *skandhas* gives rise to the desires and aversions that this self experiences. It is then a short step to form attachments to this self, and so the suffering continues. In Buddhist eyes, living a life under the delusion that we all have a self in addition to the five *skandhas* is living a lie, and it is this lie which has to be annihilated, not life itself. Clearly, this teaching has nothing to do with nihilism. Accordingly, when we speak in terms of preventing "Birth" on the Wheel of Becoming in order to break the cycle and thereby negate suffering, the birth to which we refer is not life itself, but the birth of the ego. This is the key to the end of suffering.

Dependent Origination

Furthermore, there can be no belief in a first cause in Buddhism since everything is said to depend upon something else; this cyclical concept is known as dependent origination, conditioned genesis, or *paticca-samuppada*. This concept is one of the cornerstones of Buddhist philosophy, and was acknowledged as such by Sakyamuni:

> Oh Monks, one who understands this doctrine of dependent origination understands the Dharma; one who understands the Dharma, understands this doctrine of dependent origination.

Since this principle holds that everything in existence depends upon something else, then any talk of linear causality becomes vacuous, causality must be cyclical. This thesis is discernible in the life-cycle of the apple. The apple depends for its creation upon the blossom, which depends on the bough, which depends on the trunk, which depends on the roots, which depend on the soil, which in order to create new life depends on the seeds, which come from the apple. This is the cyclical view of creation which is ongoing, has no beginning, and no end.

If we superimpose the allegory of the apple upon the theory of dependent origination, we produce a fourfold formulation:

1   If the tree blossoms it will bear fruit. So if A exists, B comes into being.
2   If the tree bears fruit, seed will return to the earth. If this arises, that arises.
3   If there is no blossom, there can be no fruit. If there is no A, there will be no B.
4   If the tree bears no fruit, seed will not fall to the earth. If this stops, that stops.

There can be nothing which stands outside this cyclical concept of creation, since everything is entirely dependent for its existence on something else. To speak of a Creator God, existing outside and entirely independent of his creation, upon whom his creation is entirely dependent, is untenable in Buddhist logic. In Buddhist thought, there can be no such thing as divine birth, since this would negate the cycle of dependence.

Accordingly, we cannot speak of *dukkha*, nor of anything else for that matter, having a first cause. What the Buddha did identify, however, is an immediate (if not the only) cause of *dukkha*. The early texts are unequivocal that this cause is *tanha*:

> It is this "thirst" (craving, *tanha*) which produces re-existence and re-becoming (*ponobhavika*), and which is bound up with passionate greed (*nandiragahagata*), and which finds fresh delight now here and now there (*tatratatrabhinandini*), namely, (1) thirst for sense pleasures (*kama-tanha*), (2) thirst for existence and becoming (*bhava-tanha*) and (3) thirst for non-existence (self-annihilation, *vibhava-tanha*).[24]

At the heart of the problem lies the false notion, caused by ignorance, that we have a permanent Self *(atman)*, and that this self has to be appeased, protected and prolonged. This introduces a craving, desire or thirst *(tanha)* to satisfy this so-called self. To this end, mankind embraces a whole gamut of ploys to satiate this thirst and thereby satisfy this supposed self. The folly is that the craving self-perpetuates not only the craving, but life itself, condemning mankind to continued rebirth on the *samsaric* cycle of aimless wandering. The greater the desire to satisfy becomes, the more mankind perpetuates the craving which is the palpable cause of suffering; this, according to the Great Physician, is the cause of all the ills of the world.

To dissociate oneself from the false concept of a self, on the other hand, has quite the opposite effect. Freedom from this belief, leads to freedom from rebirth and escape from the *samsaric* cycle. Thus for the *arahant*, the enlightened human being of Theravada Buddhism, liberation from *samsaric* bondage is assured. Since the *arahant* has no notion of an *atman* or permanent self, selfish desires are not present in his thoughts, nor do they manifest themselves in his actions. He certainly performs actions, but these actions are devoid of *tanha* and therefore do not produce *karma* (good or bad), which is responsible for rebirth. Damien Keown makes the interesting observation that Buddhist sources often speak of desire in a positive light, thereby distinguishing between excessive or wrongly directed desire *(tanha)* and desire described in more positive terms *(chanda)*. On this view, not *all* desire is wrong:

> Whereas wrong desires restrict and fetter, right desires enhance and liberate. We might use smoking as an example to illustrate the difference.

The desire of a chain-smoker for another cigarette is *tanha*, since its aim is nothing more than short-term gratification. Such a desire is compulsive, limiting and cyclic: it leads nowhere but to the next cigarette (and, as a side effect to ill health). The desire of a chain-smoker to give up smoking, on the other hand, would be a virtuous desire since it would break the cyclic pattern of a compulsive negative habit and enhance health and well-being.[25]

This is a nice point, because *any* form of desire (good or bad) will produce *karma*, and *karma* causes rebirth. This will need further examination when we look at the concept of *karma*, and particularly when we come to look at the Buddhism of Nichiren Daishonin.

The Third Noble Truth: the cessation of *dukkha* – *nirodha*

The Third Noble Truth affirms that release from *dukkha* is attainable by the elimination of *tanha*, the thirst or craving to satiate the supposed self. This extinction of craving *(Tanhakkhaya)* is known as *nirvana* (Pali *nibbana*). At this point the interested reader could well expect a description, or at very least an explanation, of *nirvana* to follow, and there is no shortage of such description and explanation to be found in those sections marked "Buddhism" in our libraries and bookshops. Furthermore, if language is the high water-mark of our civilization, it would seem reasonable to expect finite definition(s) of what *nirvana* is to be within the compass of accomplished writers.

Such definitions, though, have raised more problems than they have solved, for we are dealing here with Absolute Truth and Ultimate Reality, which are beyond language. We said earlier that if the Buddha's Enlightenment could be explained then it wouldn't be Enlightenment: the same could be said of *nirvana*. Our task is not to understand *nirvana* but to realize it.

The Fourth Noble Truth: the Path or the Way – *magga*

Having gained experience of both the sensual and the ascetic ways of life, the Buddha concluded that neither was satisfactory. Accordingly, he set out to teach a path to *nirvana* which followed neither of these two extremes, but which was actually a middle path between them, more popularly known as the Middle Way or the Noble Eightfold Path. It should not be thought that the Buddha taught this Way "one fine day" nor that the path must be walked step by step in a linear fashion. Rather, the teaching that the Buddha gave over forty-five years advocated developing these attributes contemporaneously and simultaneously as far as one is able. To illustrate his *dharma* the Buddha drew a wheel on the ground, the wheel being a well-known symbol in Indian thought. To this wheel he added eight spokes, his point being that all eight spokes must function simultaneously in order for the wheel to operate smoothly. By the same token, the Buddhist cannot pick and choose those aspects of the Noble Eightfold Path which are appealing, but must try to practise them all at once.

In the Four Noble Truths the Great Physician drew attention to man's malaise, and in the Noble Eightfold path he prescribed the cure for this malaise. The prescription takes into account man's thoughts, as well as his actions and can be divided into three broad sections, which deal with Wisdom *panna* (Skt. *prajna*), Ethical conduct *sila*, and Mental discipline *samadhi*.

Wisdom *(panna)*
1 Right understanding.
2 Right thought

Ethical conduct *(sila)*
3 Right speech.
4 Right action/morality and conduct.
5 Right livelihood.

Mental discipline *(samadhi)*
6 Right effort.
7 Right mindfulness.
8 Right concentration, or state of mind.

Right understanding (Samma ditthi)

Central to right understanding are three basic doctrines of Buddhism – *dukkha*, *anatta* and *anicca*. The student of Buddhism will have studied the concept of *dukkha* as set out in the Four Noble Truths. *Anatta* (Skt. *anatman*) is the teaching that there is no such thing as a permanent, unchanging essence in sentient beings, in other words no self, soul, or spirit which lives on long after the mortal body has died. The Buddha taught that beyond the five *skandhas*, the five aggregates which are in constant flux, there is nothing – a point exemplified in the teaching of a second-century BCE monk named Nagasena.

The concept of a permanent, immutable self, or *atman*, which constitutes the very heart of *Upanisadic* thinking, in Buddhist eyes is seen to be no more real than the constituent parts of the chariot of the Greek King Menander. The following passage from the *Questions of King Menander (Milindapanha)*, is an oft-adduced argument put forward to support the idea of the composite nature of the individual:

The King Menander went up to the Venerable Nagasena, greeted him respectfully, and sat down. Nagasena replied to the greeting, and the King was pleased at heart. Then King Menander asked: "How is your reverence known, and what is your name?"

"I'm known as Nagasena, your Majesty, that's what my fellow monks call me. But though my parents may have given me such a name . . . it's only a generally understood term, a practical designation. There is no question of a permanent individual implied in the use of the word."

"Listen, you five hundred Greeks and eighty thousand monks!" said King Menander."This Nagasena has just declared that there's no permanent individuality implied in his name!" Then, turning to Nagasena, "If, Reverend Nagasena, there is no permanent individuality, who gives you monks your robes and food, lodging and medicines? And who makes use of them? Who lives a life of righteousness, meditates, and reaches Nirvana? Who destroys living beings, steals, fornicates, tells lies, or drinks spirits? . . . If what you say is true there's neither merit nor demerit, and no fruit or result of good or evil deeds. If someone were to kill you there would be no question of murder. And there would be no masters or teachers in the [Buddhist] Order and no ordinations. If your fellow monks call you Nagasena, what then is Nagasena? Would you say that your hair is Nagasena?" "No you Majesty."

"Or your nails, teeth, skin, or other parts of your body, or the outward form, or sensation, or perception, or the psychic constructions, or consciousness? Are any of these Nagasena?" "No, your Majesty."

"Then are all these taken together Nagasena?" "No, your Majesty."

"Or anything other than they?" "No, your Majesty."

"Then for all my asking I find no Nagasena. Nagasena is a mere sound! Surely what your Reverence has said is false!"

Then the Venerable Nagasena addressed the King.

"Your Majesty, how did you come here — on foot, or in a vehicle?"

"In a chariot."

"Then tell me what is the chariot? Is the pole the chariot?" "No, your Reverence."

"Or the axle, wheels, frame, reins, yoke, spokes, or goad?" "None of these things is the chariot."

"Then all these separate parts taken together are the chariot?" "No, your Reverence."

"Then is the chariot something other than the separate parts?" "No, your Reverence."

"Then for all my asking, your Majesty, I can find no chariot, The chariot is a mere sound. What then is the chariot? Surely what your Majesty has said is false! There is no chariot! . . . "

When he had spoken the five hundred Greeks cried "Well done!" and said to the King, "Now, your Majesty, get out of that dilemma if you can!"

"What I said was not false," replied the King. "It's on account of all these various components, the pole, axle, wheels, and so on, that the vehicle is called a chariot. It's just a practically understood term, a practical designation."

"Well said, your Majesty! You know what the word 'chariot' means! And it's just the same with me. It's on account of the various components of my being that I'm known by the generally understood term, the practical designation, Nagasena."

In this light, what is commonly supposed to be an individual "living being", or "soul", which gives warrant to the affirmation "I am . . . ", is nothing more than a combination of the five *skandhas*.

In modern terms it may be prudent to cite the case of the disgruntled father who wants his daughter to forsake her studies and seek employment rather than begin a university education. The father's wishes are resisted, however, for the student is determined. Still not convinced that his daughter has made the right choice, the father demands to be shown the university, for he wants to see it for himself. As they walk through the grounds the father sees a rugby match in progress and asks if this is the university. The daughter explains that these are the university playing fields. He is then taken to the library where he asks the same question. The tour then embraces the dining halls, faculty offices, the student village, computer suites, language and science laboratories, admissions office, lecture theatres and tutorial rooms, but there is no "university" to be seen. The bewildered father leaves the campus still wondering why he hasn't seen the "university", quite unaware that the term is merely a convenient designation for its component parts. Without these components there can be no university, but even with them it is nowhere to be found. So it is with the five *skandhas* and the supposed "self". Clearly, the father lacked understanding, for right understanding is the ability to see things as they really are, as set out in the Four Noble Truths.

The third doctrine basic to understanding things as they really are is the doctrine of *anicca*. This teaches that there is no such thing as permanence, for nothing ever is; rather, everything is in a state of becoming. As surely as the five aggregates which constitute what we call a person are constantly changing, so too is everything else. Lack of understanding perpetuates suffering as we strive to hold on to that which is impermanent – life and relationships being two notable examples. Right understanding, on the other hand, negates ignorance, one of twelve causal links which perpetuate the continuous cycle of death and rebirth known as *samsara*. With right understanding of things as they really are, the craving for attachment to people and possessions which causes so much misery becomes vacuous, and suffering is negated.

Right thought (Samma sankappa)

> What we are today comes from our thoughts of yesterday, and our present thoughts build our life of tomorrow: our life is the creation of our mind. If a man speaks or acts with an impure mind, suffering follows him as the wheel of the cart follows the beast that draws the cart.
> *Dhammapada* 1.1 (trans. Juan Mascaro)

According to the *Dhammapada*, we as persons are the result of our thoughts; change these thoughts, and we change ourselves. So right thought or attitude implies that in your wisdom you want to be changed and cured. You must want to escape from believing that you are permanent, from the burden of *karma* and from the trials of craving, aversion, anger, covetousness and foolishness, all of which are *karmic* producing states of mind, all of which perpetuate the endless round of death and rebirth. Drawing an analogy between rebirth and the burning of a flame, the Buddha claimed that if a man is still aflame at death, with wrong attitudes and desires, the lamp will be re-lit in another life.

Having dealt with wisdom, the next four steps along the path concern moral conduct.

Right speech (Samma vaca)

Man's speech must be compatible with the Buddha's *dharma*, that is, he must speak the truth, his conversation must be edifying, and he must not engage in scandal and gossip. One should take care with one's words, not only for the sake of truth but to demonstrate control and discipline.

Right action (Samma kammanta)

Right action is the expectation of correct moral behaviour. Since the word *karma* means "action" (not "action and reaction" as is commonly assumed in the West) our actions must be right in order to produce the right results and so end suffering. The Buddha made clear that it is the *intention* behind the action which is of ultimate significance, not unintentional action of an incoherent mind:

> It is choice or intention that I call karma – mental work —, for having chosen a man acts by body, speech and mind. A III 415

The five moral precepts which every Buddhist should follow are outlined in the *Pancha Sila*.

Right livelihood (Samma ajiva)

Right livelihood should be maintained in accordance with the *Pancha Sila* as well as being non-exploitive and generous in spirit. Any occupation which brings harm to others, such as the manufacture or sale of arms, tobacco, poisons, alcohol, gambling, or harm to other creatures such as butchery, hunting or vivisection are anathema to Buddhists, for these are the lifeblood of suffering.

Right effort (Samma vayama)

We can only rely on our own individual effort to realize *nirvana*. This implies continuous hard effort and striving. For the Buddha, effort meant putting theory into practice, eliminating evil thoughts and cultivating good thoughts. In the *Dhammapada* the Buddha states that, "Little beautiful flowers full of colour but without scent are the well chosen words of the man who does not act accordingly." Right effort is the conscious will to overcome the undesirable and unwholesome states of mind to which we, being human, are prone, and to prevent the development of similar thoughts; to promote the development of good, wholesome thoughts and to maintain these.

Right mindfulness (Samma sati)

Right mindfulness is a mindful awareness of four main areas of consideration, bodily activities *(kaya)*; feelings or sensations *(vedana)*;

activities of the mind *(citta)*; and the arising and control of thoughts and ideas.

In connection with the body, special measures are required to rid ourselves of ignorance and enhance our mental development; concentration on breathing *(anapanasati)* being one of them. Concentration (yoga) leads eventually to enlightenment; there being stage by stage progressions which develop this. In connection with activities of the mind, we should be aware that our minds have a propensity to lean towards one or more of the three defilements – greed, hatred and delusion – and one should act accordingly to overcome this inclination. It has been well said that the only common factor *all* Buddhists have is the will to control (but not "suppress"!) the three defilements.

Right concentration – state of mind (Samma samadhi)

In this state, the Buddhist is able to free the mind from all external thoughts and images which are disturbing or unwholesome. Right concentration refers specifically to the use of meditation as a vehicle to control and discipline the mind, to lose the sense of ego. The unfocused, indisciplined mind in its normal desultory state is quite unsuited to perceive Ultimate Truth, but meditation enables the Buddhist to do just this.

Meditation, therefore, helps the Buddhist to catch ever-increasing glimpses of the Truth, until *nirvana* is achieved. *Nirvana* means "blowing out": the blowing out of the fires of greed, hatred and delusion, and hence the end of suffering. The Buddha once said of *nirvana*:

> There is a sphere which is neither earth, nor water, nor fire, nor air, which is not the sphere of the infinity of space, nor the sphere of the infinity of consciousness, the sphere of nothingness, the sphere of perception, or non-perception, which is neither this world nor the other world, neither sun nor moon. I deny that it is coming or going, enduring, death, or birth. It is only the end of suffering.

The *Pancha Sila*

Central to the ethical principles of Buddhism is the *Sutta Pitaka*, the second of the *Tipitaka* (three baskets) in the Theravadin scriptures. The basic moral beliefs are shared by both schools. The *Sutta Pitaka* includes within its collection the *Pancha Sila* or five ethical precepts of

Buddhism, and the *Dhammapada*, consisting of 423 verses of sayings of the Buddha. The *Pancha Sila* lays down specific rules of moral conduct which are really an enlargement on the fourth stage of the Noble Eightfold Path.

1 To abstain from taking life

This means abstaining from killing anything that lives. The crime is proportionate to the strength of the desire to kill. Five factors are involved here:

(i)   the presence of a living being, human or animal.
(ii) the realization or perception that it is a living being.
(iii) the intention to murder.
(iv) the action of murdering the living being.
(v)   the resulting death.

The individual who deliberately takes the life of a living being will reap dire consequences in the next life. Important also, is whether life is taken at one's own hand or by instigation. So this first precept implies pacifism. Butchering, hunting and warfare are traditionally abhorrent to the Buddhist. This presents some moral predicaments for the practising Buddhist in contemporary life.

Saddhatissa in *The Buddha's Way* has commented on this question of the application of non-violence and non-killing, particularly concerning stage five of the Noble Eightfold Path which stresses "Right livelihood". He raises certain questions:

(a)   Can one support "by working, paying taxes and accepting benefits, a government which is engaged in warfare, or actively preparing for it?"
(b)   Can one "in the name of the relief of human suffering, engage in medical research that involves sacrificing the lives of countless animals and, more subtly, can one prescribe, sell - or even use - those drugs which have been discovered and treated by means of such experiments?"
(c)   Can one destroy "possible disease-bearing" insects, or work in the preparation of materials for that purpose?

For some Buddhists today, it is debatable whether animals should be killed for food. This seems to be a question of interpretation as well as a matter of culture, many Japanese Buddhists being traditional fish eaters. Some Buddhists are strict vegetarians, others interpret the Buddha's teaching on this to suggest moderation, eating without indulgence. For the Buddha, however, one's relationship with all living things should be so close that to harm any living creature is tantamount to harming oneself. The Buddha taught that true sacrifice was not in the form of animals for worship or food, but of one's own selfish motives. The greatest sacrifice is made by the person who abstains from taking life and follows the remaining four precepts.

2   To abstain from taking what is not given

As surely as the first precept is wider than the edict "Thou shalt not kill", so is the second precept wider than the law "Thou shalt not steal". Two interesting qualifications are laid on this rule of conduct. The severity of the sin depends on :

(a)   the value of the property stolen
(b)   the worth of the owner.

Traditionally, although a Theravadin monk is allowed to carry a begging bowl, he must never ask nor beg for anything, but rely for sustenance on the generosity of the laity (who will offer him food only too willingly in order to accrue good *karma*).

3   To abstain from sensuous misconduct

This is seen in terms of (i) mental misconduct, that is, the will to enter into forbidden relationships, and (ii) physical misconduct in terms of the physical action itself. Homosexuality is completely forbidden, and taboos on females fall into two main categories :
(a)   those who are within kinship relations who are also "claimed".
(b)   those in a subservient position or "bought" women, e.g. servants, concubines, war-captives, etc.

4   To abstain from false speech

This covers all types of deception, even deceitful body language. Hypocrisy seems an apt description here. To mislead someone willingly or to misrepresent something is morally wrong. Here, again, different degrees of moral transgression are noted. For example:

If a householder, unwilling to give something, says that he has not got it, that is a small offence, but to represent something one has seen with one's own eyes as other than one has seen it, that is a serious offence.[26]

5   To abstain from intoxicants

This refers to alcohol and all drugs. The essence of this precept is that one must have control over oneself, and one's mind must not be clouded. Drugs and alcohol involve dependence on externally induced alteration of one's consciousness.

These then are the five precepts, and within them, abstention can take place at three levels.

(a)   at the intuitive level: we may feel that it is wrong to take life in a particular situation and actually refrain from doing so.

(b)   at the level of formal commitment to the principles, even at the expense of one's own life.

(c)   at the level of the saintly holy man who, on the Eightfold Path, has lost all inclinations and temptation to engage in practices which are not right.

The *Dhammapada* gives many other moral principles to be observed by Buddhists. Similar to the Christian ethic of "turning the other cheek" is the Buddhist teaching on forgiveness, "'He abused me, he struck me, he overcame me, he robbed me' – in those who harbour such thoughts hatred will never cease." The Buddhist should avoid inflicting suffering:

That action only is "well-done" which brings no suffering in its train.

An additional three precepts soon followed the original five. These *Eight Precepts* were followed by early monks and the additions included what soon came to be regarded as a prohibition on eating after midday; abstaining from dancing, singing and revelry's attendant dress and cosmetics; and abstaining from using high seats or high beds, both normally associated with the wealthy. By dividing the *Eight Precepts* into nine and adding the prohibition not to accept gold or silver even when they are offered as gifts, *Ten Precepts* were formed. Many other rules were added and accepted by the monks of early Buddhism.

Sila, Samadhi, Panna

The Buddha's teachings fall into three broad categories – *sila*, *samadhi* and *panna*. The discourses have been given this authoritative grouping by compilers who have arranged the material in a manner which gives it a cumulative order. By way of illustration, we may consider the *Samannaphala* discourse, found in the *sutta* of the same name, otherwise known as "The Fruits of the Life of a Recluse".

The discourse begins with an account of the rising up of an *arahant*. According to Theravada Buddhism, an *arahant* is a perfected being in whom ignorance, desire, wrong views and becoming have ceased. Derived possibly from *ari* "enemy", and *han* "to kill", an *arahant* is one who has "killed the enemy", the enemy being "desire". Alternative derivations include *arhati* "to be worthy of", which would render a meaning to *arahant* of "one who is worthy and deserving". An *arahant* has no sense of *I* or *mine*, but is dispassionate and totally free from attachment. *Arahants* were trained to achieve perfection in three areas – moral discipline, concentration and wisdom. In Pali, these are translated as *sila*, *samadhi* and *panna*. Having abandoned all that is foolish in word and deed, the *arahant*'s speech is considered to be a hidden treasure.

Sila

Time and again, Buddhist scriptures warn of the danger of approaching *samadhi* and *panna* without a thorough grounding in *sila*. The fact that the first of the three categories in the *Samannaphala* discourse is the section on moral discipline is quite intentional. However, It is to the *Dhammapada* we must turn for the key to Buddhist ethics:

Mind precedes all things; all things have mind foremost, are mind made.

Indeed, this is the kernel of all Buddhist teaching, *for Buddhism is essentially a mind culture*. No person can advance (nor retard, for that matter) unless the seed for thought is first in the mind. Thus, the well-disciplined, indeed morally-disciplined, mind is a prerequisite for advancement to *samadhi* and *panna*. It is not only folly, but extremely dangerous, to attempt to progress to *samadhi* and *panna* without first attaining moral discipline. By the same token, the attainment of moral discipline should be supported by cultivating *samadhi* and *panna*, for neither morality nor wisdom can exist in a vacuum.

An *arahant* is trained to feel disgust for his body. Moral discipline took the form of learning to see the body as disgusting and repulsive, composing 32 parts, the last twelve of which are:

> bile, digestive juices, pus, blood, grease, fat, tears, sweat, spittle, snot, fluid of the joints, and urine.   *Samyutta Nikaya* 1: 62

An *arahant* who holds this view of the body is hardly likely to find it an object of passion and desire!

Samadhi

Having enjoined the *bhikkhu* (novitiate) to the importance of *sila*, the *Samannaphala* discourse proceeds to a discussion of *samadhi*. *Samadhi*, the second important aspect of *arahant* training, refers to the calming of the mind, when one has withdrawn from sense stimuli. This Sanskrit word is normally translated "concentration", experienced in a trance-like state, but wherein one still has mindfulness and awareness. Evil thoughts and desires disappear, and one experiences an inner peace and harmony, a contentment with simplicity. The state of *samadhi* is often described as a flame which is totally still, quite unaffected by even the slightest breeze. *Samadhi* involves "guarding the doors of the senses". The *bhikkhu* cannot avoid *experiencing* sense stimuli, but he can avoid *reacting* to them. Once the mind can be guarded against such invasion, it can evolve. Within *samadhi* are three practices – *the eight dhyanas, the four unlimited,* and *occult power.*

The eight dhyanas

The eight *dhyanas* are the stages by which one gradually transcends the field of sense perception, until one can "touch *nirvana* with one's body". Such proximity to *nirvana* does not mean that final salvation is now achieved, for the experience lasts only while practising the *dhyanas*. In later Buddhism, the Yogacarin school of thought concentrated particularly on this aspect of Buddhism.

The Buddhist term *nirvana* means "blowing out", and endless confusion has been caused by western writers who, in their misunderstanding, have interpreted this to mean the cessation of life. They conclude that, because of its emphasis on suffering, Buddhism seems to have a negative goal of extinction. *Nirvana*, so the argument goes, is the "blowing out" of the person or soul. How *nirvana* can have this meaning when the

Buddha, in his second sermon, taught that beings have no soul, these writers never make clear. To suggest that a being with no soul can have the soul he never possessed "blown out", is linguistic nonsense. *Nirvana* does mean "blowing out", but it has nothing to do with the cessation of life: what must be blown out are the three roots of evil – greed, hatred and delusion.

Nirvana, then, should not be seen as extinction, but as *extinguishing* the self-centred, self-assertive life. This is the destruction of the separate ego through which the world takes on its illusory form. Thus in *nirvana* reality is *realized*, not lost, as "the drop slips into the sea". *Nirvana* represents communion and mergence with all that is, it is a *oneness*. The Buddha once said of this wholeness or "thusness" of things:

> There is, O monks, an Unborn, Unoriginated, Uncreated, Unformed. Were there not, O monks, this Unborn, Unoriginated, Uncreated, Unformed, there would be no escape from the world of the born, originated, created, formed.   *Udana* 80–81

The Brahmavihara

In Theravada Buddhism, the *Brahmavihara* (otherwise known as the four unlimited), consist of four sublime states of mind:

metta	—	love
karuna	—	compassion
mudita	—	sympathetic joy
upekkha	—	serenity

The importance given to the *Brahmavihara* is exemplified in the fact that this was one of the major aspects of Buddhism taken up by early Mahayanists.

Metta: Metta means "love" or "active good will". *Metta* is the first of the *Brahmavihara*, and is a sublime state of consciousness in which loving-kindness is radiated to all humanity. This is an injunction to universal love. *Metta* is concerned with every quarter of the world, and all its inhabitants, to whom love should be given. Loving-kindness must become a quality of the thinker's mind.

> So let a man cultivate love without measure towards the whole world . . . this state of mind is the best in the world.   The Discourse on Universal Love, *The Metta Sutta*

The Discourse contains the express wish for the happiness of all beings:

May all beings be happy and at their ease. May they be joyous and live in safety. All beings whether weak or strong – omitting none – in high, middle or low realms of existence, small or great, visible or invisible, near or far away, born or to be born – may all beings be happy and at their ease. Let none deceive another, or despise any being in any state; let none by anger or ill-will wish to harm another!

It is appropriate that *metta* should be the first of the *Brahmavihara*, for the Buddha taught by example that we should serve and love others. He is depicted as delaying his *nirvana* for the benefit of others and as caring for others by actively seeing to their needs.

The Buddha continued his discourse by declaring that as surely as a powerful trumpeter is capable of making the sound of his trumpet carry to every quarter of the world, so the *bhikkhu* suffused with loving kindness will not keep his own council. The discourse was delivered to one Vasettha, a young brahmin ernestly seeking the way to "union with Brahma". Vasettha is urged to radiate this loving-kindness throughout his travels – this is how to achieve "union with Brahma". Keeping to the simile of the trumpeter, the Buddha next explains how the *bhikkhu* imbues his thought with compassion *(karuna)*, sympathy for the welfare of others *(mudita)*, and equanimity *(upekkha)*. In the West, there has been a tendency to regard these three practices as less important than *metta*, since western translations of the text are only complete in the case of *metta*: such interpretation of the relative importance of the four practices has no warrant. Nor is there any place in Buddhist vocabulary for the phrase, "union with Brahma". This was a phrase introduced into the conversation by Vasettha – the Buddha merely took up the expression in a language which was familiar to the young brahmin.

Karuna: As a result of *metta*, *karuna* is generated. This, the second of the *Brahmavihara*, is best translated "compassion", and is one of the two pillars of Mahayana Buddhism, the other being "wisdom". *Karuna* is the complete identification of oneself with the suffering of others, having total empathy with the sufferer.

Mudita: *Mudita*, the third of the *Brahmavihara*, is the ideal of sharing joy and happiness. Besides one's own joy, this includes the ability to be joyful and happy because others are happy. One should share the joy of others even when one is not personally involved in the circumstances of that joy.

Upekkha: *Upekkha* is equanimity and serenity. The fourth of the *Brahmavihara* suggests a balanced, calm approach to life when one is not swayed by excitement or one's own ego. What it most certainly is not is "indifference" – rather it is the ability to be active in the world without the involvement of the ego.

Occult power

Occult power became an important expression of later Tantric Buddhism. It was said to be the result of practising the Buddha's *dhyanas.* It involved clairvoyance, knowledge of former births, mind-reading, walking on water and through solid structures, levitation and the performance of many other miracles.

Panna

In Theravada Buddhism *sila, samadhi* and *panna* are the three doctrines often used to epitomize Buddhism, but it is the last of these, *panna* (Pali) or "wisdom" (Skt. *prajna*), which is the key to Theravada Buddhism. While the *dhyanas,* the stages of trance, can take one to the door of *nirvana,* only with wisdom can one enter. *Wisdom* pervades all *dharmas* and teachings of the Buddha, and the methods for developing it are to be found in the literature of the *Abhidamma.* The most important aspect of Buddhism and the key to *nirvana* is the wisdom which shows that separate individuality cannot exist.

3

The Theravadin Doctrine

Monastic life

Everything the Buddha taught was delivered orally; throughout his lifetime he wrote nothing. Indeed, a supposedly complete record of the Buddha's teachings was not committed to writing until some four centuries after his death. Nor did his uniquely precious legacy propose any consistent system of philosophy or metaphysics, for his thrust of thought centred upon the practicalities of spiritual liberation. This omission was soon rectified, and an in-depth analysis of the Buddha's teachings began to develop which became known as the *Abhidamma* or "Higher *Dharma*". However, within a century or so of the Buddha's death, this body of theory and commentary compiled by a succession of *Sanghas* was causing disagreement. One of the seven component works which now comprise this "Higher *Dharma*" refutes more than two hundred opinions held by other Buddhist schools and identifies those doctrines peculiar to the Theravada.

Consequently, various schools of thought came into being. Within a century or so of the Buddha's demise, a group of monks calling themselves "the great *Sangha* party", the *Mahasanghika*, had left the mainstream *Sangha* to become what many scholars believe to be the seed of Mahayana Buddhism. Prior to the rise of the Mahayana around the beginning of the common era, eighteen schools had evolved, each centred about a particular point of contention concerning the *Abhidhamma*; only one of these early Indian Buddhist schools survived, the Theravada. The name derives from the elders who convened the First Great Council immediately following the death of the Buddha; Theravada means "Doctrine of the Elders". This is not to say that the term was coined at the First Great Council; as yet there was no division of opinion which would prove germane to a variety of schools.

Theravada Buddhism specifically advocates monastic life. Some

Mahayana Buddhists have raised the objection that the teaching contains little for the layman and its message is unequivocal – if a man wishes to make any spiritual progress he must become a monk. These writers object that monks do not fulfil a functional role for the benefit of the community, other than to act as recipients for the generosity of the laity, who thereby accrue good *karma*. The monk has no other function in the community; his goal is his own salvation, not to be useful in society. He will not provide religious services for the laity with the notable exception of funerals where, with his preoccupation with death, the monk will officiate and preach.

Although it is true to say that the monk is not a country parson, those who raise these objections overlook the fact that the *Sangha* is regarded by Theravadins as the ideal state of Buddhism. In fact, the inter-relation-ship between *Sangha* and community is its essential and original contribution to Theravada Buddhism. The *Sangha* relies upon the laity for its material needs, and the laity depends upon the monks for its spir-itual needs, so that the Buddha's *dharma* is both preserved and disseminated. In the East today, the acceptance of food and alms is an integral part of the relationship between the *Sangha* and the community, so much so that the main festivals and celebrations often terminate with a great *dana* or offering of food or robes for the monks. Indeed, the objection that monks are of little benefit to the community is wide of the mark:

> the criticism is somewhat overstressed. Theravada doctrine is based on *panna*, which is wisdom (Sanskrit *prajna*), but basic to Theravada Buddhism are the *brahma-vihara*, four sublime states – the suffusing of the world with loving kindness (*metta*), compassion (*karuna*), sympa-thetic joy (*mudita*), and equanimity (*upekkha*). A monk's concentration on spreading these four sublime states to the whole world . . . suggests that the monk is not so divorced from concern for the welfare of all humanity.[1]

We have already noted that there was certainly a mutually successful relationship amongst the king, the people and the *Sangha*. The *Sangha* advised the king, and at the same time advised the laity to obey the king. Meanwhile, the king not only patronized the *Sangha* but encouraged the people to support the monks. This support was considerable and shows how early Buddhism appealed to all levels of society, which is just as well, for the monks were entirely dependent on the laity for food and alms. The task of the Theravadin monk is to preserve the *dharma*, and there are still monks in the Far East today who can recite major portions of the Theravadin scriptures. This acquaintance with the *dharma* is then utilized by the monk in his teaching of the laity.

For the vast majority of Buddhists in Theravadin countries, however, the order of monks is seen by lay Buddhists as a means of gaining the most merit in the hope of accumulating good *karma* for a better rebirth. The monk's duty is to save himself and the laity sees its duty as providing for the monk's material needs in the form of offerings or *dana* in order to acquire merit to effectuate a better rebirth:

> We can define two aspects of Burmese Theravada Buddhism where conflicting views of salvation are held, namely *nibbanic* and *kammatic* Buddhism. *Nibbanic* Buddhism concern's the monk's aim to reach *Nibbana*, whereas *kammatic* Buddhism concerns the lay Buddhist's aim to achieve good *kamma* for a better rebirth.[2]

Upon the Buddha's death, teaching the Buddha's *dharma* to the laity came quickly and naturally to the early monks, all of which was done through oral recitation, there being no writing in India until the reign of Asoka, some one hundred and fifty years later.

Nor were women accorded equal respect in those times. When speaking to Ananda, the Buddha made plain that he regarded women as a distraction, "You should shun their gaze, Ananda." He appears to have regarded women with distrust, "Keep wide awake, Ananda", his disciple was warned. In the *Anguttara Sutta* it clearly states that one must be born male in order to achieve *arahantship*:

> It is impossible, monks, it cannot come to pass that a woman should be an arahant, a fully enlightened one (*sammasambuddha*). It is impossible. Yet, monks it is possible for a man to be one.[3]

The Buddha predicted that the admission of women to the *Sangha* would halve the duration of the True *dharma* to five hundred years. Nevertheless, although the Buddha imposed no less than eight vows of subordination on those women who wished to join the *Sangha*, he later conceded to Ananda that women were able to achieve Enlightenment. The *Therigatha* (Psalms of the Sisters), furthermore, attests that they did so. The Buddha's reluctance to agree to female ordination was based on the traditional role of women in the East, which had been firmly moulded by the Laws of Manu. This code of Vedic Laws explained the established structures in the Vedic society. The role of women, along with other members of the community, was decidedly one of subservience:

> Sudras, slaves and women were prohibited from reading the Vedas. A woman could not attain heaven through any merit of her own. She could not worship or perform a sacrifice by herself . . . [4]

Contrary to popular belief, the Buddha never advocated absolute equality for all members of the *Sangha*, and there was a formal subordination of the Order of Nuns to the Order of Monks. Even today, so-called nuns are not treated as the equals of the monks, as a visitor to a Theravadin monastery in England recently observed:

> During breakfast it was possible to discern the attitude to the role of the two sexes in this strange environment. The meal was taken on the floor of a large reception room with the novice nun serving the gruel and tea from big pots. The nuns obviously considered they were equal to the monks yet it was clear that they were not treated as such. Whenever a nun addressed a monk she put her hands together in front of her face in an act of veneration. The monks only did this when addressing the senior monk but never to a nun . . . The offering of the (one) meal (of the day) is made to the monks, nuns and novices as they enter in order of seniority . . . Seniority is reckoned from the date of ordination. Nuns always come after the monks.[5]

In Theravadin countries the very concept of nuns and monks being together under the same roof is contrary to tradition, and here the new ordination of nuns is not recognized.

The code of conduct and morality central to Theravada Buddhism addresses the monk; there is little to interest those who live outside the monastic life. It is a code of discipline *(Vinaya)* for those who have renounced the world, a way of life regarded in every way superior to that of the layman. Spiritual progress, let alone *nirvana,* is only for those who have forsaken the world, and the *Vinaya* expressly forbids monks to live under the same roof as a woman, do their own cooking, work, or handle money.[6]

The path of the Theravadin monk is severe. His religious life is dictated by two hundred and twenty seven rules of conduct outlined in the *Vinaya,* which undoubtedly reflects the nature of the early Indian *Sangha*. It is also self-centred in as much as each monk has to work out his own salvation, for only by becoming a monk can *nirvana* be realized:

Verily, I say to you, O monks
All conditioned things are transient
Work out your own salvation with diligence.
Mahaparinibbana Sutta

The *Vinaya* requires a monk to beg for his food, which must be eaten before midday. (More properly, he should make himself available to be *offered* food, for he is not allowed to ask. Recently, a monk at a Theravadin monastery in England invited a nun to *offer* him an aspirin for his headache; clearly, to *ask* for an aspirin would breach the rules). The monk who contravenes this rule and eats after midday is an embarrassment to the monastery, for in order to retain the support of the laity the monk must be seen to be conforming to the rules. His possessions, which must not exceed eight in number, are similarly specified and include a three-part robe and a loincloth to wear, a begging bowl and water-strainer for food and drink, a razor to remove facial hair, and a needle to sew together the rags which make his clothes. Contrary to a misconception which persists in the West, the monks do not take a vow of poverty. Traditionally, it is the laity who supplies these few possessions, though it is not unknown for well-meaning benefactors to become over-zealous in their generosity and, ever-mindful of a better rebirth, bestow ostentatious material gifts which are an embarrassment to the monks.

The monk may leave the monastic life at any time he chooses without fear of criticism. By the same token, the monks may be joined in the monsoon season by a laity who will forsake waterlogged roads for the Five Precepts, and live with them in the monastery. This is less evident in Sri Lanka, where social prejudices discourage the leaving of the *Sangha*, and the monks there have formed what amounts to a priestly caste. In other Theravadin countries there is, of course, what could be described as a hard-core of permanent monks who exert a strong influence on the administrative and organizational development of the *Sangha*, but there is also a (usually rainy) seasonal influx of laity. In Burma, which has an average of some one hundred and twenty thousand practising Buddhists, the advent of the rainy season heralds the development of the religious experience of a large proportion of the laity:

Women are at least partly excluded from these experiences, for the tradition of valid ordination of nuns is considered as having ended in AD 456 in Theravada Buddhist countries. Women cannot therefore be nuns (*bhikkhuni*) but only *meithila-shin*, lay members who have taken at least ten vows and who wear the monastic robe. Though the revival of Buddhism has brought more women and girls into this community of women ascetics than before, the number is still very limited.[7]

In fact, the requirement for nuns to be ordained not only by monks, but also by ordained nuns (who, by that fact, don't exist!) means that there are no authentic Theravadin nuns.

The monastery or *vihara* could be anything from an individual hut to a vast, even *wealthy* complex with many acres of land, which seems far removed from the organizational structures envisaged in the *Vinaya Pitaka*:

> Nonetheless, the viharas also provide a common meeting place for the monastic community and laity, a place for Dharma instruction, personal training and inspiration.[8]

The advent of the monsoons, which prevents any serious travel, also encourages an increase in meditational practice, so important to monastic life. When not in meditational retreat, working out their own salvation, the monks are to be found reciting the *Vinaya Pitaka* in unison, such is its importance, or engaging in rigorous debate: "indeed, the word *thera*, while normally meaning 'monk', can have the nuance of meaning 'view' or 'debate'."[9]

In early Buddhism, ordained monks were considered to be *arahants*, enlightened beings who thereby were assured of final release from the *samsaric* cycle, the endless round of death and rebirth. This is not assumed to be the case in monasteries today, however. Nor in Theravada Buddhism is there any concept of an omnipotent Creator God, so central to the theistic religions of Judaism, Christianity and Islam; nor, for that matter, any manifestation of the totally trancendent Absolute, the Ground of all Being in Hinduism, to whom the monk can turn for support. Spiritual progress towards liberation from *samsara* is a solitary pathway for the Theravadin monk and has to be made without divine inspiration, for there is no belief in an omniscient, omnipresent, supramundane Being. There is certainly the acceptance that there are gods in Buddhism; equally certainly there is no suggestion that any are particularly important, at least to the staunchly atheistic monastic view.

While gods such as the Vedic deities of Hinduism are accepted as having existence, they are seen as fellow wanderers in the *samsaric* cycle of existences just like ordinary mortals. The only difference is that their *kamma* is good enough to place them in a birth in a heavenly, and not earthly, realm. However, it must be said that such minor divine beings often supply the focus for propitiatory requests from lay Theravada Buddhists at auspicious times in life and at times of need or trouble, and fulfil a particularly anthropomorphic and perhaps theistic role in a religion devoid of an omnipotent creator God.[10]

Even if there is a tendency amongst the laity to regard the Buddha as the object of devotion, the Buddha was never considered to be in any way divine by the Theravadin monastic tradition. He is not thought to have lived on after his death in some miraculous way, nor was he resurrected; since there is no concept of a permanent unchanging *atman*, self, spirit or soul (call it what you will), in Theravada Buddhism, there is no suggestion that the Buddha's demise was accompanied by the fusion of his former self with the cosmic soul or spirit of the universe, the Brahman: atman synthesis central to *Upanisadic* Hinduism. On the contrary, the Buddha's death, his final or *parinirvana*, was precisely that, and he simply ceased to exist according to orthodox monastic thought.

With no concept of a divine being of any kind to whom the Theravadin monk may turn in praise or prayer, his concern lies with the working out of his own salvation along his spiritual path to *nirvana*, a path which has the three defilements of greed, anger and delusion firmly indicated as its boundary markers. The Buddha's promise in the *Majjhima Nikaya*[11] that a rebirth in heaven was assured to those who had faith in and love for him, however, held more meaning and attraction for the laity than the incomprehensible *nirvana*

Puja

The Buddha's legacy was not eternal life but his *dharma*, his teaching, and in *puja* the Buddha's teaching is both honoured and respected. This is the meaning of the word in Theravada Buddhism, for although *puja* can also mean "worship" there is no question of the Buddha being worshipped in the monastic tradition; nowhere in the Pali scriptures is it ever claimed that the Buddha was in any way supernatural. Instead, the *dharma* is honoured in temples and shrines throughout Theravada countries by prostration and the three times repetition of the Three Jewels, which raises an interesting point, as Basham has noted:

soon after his death his followers evolved the "Three Jewels", which form the basic profession of faith of Buddhism, and which every Buddhist, both monastic and lay, repeats to this day: "I go for refuge to the Buddha; I go for refuge to the Doctrine (*Dharma*); I go for refuge to the Order (*Sangha*)." Though the theorists might explain away the first of the Three Jewels, on the obvious interpretation "going for refuge to the Buddha" implied that the Master, as distinct from his teaching, was in some way still present, and able to help his followers.[12]

Be this as it may, it is certainly the Buddha's *dharma* which is honoured in *puja*, with the bringing together of the palms of the hands, and their being raised first before the forehead, then the mouth, before finally returning to the chest. This symbolizes the honouring of the *dharma* with mind, word and body, and is accompanied by bowing, kneeling and prostration. The Buddha's *dharma* is disseminated to all corners of the world, which is symbolized by the fragrance of incense, while the darkness of ignorance is overcome by the light from burning candles which depicts enlightenment. Flowers or flower petals portray the fragility of all life and all three – flowers, candles and incense – feature prominently as offerings that are brought by a laity which frequents the temples and shrines of Theravada countries, again with thoughts of accruing good *karma* and hence a better rebirth firmly in mind.

According to orthodox Theravadin tradition it is unacceptable to have monks and nuns together under the same roof, so the question of doing *puja* together would not arise in Theravada countries. Elsewhere, western attitudes have made their mark though equality of the sexes in *puja* is still some way off:

> We found this tendency to subordinate the nuns most evident in the way that *puja* was conducted. Every evening between 7.30 p.m. and 9.00 p.m. there was meditation in the shrine room for all. While the monks knelt on the raised platform around the Buddha the lower area below the statue and the rear of the room was occupied by visitors, nuns and novices.[13]

Meditation (*bhavana*)

The two fundamental types of meditation are *samatha* and *vipassana*. The former concentrates on mindfulness of body, feelings, mind and mental states and aims at detaching the mind from responses to sense stimuli through four stages of *jhana* (Sanskrit *dhyana*), which is meditation, until the level of pure consciousness of *samadhi* is achieved, then beyond *samadhi* to four formless states where dualities cease to exist. *Vipassana* or "insight" meditation is more psycho-analytically based, analysing the nature of the self in the context of the fundamental tenets of Buddhism.[14]

Perhaps no section of the Buddha's teaching has been more misunderstood than his words on *bhavana*, which is best translated as "culture" or "development". Buddhism is a mind-culture, and the purpose of meditation is to cultivate an attitude of mind; it has nothing to do with turning one's back on life and sitting in isolated splendour while in some form of mystical trance or the like. So little understood was the Buddha's teaching on meditation that at one time it degenerated into a ritual of burning candles and reciting formulae.[15] Great Master Tendo Nyojo once said:

> Learning meditation is to cast off body and mind. It is not necessary to burn incense, prostrate oneself, recite the name of the Buddha, perform repentance or chant sutras. If you concentrate on meditation, your main purpose will be attained.[16]

The Buddha taught that the pre-Buddhist form of meditation known as *samatha* was mind-created and did not give insight into the Ultimate Reality. Although the Buddha did not eschew *samatha* from Buddhist meditation, he nevertheless considered it to have limited value. For the Buddha, the aim of meditation is to effectuate the attainment of highest wisdom which alone recognizes the True Reality and brings about the realization of Ultimate Truth, *nirvana*. The cultivating process involves the overcoming of all negative and impure thoughts (such as lust, anger, indolence and negativity), and the development of pure and positive qualities (such as concentration, energy and confidence); this is "insight" meditation, *vipassana*, which has as its foundation mindfulness, awareness, vigilance and observation.

The Buddha's discourse on meditation known as the *Satipatthana Sutta*, or "The Setting-up of Mindfulness", has four main sections which direct their attention in turn to our body *(kaya)*, feelings and sensations *(vedana)*, the mind *(citta)* and, lastly, moral and intellectual subjects *(dhamma)*. In every instance, being mindfully aware of what is happening at the present moment is a fundamental principle; "The Mindfulness or Awareness of in-and-out breathing" *(anapanasati)* is a case in point. Seated in a specified (by the text) posture, with legs crossed and body erect, the meditator is enjoined to become mindfully aware of an action which we, of necessity, do all the time – breathing in and breathing out. Although one of the simplest practices, it is one which in time will develop considerable powers of concentration and reap all its attendant benefits, even the realization of *nirvana*. The key word here is "develop", for, at first, the mind will flit here and there and do anything other than concentrate on one's breathing; as always, the ego will be determined that it and nothing else, remains the centre of attention.

By the same token, forgetting ourselves completely and losing ourselves in what we are doing also enhances mental development, a fact which has not escaped the attention of Zen Buddhists today. To a detached observer, however, it would appear that so many of us almost crave an out-of-body experience, so determined are we to concentrate on anything other than the task-in-hand. Rather than apply ourselves totally to what we are doing at the present moment, we would far prefer to deliberate over the past and anticipate the future, in dejected or enthusiastic tones, dependent upon our mood. In the famous Simili of the Raft in the *Majjhima Nikaya*, the Buddha questions whether a man who has just crossed a flood on a wooden raft he has built would be likely to put it on his head when he reaches the other side and carry it with him. The point the Buddha is making is that even profitable states of mind created by morality and meditation (let alone unprofitable states of mind) are not to be held on to, but rather should be allowed to pass away, as surely as the man would have left the raft. The benefits of living in the present moment in a totally unselfish and unselfconscious way, moreover, are graphically recorded in an anthropological field-study of meditating forest monks in Sri Lanka conducted between 1972 and 1975.[17] Whether the monks were applying themselves to their daily round of study, eating, meditation and exercise, or committing themselves to long-term projects such as founding forest hermitages, their application was total and disinterested, without any thought of recognition for themselves, nor indeed any interest in the outcome of their efforts. Described by the researcher as "radiant" and "without remorse", the monks poured all their energies into the task-in-hand, and were both absorbed in and fascinated by whatever they happened to be doing at the present moment. A visitor to a Theravadin monastery in England encountered the same attitude in the kitchen:

> when helping to prepare the one meal of the day for a community of around twenty people, the writer thought it might be a good opportunity to ask the novice nun, who was the only other helper in the kitchen, everything she wanted to know about Buddhism. However, the reply was,

I cannot talk now as I must concentrate on the task in hand.
Every action required mindfulness whether it was how carefully the
vegetables were chopped or how the waste should be disposed of.[18]

All too often, we find ourselves resentful of the task-in-hand (even if
that task is eating a meal) because this is preventing us from tackling our
next assignment. Accordingly, we direct our attention not to what we
are doing, but to the next task, and when we eventually do that, to the
next, and so on. This frenetic behaviour leads nowhere other than to
frustration and, far from evolving, the mind resembles some farmyard
dog on a chain, which surges first this way and then that, without ever
making any real progression. Much of the problem is one of ego,
whereby we are convinced that only we know what is really important,
and so we place unbelievable strain upon ourselves, rushing through
those chores we believe to be less important, like eating properly, and
spending time with those we love, so that we can get on with that which
we alone know to be all-important.

Once the mind is weaned away from this treadmill of ignorance, and
through Right Mindfulness and Right Concentration comes to terms
with the Buddha's teaching that there is no permanent unchanging self
(anatta), anymore than anything can be said to be permanent or unchanging *(anicca)*, then belief in an ego which has to be constantly
satiated becomes vacuous. This is no easy task, and can be accomplished
only with regular daily practice and perseverence. This lack of subjec-
tivity is also advocated in the texts when they come to discuss the
association between meditation and the mind. Observing the state of
mind we are in at any given time, as the mind meanders its way through
its galaxy of mood swings, embracing in turn both positive and negative
thoughts, should be done objectively and dispassionately. As a scientist
views a subject-study without passion, so should we observe our minds,
without pride or criticism, and without any thought of having owner-
ship of the anger, worry, or love, which becomes voiced in the words,
"*my* worry" or "*I* am worried". With such a detached view, we become
able to analyse the reasons why the emotion in question dominates our
thoughts and act accordingly. The Buddhist may also meditate on ethical, intellectual and spiritual subjects in order to cultivate these qualities.
Accordingly, the Theravadin monk engages in highly developed meditational practices such as concentrating on one aspect of the
Brahmavihara at a time, which will assist the mind to evolve and the ego
to dissolve. On the full- or quarter-moon the Theravadin monk will
undertake an all-night vigil, which is a feat of endurance in itself:

The hours of silence to midnight seemed endless and efforts to meditate waxed and waned. This was in fact to be the hardest part, for on the dot of midnight in came the novices with a tray of steaming hot chocolate, bramble tea and plates piled with cubes of cheese and chocolate. The senior monk then explained that the Buddha decreed that *medicine* is allowed at certain times so long as it requires no mastication. After this welcome break and discussion the meditation recommenced but in the chanting of mantras some of which reflected the Mahayanist tradition. This served to reinforce the view which the senior monk was at pains to convey that, *There really is no difference between the Hinayana and the Mahayana schools.*[19]

Theravadin festivals

The extent to which festivals are given prominence in world religions varies greatly. Some faiths, such as Judaism, use festivals to relive, indeed re-enact, their sacred histories; the festival of *Sukkot*, in which Jews remember the times spent in the Wilderness by building and inhabiting shelters in their gardens today, is but one example among many. Other faiths certainly have their own festivals, equally certainly they are not all festival-conscious religions; Islam is a case in point. This variation in importance accorded to festivals is conspicuous in Buddhism also. Given the emphasis placed on ritual by the schools of Tibetan Buddhism, it is small wonder that festivals feature prominently in this tradition. In Zen Buddhism, too, a whole range of festivals is celebrated, while other Japanese schools, such as Nichiren, completely ignore all of the traditional Buddhist festivals and observe instead commemorative days such as the 12 October, when Nichiren Daishonin first inscribed the *Dai-Gohonzon* in 1279.

Within the Theravadin tradition, the intent of the laity to accrue good *karma* in order to achieve a better rebirth, when it would become possible for them to enter the monastery as a monk, finds expression in a variety of festivals in which monks and laity come together for a time, originally for monastic recitation of the *Vinaya*. These are not random times, however, for the first and fifteenth days of the month, when the moon is first new, and then full, are the crucial *uposatta* days. The term *uposatta* means "entering to stay" and, appropriately, these days mark the beginning of a period of time when the laity enter the monasteries to stay with the monks, nowadays reaffirming their acceptance of the Buddhist Precepts and joining the monks in fasting, meditation and devotion, albeit on an impermanent basis.

Theravadin Buddhists celebrate the birth, Enlightenment and death of the Buddha in an important three-day festival called *Wesak*, which coincides with the full moon and is named after the month which falls in May/June. Light is a prominent feature of this festival, since light is representative of Sakyamuni's Enlightenment, and in Sri Lanka *Wesak* is often known as The Festival of Lights. Indeed, on *Wesak*, lights are conspicuous everywhere, illuminating homes, temples, *bodhi* trees, images of Sakyamuni (together with flowers and incense) and home-made lanterns. Flowers also feature prominently in *Wesak*, emphasizing the transitory nature of all life, but all life is nevertheless respected at this time and care is taken to ensure that no living thing is harmed. Homes and streets are decorated, *Wesak* cards are sent and the monks and the poor receive gifts from the laity. In Thailand, garlands of flowers bedeck spotless homes as well as streets and temples, where the largest of the newly-cleaned Buddha statues is transported outside to a temple court-yard replete with clean sand. There, on a raised platform, the Buddha image is encircled by moving lights carried by Thai Buddhists, who circumambulate the local monastery three times to symbolize the Three Refuges.

One time when weddings and festivals are *not* celebrated is the rainy season, called *Vassa* (or *Asala* in some Buddhist countries). *Vassa* occurs from July onwards when monsoons make travel extremely difficult. However, these inclement weather conditions lend themselves admirably to study and meditation; accordingly, this is also the time when lay Buddhists may choose to live in the monasteries with the monks, who are given special offerings. *Vassa* is a time for stricter religious life, and initiation, ordination and renewal of vows are common. What *is* celebrated is the end of *Vassa*, for this is considered by Buddhists to be the period when Sakyamuni returned from heaven after preaching the *dharma* to the gods. His return is heralded with a profusion of lights which form what amounts to a "flightpath" to earth, often in the form of lanterns, as in Burma.

Another three-day festival is the Buddhist New Year, where religious and cultural traditions combine. On the religious front, respected Buddha images are washed and adorned in robes for the monks; Buddhists take the Three Refuges and the Five Precepts on the last of the three days, and good *karma* is thought to accrue by the release of captive animals, fish and birds. On the secular front, as one would expect, the New Year heralds a time for merry-making and less-serious pastimes, when water becomes the medium to spray and sprinkle, even drench, almost anyone who happens to be in Sri Lanka or Thailand at the time. Traditional dance, shadow-puppet plays and kite-flying are conspicuous. Sacred and secular combine when everyday activities such as cooking, eating and bathing are given religious significance, and honoured Buddhists are offered bowls of cool water.

In the festival of *Kathina*, meaning "cloth", which is celebrated in October/November, gifts, especially of new robes, are made to the monks in gratitude for their preserving the religion. In Bangkok, the monks are presented with a robe by the King, who is rowed out to the Temple of Dawn *(Wat Arun)* in a boat. *Kathina* may only begin when five monks who have observed *Vassa* correctly are present, and four of the five must have done so in the same temple. Clive Erricker gives mention to one special robe which features in *Kathina*:

> The robe is made according to ceremonial prescription, by sewing patches together in such a way as is said to imitate the patchwork of the paddy fields familiar to the early monks on their travels.[20]

The robe is sometimes woven by young local girls; at other times it is made by the monks themselves, who give it to the laity to make the official presentation. In either circumstance, these events mark the continued interdependence of the monastic order and the laity, with the former offering spiritual guidance and teaching to the latter, with the reminder that kindness and generosity brings merit, and the laity accordingly satisfying the basic needs of the monastic order.[21]

A particular feature of Sri Lankan festivals is the processing through the streets of sacred relics accompanied by much revelry. These processions are known as *perahera* and commemorate such times as the arrival of Buddhism in Sri Lanka during the days of Asoka. In the Festival of *Esala perahera*, named after the month (July/August), a tooth which is reputed to have survived the cremated remains of Sakyamuni is purportedly transported through the streets of Kandy on the back of a royal elephant.

The festival lasts for fifteen nights and becomes progressively more ostentatious, culminating in a procession of one hundred elephants attended by VIPs, illuminated by fireworks, and complete with dancers, drummers and musicians.

Other Theravadin festivals include *Asalha Puja*, which commemorates the Buddha's First Sermon in the Deer Park near Benares (in Tibet, this festival had the spread of the Buddha's *dharma* re-enacted in the processing through the streets of Buddhist scriptures written on long wooden blocks). Another festival of lights in Thailand is *Magha Puja*, when the lighting of 1250 candles in some Eastern temples commemorates the Buddha's prediction of his impeding death three months hence before 1250 disciples. This full moon festival also marks the choosing of two of Sakyamuni's chief disciples as well as the establishment of the *Vinaya*, which formed the structure by which the early monks could live.

4

The Mahayana Doctrine

The rise of the Mahayana

Paul Williams reminds us that, "The origins of the Mahayana are obscure in the extreme, and it is difficult to give a satisfactory explanation of why this widening happened."[1] Nevertheless, when the Buddha failed to bequeath any consistent system of philosophy or metaphysics in his precious legacy, he could hardly have imagined that this omission would be at least indirectly responsible for one of the most far-reaching schisms in the history of Buddhism. The two centuries that acted as bookends to the turn of the millennium, appropriately bore witness to an India which was changing from an oral to a written culture, a change which would give a hitherto unknown finality to a standardized form of the Buddha's *dharma*.

What was hailed by the Abhidharma scholars as an in-depth analysis of the Buddha's teaching had already found acceptance in the *Tipitaka*, and this so-called "Higher *Dharma*" had gained its rightful (according to Abhidharmists) place in the early canons alongside the *Vinaya* and *Sutta Pitakas*. This state of affairs curried no favour with opponents of the Abhidharmists – and there were many of them – who found no warrant in the claim that this "Higher *Dharma*" was actually (directly or indirectly) the teaching of the Buddha. Accordingly, these opponents of the Abhidharmists began compiling their own *sutras*, which were anti-Abhidharma in polemic, and heralded as the long-lost words of the Buddha and his disciples which had only just come to light. Another light which now appeared on the horizon was the first chink in a rift which would become a major split: the acceptance or rejection of the new *sutras* as authoritative.

Those conservatives who saw themselves remaining politically correct, refusing to accept the new *sutras* as authoritative, were given the pejorative title "Hinayana" by their opponents, meaning that theirs was the "inferior way" to salvation. The other major school of Buddhism which was now evolving coined for itself the title "Maha" (Great) "yana" ("vehicle" or "way"), a title which it accepted with no little pride. The Mahayanists were by no means confined to opponents of the Abhidharma, however, for by this time the latter had joined forces with numerous new theistic religious movements which were now embracing India. Cultic and doctrinal elements from the cult of Visnu, as well as Hellenistic and Zoroastrian saviour cults, were beginning to make their impress on Mahayana Buddhism. In the words of Harsh Narain, "In short, the Buddhist mind is divided against itself on more than one point and in more than one respect."[2]

Accordingly, it comes as no surprise to learn that Mahayana Buddhism is characterized by considerable variety in both belief and practice. In some ways it continues with the same basic tenets of Theravada Buddhism in its acceptance of *dukkha*, *anatta* and *anicca*, the three marks, as they are called, of Buddhism. And there are many who would see Mahayana as deviating little from the older school. But there are also variations which have led to an overt theism and devotionalism, belief in an Absolute (notwithstanding the difficulties of interpretation), and even belief in a permanent inner *essence*. The designation *Mahayana*, then, is a broad one and must serve as something of an umbrella term. In many ways, Mahayana is a flowering of the early Buddhism tradition and came about as a result of the more liberal ideas put forward by some of the monks, in particular, the *Mahasanghikas*, as we have seen. But what really enabled Mahayana Buddhism to flourish was the belief in a continuing revelation of literature. While Theravada Buddhism accepts only the Pali Canon of the *Tipitaka*, Mahayana was prepared to accept other works as part of revealed literature, that is to say, literature which could be accepted as authoritative because it was written as a result of spiritual experience of the Buddha's *dharma*, or which supposedly could be traced back to the Buddha himself. Such literature was recorded in what are called *sutras*, teachings which were believed to express the Buddha's *dharma*, but there was a difference!

Because they were the product of a written rather than an oral culture, they were much longer and more luxuriant in style than the short, spare discourses of the early schools. In fact their style is a major defining characteristic of the movement. Their surrealist locales, measured in mind-boggling dimensions and filled with dazzling apparitions; their immense, all-star casts of characters; and the sheer extravagance of their language all serve to reassert the primacy of the visionary, shamanic side of Buddhism that had been generally neglected by the Abhidharmists.[3]

Many do not make easy reading and their complex teachings and dialectic (testing of truth by logical disputation) have been the subject of endless commentaries by both enlightened and not-so-enlightened Buddhists. Sometimes, the commentaries themselves become sacred works. *Sutras* are always traced back in lineage to Sakyamuni Buddha himself, to another buddha, or to someone with spiritual authority, and are therefore believed to have continued in oral tradition in the early part of their history.

The most important literature for Mahayana Buddhism is called the *Prajnaparamita* literature. This began as a basic text formulated in the last century BCE and the first century CE, and was later expanded into a number of *sutras*. *Prajnaparamita* means "Perfection of Wisdom". The word *prajna* "wisdom" is an important one in Buddhism for it is one of the pillars of both the Theravada and Mahayana traditions. Mahayana Buddhism is based on the two pillars of *prajna* and *mahakaruna* (great compassion): I shall return to the latter later. Although in ordinary usage it can refer to intellectual analysis, *prajna* here refers to the kind of wisdom which is ultimate wisdom, knowledge of reality and the way things really are. Because it is *ultimate* knowledge, in this sense it is *perfect* wisdom. In Buddhism such wisdom, for most schools, is the key to *nirvana*. The *Prajnaparamita* literature, therefore, praises the highest and perfect wisdom which leads to *nirvana* while also setting out the perfections, the *paramitas*, of the path to the realization of *nirvana*. There are six of these – giving, morality, patience, vigour, concentration/meditation and, underpinning all, wisdom. These *paramitas* can only *be* perfect when they are accompanied by perfect wisdom. So the *Prajnaparamita Sutras* claim that perfect giving, morality and so on can only come about with the acquisition of ultimate wisdom, knowledge of the true state of things.

Scholars are not of one mind concerning the nature of the teaching of the *Prajnaparamita* literature. Some, such as Paul Williams, believe it extends the Buddha's teaching of no-self to confirm that total emptiness, *sunyata*, is the reality of all things, but would deny any concept of an indescribable Absolute along the lines of the Brahman of the *Upanisads*. Far from being beyond description, unlike Brahman the Absolute of the *Prajnaparamitas* abounds with good qualities which are clearly defined.[4] Be this as it may, there is no escaping the fact that in the *Mahaparinirvana Sutra*, the word *atman* (Self) – an anathema in Buddhist thinking – is used quite categorically. Perhaps this was a device, a "skilful means", used by the Buddha in order to gain a following of Hindus and others who would be thoroughly familiar with the *atman* concept, and thoroughly uncomfortable without it, though this, in a sense, is admitting to Hindu influence on Buddhism. On the other hand, it could be part of the Middle Way strategy, to recover followers who were going to the extremes:

> Early Buddhism had spoken of the four cardinal errors of seeing perma-nence where there is impermanence, happiness where there is only suffering, self where there is no self, and purity where there is impurity. This *sutra* is quite categoric in asserting that the error here lies in looking in the wrong direction – in other words that there is an equal error in seeing impermanence where there is permanence, suffering where there is happiness, no-Self where there is Self, and impurity where there is purity, in failing to see the positive element in Buddhahood which contrasts with the negative realm of unenlightenment.[5]

Critics, even of Pali texts such as the *Udana*, have long tried to equate *nirvana* as the Ultimate Reality with the Hindu Brahman: *atman*,[6] a view which has gained little support in Buddhist circles, but what of the *Prajnaparamita* literature? Harsh Narain considers that, "it would be preposterous on our part to read the Absolute into *Prajnaparamita*, as some scholars are tempted to do today. To read into it anything what-ever would mean determining it, and all determination is negation on the Madhyamika view."[7] However, David Kalupahana is unequivocal that the Absolute here *is* indescribable,[8] presumably because every posi-tive statement made about it is immediately negated by another.[9] On his view, the theory of an Absolute, which originated only after the death of the Buddha, gained momentum until it reached its culmination in the *Prajnaparamita* literature,[10] where it took on the role of a totally tran-scendent Absolute, a revolution in early Buddhist thought![11] Professor Murti agrees:[12]

> Words do not denote the absolute in any recognisable sense. The Absolute is incommensurable and inexpressible; it is utterly transcendent to thought – Sunya.

> "Appellation ceases with the absence of the objects of thought: The absolute as the essence of all things is not born, nor does it cease to be."

Indeed, Edward Conze, goes so far as to say:

> The Mahayana writings, and in particular the Prajnaparamita Sutras, are almost exclusively concerned with the problem of the Unconditioned, nothing but the Absolute over and over again.[13]

For Conze, the underlying theme of nearly all Mahayana Buddhism is the common belief in the Absolute. The only thing which prevents realization of this is the lack of wisdom, that is the lack of the wisdom which takes us beyond the dualities of life to a point where we see all things as just one emptiness, and which condemns all forms of multiplicity.

The original writers of these Mahayana texts were not at all pleased that their writings were seen to contain the Brahman of the *Upanisads* in a new form. The authors of the *Lankavatara* strenuously denied that the womb of Tathagatahood, which will be discussed below, was in any way equatable with the "eternal self", the Brahmanical *atman* of *Upanisadic* thought. Similarly, the claim in the *Nirvana Sutra* that the Buddha regarded Buddhahood as a "great *atman*" caused the Yogacarins considerable distress. The problem is that the texts themselves are ambivalent and contradictory; in chapter 12 of the *Srimala-devi Simhanada Sutra* there is both a perfection of permanence and a Self, while the *Lankavatara Sutra* attests that there may appear to the ignorant mind a Self or an Eternal Creator, but this is really emptiness.[14]

Though most scholars equate the wisdom of Mahayana Buddhism with knowledge of the total lack of plurality and dualities in all things and their commonality in emptiness, the fact that scholars are not of one mind over the *Prajnaparamita* literature highlights its complex nature, where contradiction is piled upon contradiction. We ourselves should be careful not to oversimplify the issues involved. Composed over many generations, the *sutras* are complex and far from clear, despite their ultimate goal of setting out a path to *nirvana*.

Mahayana *sutras* were still being composed as late as the eighth century CE and their development is a complicated one. It is possible to discern, however, a growing hostility towards early Buddhism throughout their composition. In the early Mahayana *sutras*, such as the *Small Perfection of Wisdom Sutras*, there is no antipathy towards the Hinayana: indeed, popular figures from early Buddhism are to found amongst the cast. As it became increasing obvious to the Mahayana writers that the anticipated wholesale forsaking of early Buddhism for the Mahayana was not to be, hostility grew. The *Vimalakirti-nirdesa* openly ridicules the *arahants*, while the still later *Lotus (Saddharmapundarika) Sutra*, composed about 200 CE, is even more inimical. By the time of the *Mahayana Parinirvana Sutra*, written about 200–400 CE, it was clear that it was time for the two traditions to part company:

According to this Sutra, whoever maligns the Mahayana teachings is destined for severe punishment, even execution. Thus what began as a small rift between the two courses in 100 BCE gradually widened until by 200 CE it had become a clear break.[15]

The *Lotus Sutra*, "The Lotus of the True Law", is one of the most influential in the whole of Mahayana literature. The Nichiren schools, for example, place great store in the fact that the *Lotus Sutra* attests that all of the Buddha's previous teaching was provisional, since humankind could not have coped with being taught the highest truths in one fell swoop, and that the *Lotus Sutra* crystallizes these highest teachings. The *dramatis personae* of the *Lotus Sutra* include buddhas and *bodhisattvas* as well as humans, and its message is unequivocal: Buddhahood is for all humanity, indeed, it is humankind's natural state. The great drama played out in the *Lotus Sutra* finds Sakyamuni Buddha as the cosmic Buddha in human form helping others on the same path to Enlightenment that he himself treads.

The main *Prajnaparamita* text is the appropriately named *Mahaprajnaparamita Sutra*, "The Great Perfection of Wisdom", which contains much of the literature extant in shorter texts, the *Diamond* and *Heart Sutras* being cases in point. On the basis of the *Prajnaparamita* literature, as well as other *sutras*, two important schools of thought arose, *Madhyamika* and *Yogacara*. In many ways, these two schools complement each other, the *Madhyamika* concentrating on *prajna* and the *Yogacara* on *dhyana*, meditation. It is to these two important schools that we now turn.

The *Madhyamika* school

As Mahayanists, the Madhyamikas happen to be as positivist, dogmatic, and devotional in religion as devotees of any other faith. They are second to none in their religious fervour. The canonical injunctions to worship *Prajnaparamita* as a goddess with flowers, incenses, garlands, unguents, aromatic powders, cloths, umbrellas, flags, buntings, bells, illuminations, etc. and Nagarjuna's prayer to *Prajnaparamita* are instances in point.[16]

Although, during his lifetime, the Buddha denied that he was either a god or a man,[17] in the context of early, orthodox Buddhism, the Buddha was never given any supernatural, divine qualities. It would appear that his words were taken to mean that he was an ordinary human being who had transcended the confines of *samsara*.

Theravadin doctrine has never wavered from the position that the Buddha is dead and no longer active in the world; in moments of great crisis some individuals do pray to him for help, but that is the spontaneous outburst of emotion and in their calmer moments they know that it can do no good except as a psychological relief to themselves. Buddhist saints, other Enlightened beings – they are commonly known as *arhats* – are similarly dead and of no influence on the world.[18]

Yet even in the orthodox Pali Canon there are times when the Buddha is given a cosmic dimension which suggests his ongoing nature.[19] Moreover, while it is generally accepted that early Buddhism recognized only one Buddha in this aeon, there are occasions in the early texts when the *arahants*, the perfected ones, were also called *buddhas*. Indeed, the Buddha himself said that the only difference between himself and other enlightened monks was the fact that he was a teacher. This concept of a wider possibility of Buddhahood for many was also something taken on board by the Mahayana tradition. It is these two factors of the different concept of the Buddha and the lack of exclusivity of buddhahood which underpins much of the Mahayana tradition. This we shall see in both the *Madhyamika* and the *Yogacarin* schools.

Described by Professor Murti as *The Central Philosophy of Buddhism*,[20] the *Madhyamika* tradition remains to this day the official philosophy of Tibetan Buddhism, and in Tibet is considered to be the true philosophical basis of the Mahayana.[21] It was founded in the second century by Nagarjuna, an exceptionally skilled philosopher, second only in importance to the Buddha himself and sometimes even called the second Buddha. He and his disciple Aryadeva set out to interpret the Buddha's teaching in the light of what they understood the "Middle Way" to be. Legend has it that Nagarjuna, a great master of alchemy, medicine and doctrine, was given the *Prajnaparamita Sutras* by the *nagas*, the sea serpents, in reward for his wisdom. An outstanding philosopher, mystic and monk, Nagarjuna aimed at demolishing the so-called logical arguments of his Buddhist opponents by demonstrating the weaknesses in their argumentation. Most philosophical schools seek to do this in order to advance their own particular logic, but Nagarjuna set up no rival philosophical thought to replace the cleverly demolished arguments of others. This was because he understood the Buddha's *dharma* as teaching the emptiness of all things – all things are empty of an independent identity and that includes philosophical argumentation also!

Madhyamika means "middle", or "middle position" and refers to the

Middle Way of the Buddha. This concept of a "middle way" is meant in a number of senses. We could say that it embodies the middle point between any dualities, the point at which those dualities cease to exist, the point where dualities are *empty*. Then, for Nagarjuna, the Buddhist *sutras* pointed to the emptiness of all things; they neither exist nor do they not exist, they are simply empty and it is this, he believed, which was the true *dharma* of the Buddha. The *sutras* also pointed to a middle position between eternal existence on the one hand, and total annihilation on the other. There were many Buddhists who understood *nirvana* as the former, the ending of *samsara* and the beginning of an eternal bliss, while others understood the Buddha's words to mean total extinction in every possible way when *nirvana* was reached. Nagarjuna insisted that *nirvana* was neither of these; it is a mid point between eternalism and non-existence.

These ideas of the ultimate emptiness of all things were based upon the Buddha's teachings on *conditioned arising*, or *dependent origination*. Whatever we look at in life or whatever we experience is always dependent on, and relative to, other factors; nothing is able to exist because of its *own-being*, called *svabhava* in Sanskrit. Nothing exists independently of other things and if things cannot exist in this way and they cannot be said to have any inherent nature of their own, then it is difficult to say that they *really* exist at all. Moreover, nothing can be a thing by itself, it can only be seen as something in relation to another thing: we can never know what good is without knowing its opposite, for example. So nothing exists which is a separate entity with its special *own-being*. Everything thus shares *non-nature*, emptiness of nature, as its true nature. Modern physics has suggested the same, for what we consider to be matter is now understood to be a field of interacting and interdependent particles.

This kind of thought is very much in line with the standard Buddhist teaching of the impermanence of all things: nothing can possess an unchanging essence, nothing ever *is*, for all is subject to change and is in a process of becoming which never becomes. Importantly, the self, too, is ultimately of the same changeable, non-permanent nature. It has no *svabhava*.

Both mind and body are constantly changing so how could there be a permanent self capable of claiming "I am this"? Many would claim that the self or *I* is made up of a continual series of selves present in all the moments of life in a continuum, but this would mean that the self is not one thing but many things, a collection of things and a collection of things in which some aspects of that collection have ceased to exist! So what is the self other than a changing, interdependent and relative thing which lacks any permanence and *svabhava*, own-being?

Sunyata

The concept of "emptiness" as the true nature of all things is called *sunyata*, and it is this teaching which is the hallmark of the *Madhyamika* school of thought; indeed, it is the main teaching of the *Prajnaparamita Sutras*. *Sunyata* is the absence of *svabhava*, own-being, in all things, and is experienced through *prajna* as an ultimate truth of the universe. Nothing can have *svabhava*, for everything is dependent on other causes and conditions for its existence. Nothing can exist of itself. When all life is understood from the point of view of *sunyata*, the emptiness of *svabhava* in all things, then it is senseless to grasp at anything in it and this factor concords with the second of the Four Noble Truths, that craving is the root cause of suffering in life. We behave as if things have permanent, inherent existence and try to grasp at them and keep them permanently in order to be happy. Nagarjuna claimed that regarding *sunyata* as the true state of all existence is the very wisdom which needs to be acquired in order to cease such craving and grasping, and so realize *nirvana*.

So truth cannot be found in something that is, or something that is not, it can only be found in the middle point between these two dualities. Indeed, this is why Nagarjuna made no assertions of his own and confined his philosophy to demolishing the arguments of others. By gaining knowledge of this middle point between dualities, finite definitions are transcended. The doctrine of *sunyata*, then, teaches the emptiness of all things in order to free the mind from its misconceptions about the finite world. This is the key teaching of *Madhyamika* and a central concept of the *Prajnaparamita Sutras*. So important is the concept of *sunyata* to the *Madhyamika* school of thought that the school was actually known as the *Sunyata-vada*. This emptiness, however, is neither nothingness nor a particular essence characteristic of all things; it is much more the idea that ultimate reality is something which cannot exist in finite things or in ideas, even the idea of emptiness itself. If, then, there is any ultimate truth, it is both inexpressible and inconceivable. It is debatable, however, if *sunyata* is even emptiness of emptiness, whether it could be regarded as a kind of metaphysical ultimate reality: scholars are divided on this issue.

Dharmas

Early Buddhism accepted that within existence there were, in fact, ultimate existents, essences or own-beingness of things. We could say that hardness, coldness and the like are essences found in certain things in life. Both these essences and phenomenal objects are called *dharmas* in Buddhism, but whereas the old school considered some *dharmas* to have *svabhava*, *Madhyamikas* maintained the doctrine that *all dharmas* are ultimately *sunya*, empty. This is expressed in Sanskrit as *svabhavasunya*. It is precisely because all *dharmas* are subject to conditioned arising that they cannot possibly have a permanent essence and are thus empty of *svabhava*. This is not to say that *dharmas* do not exist; it would be nonsensical to say that tables, chairs and people are not really there. What is claimed is that there is no *essence* in any of these things; they are *sunya* because they are impermanent, dependent and relative things at the conventional level only. Thus, *sunya* and conditioned arising or *dependent origination*, as Buddhists term it, are really one and the same.

So all *dharmas* ultimately do not exist because they are dependent on so many other factors for their existence and cannot exist in their own right. They exist merely at the nominal level; we give names to things in order to make sense of our world and environment, but this does not mean that *reality* can be given to such things just because we have terms for them. The reality of these *dharmas* is the inexpressible nature of *sunya* and there is no property in any *dharma* which is essentially its own other than this emptiness.

If we now turn all this round to look at what *really* exists we would have to say that it is only emptiness. This is the only *dharma* which does not arise from something else; it simply is. It is thus unborn, unoriginated and unformed. The Buddha himself stated this clearly:

> There is, O monks, an Unborn, Unoriginated, Uncreated, Unformed. Were there not, O monks, this Unborn, Unoriginated, Uncreated, Unformed, there would be no escape from the world of the born, originated, created, formed.   *Udana* 80–81

This is true *dharma*; the true nature of things is their own emptiness. Everything else is like the phenomena we see in dreams which we think are real only to realize on waking up that they were not. Just so, realization of the *sunyata* of all existence is the ultimate wisdom which puts conventional reality into its true perspective. And just like the things we see in our dreams are fleeting, so are conventional phenomena, they are just as unreal and as fragile; we cannot depend upon them. Thus, insight into the emptiness of all *dharmas* is the purpose of *prajna*. This teaching of *sunyata* is not just emphasizing the middle point of all dualities and therefore their annihilation, it is encouraging the evenmindedness and equilibrium in life which must follow if all existence is seen in this way. This, to the *Madhyamikas*, is what the Buddha really meant by the *Middle Way*.

It is in particular relation to the concept of the self that this doctrine of *sunyata* needs to be seen, for the self, too, is an impermanent *dharma*. There can really be no sense of "I", "me", "mine", "belonging", "owning", "possessing", "inner-self", or "soul", because these are all *dharmas* which are subject to the same dependent origination or conditioned arising as everything else. Thus, in many ways, the *Madhyamika* tradition is true to the basic Buddhist doctrine of impermanence, and in some ways takes it further in seeing *all dharmas* as empty, even going so far as to say that Buddhahood is empty, *nirvana* is empty, and even *bodhisattvas* are empty.

Bodhisattvas

Because dharmas have no own-being, there is nothing bound in samsara, nothing freed in nirvana, nothing is observed to arise, nothing is observed to cease. There are no beings to save from samsara, and yet the bodhisattva remains firm in his vow to save all beings. The world is a phantom conjured up by karmic action, the magician, but the phantom maker is itself maya (a phantom).[22]

The true ideal of Theravada Buddhism is the *arahant*, the being who, through wisdom, has worked out his own salvation and realized *nirvana*. The Mahayana, however, is based upon two pillars, wisdom *(prajna)* and great compassion for all humanity *(mahakaruna)*. It is the *bodhisattva* ideal which epitomizes these two pillars. Mahayana Buddhism sees no value in a *nirvana* or Buddhahood which is realized for purely selfish ends, and so the Mahayana Buddhist who realizes *nirvana* will delay final *nirvana*, *parinirvana*, and stay in the world as a *bodhisattva*, to help (ultimately *all*) others achieve enlightenment. Since *nirvana* and *samsara* are regarded as the same in the Mahayana tradition, the *bodhisattva* is able to realize *nirvana*, but remain in the world of *samsara* for the benefit of others. In so doing, the *bodhisattva* will accrue a vast store of *karmic* merit.

A *bodhisattva* in Theravada Buddhism is one on the way to *nirvana*, to becoming a buddha. This definition is possibly retained in the Mahayana tradition in the sense that we can talk of the *bodhisattva* path to Buddhism, and the stages that a *bodhisattva* passes through on that path. The heart-felt necessity for full Buddhahood by aspirants who walk that path is known as *bodhi-citta*, the arising of the thought of enlightenment. The stages by which *prajna*, wisdom, is achieved are described in the *Diamond Sutra*. The very fact that there is a path for *bodhisattvas* suggests that there are different levels of *bodhisattvahood*. Some have only just begun on the path while others have reached the end of it. For those towards the end of the path, the wisdom attained through *nirvana* brings knowledge that there are really no beings to be led to enlightenment at all, for all is *sunyata*, yet, because of the massive compassion of these *bodhisattvas*, their *mahakaruna*, they choose to help others who are trapped in the *samsaric* world to gain this kind of knowledge also. These two concepts of *prajna* and *mahakaruna* are the two pillars of all Mahayana Buddhism. Because the *bodhisattva* knows that all *dharmas* are empty, he or she can become involved with any part of the *samsaric* world and can be reborn even into the animal kingdom or into one of the hells.

The distinction between buddhas and *bodhisattvas* is not always a clear one. There are many buddhas, but it is not suggested that they have opted for *parinirvana* and can no longer function as aiding all others to *nirvana*. This is particularly evident in Tibetan Buddhism. Then, there are many enlightened *bodhisattvas* with the same functions as buddhas. However, other *bodhisattvas* are still on the path to *nirvana*, aiming to fulfil their vows of bringing all to *nirvana* and perfecting their generosity, morality, patience, vigour, meditation and wisdom – the six perfections or *paramitas* of the *bodhisattva* path. What is important with the *bodhisattvas* is their *upaya*, their "skill in means", for this is the special knowledge they have which enables them to know exactly what is right in any situation in order to help someone on the path to enlightenment. There are ten stages on the *bodhisattva* path, the tenth stage (before the *bodhisattva* becomes a buddha) bringing the *bodhisattva* to the *Sambhogakaya* level of the *Trikaya* which will be discussed below, and it is at this level, in particular, that the *bodhisattvas* become objects of devotional worship with all the qualities necessary for the salvation of individuals and of the universe itself.

At the *Sambhogakaya* level the number of *bodhisattvas* is legion, and different Mahayana schools will favour different *bodhisattvas*, which goes at least some way to explaining the great diversity in belief and the sheer number of different strands to the Mahayana (there are twenty-one different Nichiren schools alone). In the extravagant language of the expanded Mahayana *sutras,* surrealist world systems or buddha-fields are envisaged, each presided over by a buddha, such as Amitayus, sometimes with an attendant *bodhisattva* in charge of a *Pure Land.* All Mahayana sects have *bodhisattvas* (though the Nichiren schools don't give them personal names), but not all *bodhisattvas* have a Pure Land.

Since the doctrine of *sunyata* (emptiness) is applicable to all things, all form is devoid of own being *(svabhava)*; everything is empty of inherent existence, and, in this sense, all dualities cease to exist.

On this view, reality is best described as a multiplicity of non-duality (though Conze[23] saw the Perfection of Wisdom literature as condemning all forms of multiplicity), since though all form is different in appearance, it is non-dual in the sense that emptiness is form, and all form is emptiness. As surely as *samsara* and *nirvana* are seen to be no different in this light, since both are empty of *svabhava,* the same can be said of humans and *bodhisattvas*; both are ultimately the same, devoid of *svabhava* and, as the *Diamond Sutra* makes clear,[24] ultimately unreal:

> But since we live in an "unreal" world, and continue to differentiate between this and that through our ignorance and ego-bound personalities, *bodhisattvas* provide an ideal at which to aim, a source of help, support, and transferable merit, and *nirvana* remains an ultimate goal in an ignorant *samsaric* world, in the realm of relative but not absolute reality. *Bodhisattvas,* though ultimately as unreal as a human being, are the means by which those on the Buddhist path can learn to pass from the unreality of life to the reality of enlightenment in *nirvana.*[25]

The concept of reality

From what we have seen, it could be claimed that reality can be divided into two areas, reality at the conventional level and reality at the ultimate level. Conventional reality consists of the sense impressions which we have continually which help us to make sense of the world in which we live. At this level of conventional reality we discriminate between subject and object, between ourselves and the objects we see, thus building up a picture of reality. So *Madhyamika* Buddhism does not say that phenomenal existence is not really there. It would be absurd to suggest that things do not exist, that the table, chair and people have no reality at all. In fact, if conventional reality were not a tangible phenomenon there would be no point to Buddhist practice in order to attain enlightenment, there would be no point in the *bodhisattva* vow, and so on. However, as the individual's consciousness rises and he or she becomes more enlightened, there follows a different perspective of such conventional reality, for its very impermanence suggests that it cannnot, *ultimately*, be real. Moreover, we make distinctions between things in order to build up our knowledge of the world, but this is very much an artificiality; the interrelatedness, impermanence, and dependent origination of things are not so readily understood, so that all knowledge at the conventional level is something of a distortion.

Conversely, *Madhyamika* Buddhism advocates another level of reality, that of absolute or ultimate reality. This is the way things really are, the way things are seen by the enlightened, and what they see is the common emptiness of all *dharmas*. This is unconditioned reality, the unborn, unoriginated, uncreated and unformed. This is a total non-dual reality, a reality beyond all discrimination and is what Buddhism calls *suchness* or *thusness*. This is *tathata*, the thusness or suchness of something which is equivalent to its emptiness and its true reality.

Nirvana

Realization of *tathata*, suchness, is realization of *sunyata*, the emptiness of all *dharmas*, and this is *nirvana*, the middle point between all dualities, the Buddha's Middle Way. *Nirvana* is the point at which discrimination between subject and object disappears so that conventional reality is lost and only absolute or ultimate reality is experienced – the thusness of all things. With *nirvana* the mind has gone beyond conceptualizing activity, beyond the limitations of language, beyond dependent origination. But since the mind is beyond conceptualizing and discrimination of dualities, then it must also not conceptualize or discriminate over *nirvana*. *Nirvana* itself is also viewed as *sunyata*; it neither exists nor does not exist. Moreover, since *sunyata* is the point at which all dualities meet in emptiness of dualities, and is the common lack of *svabhava* in everything, then *nirvana* and *samsara* must be exactly the same; they share the same lack of *svabhava*. *Sunyata* is non-differentiation between subject and object, between all polarities and therefore we cannot say that *nirvana* is the opposite of *samsara*, or is what happens or is attained when *samsara* ceases. *Sunyata* takes away differences, so *nirvana* and *samsara* are identical.

Important to recognize here in this identification of *nirvana* and

samsara is that all *dharmas* are characterized by *sunyata* as ultimate
reality, and if *sunyata* is *nirvana* then all *dharmas* are *nirvana* in their
true state. This suggests that *nirvana* is not something which has to be
attained but is something that everything is anyway and which has only
to be revealed or uncovered. So all *dharmas* are *nirvanic* from the beginning. This doctrine is an important one in the *Prajnaparamita Sutras*
because it suggests two very important things – first, that all beings
possess Buddhahood because all beings have the same ultimate reality
of *sunyata* which a buddha has, and secondly, that *bodhisattvas* can be
involved in the world of *samsara* working for the enlightenment of all
beings and helping them to uncover their Buddhahood for the simple
reason that *samsara* is *nirvana*.

The Absolute

The extent to which *Madhyamika* accepts the concept of an Absolute in
the sense of a totally transcendent, indescribable Ultimate Reality is
debatable. As we saw earlier, some scholars see considerable evidence
for this in the *Madhyamika Sutras*. Indeed, the Buddha's claim in *Udana*
80–81 that there is an Unborn, Unoriginated, Uncreated and Unformed,
suggests an unconditioned permanence to ultimate reality which would
justify the acceptance of an Absolute in Mahayana Buddhism. Edward
Conze had no doubts that that which was once an incomprehensible
abstraction in the *Prajnaparamita Sutras* became, in the course of time,
much more than this:

> But it is a fact of observation that in the course of their spiritual struggle
> people actually come to a stage where this abstraction miraculously comes
> to life, gains a body, fills, sustains and irradiates the soul. It is then that
> these writings become interesting and meaningful.[26]

On this view, the Absolute is *the Dharma*, sometimes called the
Dharmakaya, and is equatable with Buddhahood. Arguably, it became
the goal of Mahayana Buddhism and the standard by which conventional reality is measured.

Upaya: skilful means

Common to Buddhism is the concept of *skilful means*, that is to say, the skill-in-means of bringing about *nirvana*. The skilful means vary from one Buddhist school to another, but in *Madhyamika* Buddhism the *sutras* themselves are regarded as skilful means which help people to progress on the Buddhist path. Indeed, the *bodhisattva* doctrine itself is thought by some to be no more than a skilful means. Ultimately, however, they are as empty of *svabhava* as any other *dharma* in existence; they are only provisional, aids on the path to ultimate truth.

As the emptiness approach began to lose its novelty, new Mahayana Sutras began to break from the earlier emptiness Sutras and treatises by turning emptiness, viewed as a perceptual mode, into a metaphysical absolute, termed the *Dharmakaya* (literally Dharma-body) . . . the new Sutras recast the term to denote both the potential for Awakening and also the source from which all things spring. In contrast to this metaphysical absolute, emptiness as an attribute of dharmas seemed to become more and more akin to nihilism. The resulting dichotomy formed the dialectic that gave rise to a new school in the Mahayana, the Yogacara.[27]

The *Yogacarin* school: *Cittamatra*

The *Yogacarin* school of thought represents the second most influential development of Mahayana Buddhism. Its ideas probably stem back to about the second century CE but it became a separate and distinct school in the fourth century under its founders, two Mahayana monks, Asanga and, a little later, his brother Vasubandhu. The word *yogacarin* means "practitioner of yoga" and tells us immediately that the emphasis of this school is very much on meditation and inner experiential knowledge. The school is thus sometimes called *Vijnavada*, the "Way of consciousness", but also *Cittamatra*, "Mind Only", for reasons which will become clear below.

The *Yogacarin* school accepted later scriptures than the *Madhyamikas*. When the Buddha taught his first sermon it was depicted by a wheel which he drew in the sand. Later, *Madhyamika* Buddhism came to accept that the turning of the Wheel of *Dharma* a second time, had produced the kind of *sutras* of the *Prajnaparamita* literature. To the *Yogacarins*, all this literature was nothing but the *skilful means* of the Buddha in raising the level of consciousness of his hearers. The *real* teaching, they felt, came from a third turning of the Wheel of *Dharma*. This superlative teaching was to be found initially in a *sutra* called the *Samdhinirmocana* though there are several others. As the result of the third turning of the Wheel of *Dharma*, the third teaching was, the

Yogacarins felt, that which should replace all other. Legend has it that the *bodhisattva* Maitreya took Asanga to one of the Buddhist heavens to teach him five new *sutras*. For many years Asanga had tried in his meditations to visualize Maitreya, without success. In despair, he gave up, but coming across a suffering dog in the roadside, full of compassion, he stooped to help it. The suffering dog became Maitreya himself, for Maitreya is to be found only where there is compassion.

The differences between *Madhyamika* and *Yogacarin* beliefs lie mainly in their perceptions of reality. *Madhyamika* saw all *dharmas* as empty, while the *Yogacarins* saw all phenomena as mental constructions, objects of the mind. The *Madhyamikas* emphasized *prajna*, wisdom, in their analysis of reality, while the *Yogacarins* emphasized *samadhi*, meditative concentration: it was Asanga, in particular, who promoted this aspect. Both schools of thought firmly believed that they were promoting the Buddha's Middle Way; however, the *Madhyamikas* accused the *Yogacarins* of being too substantialist (seeing too much existence in substances, in this case the mind) while the *Yogacarins* accused the *Madhyamikas* of being too nihilist (rejecting all existence). However, we should not see the two schools as totally opposed to each other, for in many ways the *Yogacarins* took the *Madhyamika* teaching on emptiness as the basis on which to build their philosophical system: thus the *Yogacarins* are successors of the *Madhyamikas* rather than opponents.

Reality

"All dharmas are preceded by mind (*manas*), chieftained by mind, made of mind" (Dhp.1). Neither the Abhidharmists nor the Madhyamikas, however, had ever satisfactorily worked out the mechanics of how the mind gave rise to dharmas, and this was precisely what the Yogacarins proposed to do.[28]

The *Yogacarin* conception of reality consisted in refuting the belief that perception could in any way be a reliable medium for saying that things really exist. After all, what we see in dreams or in a mirage can produce the same reactions as if we see these objects in real life. How do I know that the objects I take to be real in life are no more products of my imagination than the dreams I have? Vasubandhu argued that, just as we have to wake up to know that we have been dreaming, so we have to experience the highest states of yogic meditation in order to know that our ordinary perception of the world is a false one.

Whereas *Madhyamika* philosophy categorizes reality into two kinds, conventional and ultimate, *Yogacarin* philosophy divides reality into three. First, there is the imagined level of reality at the conventional level which is the delusional perception that there are separate things in the world which have *svabhava*, own-being. This is the level of ordinary knowledge in which we categorize things and make imaginary distinctions between subject and object. At this stage we think that everything is exactly as it is when it is perceived by us without any distortions of our own mind. All we really see is a *conceptualization*, not the real thing at all. Whatever we look at, we project our prejudices, memories, fears, expectations, beliefs and so on, onto that object, so we can only see it in terms of our mind conceptions about it. Second, there is the experience of reality as a flow of perceptions which is dependent on, and relative to, a multiplicity of conditions. This is the level of reality at which we at least understand in theory that nothing has *svabhava* or independent existence. Third, there is the perfected knowledge of reality which sees no distinction between subject and object and nothing with *svabhava*. It is by the process of yoga, the *Yogacarins* believed, that delusional reality could be overcome. Since all is really empty of *svabhava* there is emptiness in every object seen and if every object is empty then the subject *I* has nothing to see and is also empty: distinction between object and subject vanishes and the middle point is reached, thusness is experienced.

So what we see as objects are really our mind-perceptions projected onto the world. We busily divide things into categories, make value judgements about them and build up a picture of reality which is totally different from that of everyone else and which we assume to be real. It is this kind of consciousness which gives reality and permanence to the self, a sense of *I* and a desire to grasp at other things which we consider to have the same kind of reality. In reality, "things" are free from any kind of discrimination brought about by the mind or by language, they are free from dualities and free from any distinct *svabhava*. Despite the tripartite division of reality, these conclusions of the *Yogacarins* concerning reality are really not very different from the *Madhyamika* perspective. The non-substantiality of all *dharmas* is still upheld.

Later developments of this *Yogacarin* view tended to lean towards an ultimate or supreme consciousness which became an Ultimate Reality or Absolute. This was particularly the case in Far Eastern Buddhism. Realization of ultimate reality, whether regarded as a totally transcendent Absolute or not, is realization of *thusness*, of *nirvana*, for when there are no distinctions between subject and object, there can be no craving, no desires and no aversions and therefore no ego: there is nothing to which *karmic* energy can be attached. But *samsara* is not abolished: it is seen simply for what it is.

Cittamatra: mind only

The *Yogacarins*, then, represent an *Idealist* school of thought, accepting that external objects are nothing but mental fabrications. Hence, they are often called the *Cittamatra* school, "Mind-Only". While there are many different sub-schools of thought here, they are all linked by acceptance of reality as stemming only from consciousness and belief that objects are conceptualizations of the mind. In particular, the mind-only concept emphasizes the delusion of subject—object differentiation. Everything we experience is really just a fluctuating flow of perceptions, a continuing series of experiences of colours, textures, shapes, feelings and so on. How can we say that something is real, given this ever-changing flow of perceptions? Again, this is not saying that things are not there, but only that things are not there in the sense in which the mind itself conceptualizes them. So what the *Cittamatra* tradition teaches is that what we experience in life is a flow of perceptions which make objects themselves ultimately unreal. What *is* real is consciousness which is devoid of subject—object differentiation, the suchness of non-duality. If there is no object to be discerned then there will be no self to discern it. The *Yogacarins*, however, unlike *Madhyamika*, actually suggest the reality of the *mind* or *consciousness*: Mind-Only is absolute, ultimate reality, but to experience this, subject—object differentiation must be lost and ordinary worldy experience transcended.

Seed consciousness

In conjunction with the concept of *cittamatra*, the *Yogacarins* put forward the idea of store consciousness or seed consciousness (*alaya-vijnana*). This is a kind of collective unconscious which stores within it all the seeds of potential phenomena. The mind projects these seeds from their unconscious level into manifest existence, taking the resultant manifestations to be real. So really, these objects arise in the mind and are no different from the subject. The seeds which are found in the substratum consciousness, the unconscious storehouse of the seeds, are affected by the neutral, positive and negative *karma* of past existences, which are the motivating factors for the ripening and projection of these seeds into fruition in manifest existence. This substratum consciousness, then, underpins and informs the *samsaric* process. The *Yogacarins* described this process of releasing seeds from the substratum consciousness as "perfuming" the seeds with *karmic* actions to cause their release. The whole substratum consciousness is an impure form of consciousness producing the flow of experiences, the imagined level of reality which we noted earlier. Interestingly, the *Yogacarins* believed that some people possessed seeds for Buddhahood while others did not, and they even believed that some sentient beings could lack the seeds for any kind of goodness at all: such people they believed could never become enlightened. Yet there were others who saw a pure consciousness at the very root of every mind, a pure consciousness which was common to all and which was beyond all dualities and equatable with *nirvana*, rather like the ocean bed which is undisturbed by the waves above.

Yoga

The practice of yoga is at the heart of the *Yogacara* belief, as its name suggests. It was this practice with which they tried to transcend the phenomenal world and overcome the subject – object discrimination which led to a false view of reality. Yoga, the skilful means of the *Yogacarin*, led to pure, undefiled consciousness, the ultimate reality. This is an ultimate reality which, in true *Madhyamika* belief, shows the emptiness of all things, the *suchness* of all as true reality. What is different in the *Yogacarin* conception, however, is that emptiness is given *positive* identity; it becomes Absolute, the innate existence within emptiness.

The Doctrine of the *Trikaya*

The *Yogacarins* are credited with the development of one of the most important concepts within Mahayana Buddhism: the doctrine of the *Trikaya*, or three bodies of the Buddha. The theory was formulated in answer to a paradox which confronted Mahayana Buddhism. Whereas the true ideal of early Buddhism was the *arahant*, this was replaced in the Mahayana by the *bodhisattva*. Yet if this was the true ideal, why did Siddhartha Gautama not become a *bodhisattva*, rather than a buddha who selfishly passed away at *parinirvana*? This objection was addressed in the Yogacarins' concept of the *Trikaya*:

Gautama was not in fact an ordinary man, but the manifestation of a great spiritual being. The Buddha had three bodies – the Body of Essence (*dharmakaya*), the Body of Bliss (*sambhogakaya*), and the Body of Magic Transformation (*nirmanakaya*). It was the latter only that lived on earth as Siddhartha Gautama, an emanation of the Body of Bliss, which dwelled forever in the heavens as a sort of supreme god. But the Body of Bliss was in turn the emanation of the Body of Essence, the Ultimate Buddha, who pervaded and underlay the whole universe . . . the Body of essence was identified with Nirvana. It was in fact the World Soul, the Brahman of the Upanisads, in a new form.[29]

The development of this tradition partly stems from the *Madhyamika* school of thought where there was a tendency to project *sunyata* as an ultimate reality, termed the *Dharmakaya*, *Dharma*-body. The *Dharmakaya*, apart from representing the Buddha's wisdom embodied in his teaching, came to be seen as the very essence of the Buddha, his true nature. And since all beings are ultimately *sunyata* also, then they share the same essence as the Buddha and have the potential to realize this Buddhahood too. Another factor was the developing tendency at this time for monasteries throughout India to be regarded as residences of the Buddha. The doctrine of the *Trikaya* attempted to account for the Buddha's ubiquity.

The *Dharmakaya*

For some, though not for others, the *Dharmakaya* is the totally transcendent Absolute of Buddhism, the ongoing essence of the Buddha and the flow of Buddha-qualities within the universe. It is seen as the support of all *dharmas* and is unborn, unoriginated, uncreated and unformed. It is ultimate *thusness*, *tathata*. It is also the essential nature of the cosmos. It is permanent, unchanging and indescribable for, as *sunyata*, it is empty of all qualities. It is also empty of all dualities. It is the middle point because it neither exists in the conventional sense of the term, nor does it not exist in a nihilistic sense. It is also the middle point because it is one with all things, but it is also the manifold expressions of phenomena in the universe. While being Unmanifest, it can manifest itself in the other two forms of *Sambhogakaya* and *Nirmanakaya*. It is the ultimate nature of all buddhas and all reality. It is pure consciousness and is the *dharma* which the Buddha taught. It is the *nirvana* which is realized when the self is lost.

The *Sambhogakaya*

The *Sambhogakaya* is the "Enjoyment-Body" of the Buddha. It is the Yogacarin innovation in the doctrine of the *Trikaya*. It is physical in the sense that it can be seen by very advanced *bodhisattvas*, but it is not material in the sense of an earthly body. It is a projection of the *Dharmakaya*, and therefore is ultimately identical to the *Dharmakaya*. It is this form of the *Dharmakaya* to which devotion can be directed and it is on this level of the *Sambhogakaya* that other buddhas exist, teaching advanced *bodhisattvas* and working for the liberation of all sentient beings from *samsara*. In some ways, the *Dharmakaya* expressed in this form is more like the describable deities of many religions. It is therefore the aspect of the *Dharmakaya* which can be the object of faith. Such buddhas in the *Sambhogakaya* form are said to be as numerous as the grains of sand on the banks of the Ganges. Many preside over their own Buddha-land, Pure Lands, as they are called, lands which are brought into being by the immense good *karma* stored up by the buddhas. Though ultimately unreal and mind-only, they serve as a skilful means to guide the faithful. Because they can be visualized and anthropomorphized, the buddhas at the *Sambhogakaya* level supply the focus for considerable outward theism in Mahayana Buddhism.

The *Nirmanakaya*

This is the Buddha in earthly form. It is called the "Transformation Body" and is manifest in whatever forms are necessary for the promotion of the enlightenment of all sentient beings. Siddhartha Gautama was only one such manifestation. Although this *Nirmanakaya* is believed to be a projection of the *Sambhogakaya* level, it is ultimately identifiable with the *Dharmakaya*. It can be projected in any form, in any time, in any place and in any number of forms at the same time. The purpose of the *Dharmakaya's* manifestation as Siddhartha Gautama was merely so that the *dharma* could be taught; therefore the *Nirmanakaya* form is regarded as ultimately unreal.

Tathagatagarbha

The doctrine of the *Trikaya* was given a particularly distinctive interpretatation in the Buddhism of the Far East in the *tathgatagarbha* school of thought. *Tathagata* means "thus come" (or "thus gone"), meaning one who has arrived (at *nirvana*) (or one who has gone from *samsara* to *nirvana*), a buddha; while *garbha* means "womb", or "embryo". This refers to the idea that every sentient being has within it the embryonic potential of Buddhahood, a potential called *Buddha-nature*. Potentially, everyone is a *tathagata* with the ability to become the *Dharmakaya* by realizing the *Buddha-nature* within. This *Buddha-nature*, then, is equatable with the *Dharmakaya*, or *tathagatagarbha*. These ideas could be interpreted as a fourth turning of the Wheel of *Dharma*, a new teaching. It was a teaching which became particularly popular in the Far East. It was a teaching which presented the *Dharmakaya* being identified with all things, even the world of *samsara*. Thus, each entity in the universe and all *bodhisattvas* are as one. The *tathagatagarbha* is not separate from the world of *samsara*, but is its very basis. Both are just different perspectives of the same reality, the distinctions between them disappearing when *nirvana* is realized. *Tathagatagarbha*, *Buddha-nature*, or *Dharmakaya*, then, are still the point at which subject—object differentiation disappear, the point of non-duality.

There is in the concept of *tathagatagarbha* a certain amount of dynamism; the concept seems something of an active one in the sense that it is almost working within the cosmos to effect the liberation from *samsara* of all sentient beings. The *bodhisattvas* are part of this dynamic process, a process of active soteriology. So the *tathagatagarbha* is also the *dharma* of the Buddha and the *prajna* which allows enlightenment, as well as the *mahakaruna*, the great compassion through which the *bodhisattvas* operate in the world. This is a much more positive view of reality than that in earlier thought and is a very optimistic view of the cosmos and human nature. Yet there is still the conformity to the "Middle Way" as we have seen in other Mahayana teachings.

Buddha-nature

The course of time saw the emergence of new movements based on the concept that within every human heart there is a potentiality which, though clouded by attachments, is shared by all, and can be realized by layman and monk alike – the Buddha-nature. The teaching that Buddha-nature is the hidden essence within all sentient beings is the main message of the *tathagatagarbha* literature, the earliest of which is the *Tathagatagarbha Sutra*. This short *sutra* says that all living beings are in essence identical to the Buddha regardless of their defilements or their continuing transmigration from life to life. Thus all sentient beings are capable of full Buddhahood, and later *sutras* were keen to express this theme. It was a concept which contrasted with the *Cittamatra* tradition which claimed that some were too evil ever to attain enlightenment; they were "no-hopers", *icchantikas*. As in the earlier traditions, there is present the idea that enlightenment, or *nirvana*, is not something which has to be achieved, it is something which is already there, but is just covered over with defilements. In one *sutra*, the *Ratnagotravibhaga*, this concealed Buddhahood is compared to a beautiful statue of the Buddha which is covered over with dirty rags, to gold in ore, or to the seed in fruit; it is always there, it just has to be revealed. In a way, it means that everyone is really a Buddha *now*.

The *tathagatagarbha* thought continues the tradition of regarding *nirvana* as *thusness* or *suchness* and this is identical to Buddhahood and is the point at which subject—object differentiation disappears. It is the point of non-duality, and is permanent and unchanging, the essence which is not subject to the flux of life. Yet, as we have seen above, it has a certain dynamism in *prajna*, *mahakaruna*, and the *dharma*, all of which ultimately equate with the *Dharmakaya*. This suggests that the *Dharmakaya*, which is Buddhahood, is both Unconditioned and is present in the conditioned world. It is Unmanifest and manifest and, as in other Mahayana traditions, it is both *nirvana* and *samsara*. To reveal Buddha-nature is to reveal *sunyata* and *thusness* and to discover the true nature of reality, a reality which does not divide sensory experience into categories of subject and object.

From what we have seen, it has to be said that Buddha-nature is a permanent essence. It is beyond ego and the self-assertive personality and beyond desires, aversions and dualities, but it nevertheless exists as a permanent element in the self, and some texts of the *tathagatagarbha* literature, such as the *Mahaparinirvana Sutra* actually refer to an *atman*, though other texts are careful to avoid the term. This would be in direct opposition to the general teachings of Buddhism on *anatta*. Indeed, the distinctions between the general Indian concept of *atman* and the popular Buddhist concept of Buddha-nature are often blurred to the point that writers consider them to be synonymous. This occurs because the concept of Buddha-nature is given *svabhava*: the concept of *anatta* is still accepted as the doctrine of no-self in terms of the five *skandhas*, but when non-duality of Buddhahood is realized, for this school of thought, the true self, *atmaparamita*, is revealed. It is still characterized by *sunyata* but *sunyata* itself is given *svabhava*, "own-being", a positive permanent self. It is doctrines such as these which have suggested an underlying monism for these particular Buddhist philosophies.

> The grand equation of the purified store-consciousness, the perfected level of experience, the womb of Tathagatahood, and the Dharmakaya created a number of problems for the Yogacarins. One was the accusation from other Buddhists that this equation was little more than a recasting of the Upanisadic equation of the essential self with Brahman, the universal principle underlying the cosmos.[30]

The Spread of Buddhism

The centuries which followed the Buddha's demise saw those teachings which had taken root during his lifetime spread throughout India, living alongside, rather than ousting that kaleidoscope of religious beliefs which today rejoices in the name of Hinduism. Buddhism spread westwards into modern-day Pakistan and Afghanistan, before continuing into Iran and Turkestan. Under the patronage of the Indian Emperor Asoka and successors such as Kanishka, it was Buddhism's turn to rejoice. As early as Asoka's reign (third century BCE) Buddhism had moved as far south as Sri Lanka, where it remains to this day. For his part, Kanishka enjoyed ruling vast areas of land from the Indian plains to the Aral Sea, and Buddhism enjoyed his patronage.

In central Asia itself, the exportation of silk from mainland China to north-west India lent its name to an international trade route to the north of Tibet. Along the Silk Road, as it was called, Buddhist merchants from India, together with wandering monks, disseminated the Buddha's *dharma* along the route, carrying it into the heartland of China; consequently, Buddhism was known in central Asia from the second century BCE. Two centuries later, both early and Mahayana Buddhism were to be found in some of the city-states (a situation which obtained until Buddhism was ousted from central Asia by the Turks in the tenth or eleventh centuries), and by this time Buddhism had also established itself in what are now known as Burma and Thailand. In the fourth century, Buddhism spread from China to first Korea and then Japan, where it is popular today.

The reader might, at this point, be forgiven for thinking that, given its origins, Buddhism today is rife throughout the Indian sub-continent, perhaps even vieing with Hinduism for the honour of being hailed as the "national" religion of India. Of course, nothing could be further from the truth. By the thirteenth century, Buddhism had all but disappeared from the Indian sub-continent, if we exclude the Himalayas and Sri Lanka.

A major influence on its demise was the propensity of an ever-expanding Hinduism to readily appropriate beliefs and practices from other faiths. Mahayanist scholars were openly critical of Hinduism, but to the laity there must have seemed many similarities between the Tantric and devotional cults of the two faiths. Hinduism continued to adopt and adapt and Buddhism influenced the Hindu practitioners in many areas:

> The devotees of the god Visnu came to frown on animal sacrifices and to practise vegetarianism, while some Saivites (followers of the god Siva) viewed caste-distinction as being of little relevance to religious practice . . . Hinduism could not ignore the Buddha; so by around the sixth century, it recognized him as the ninth incarnation of Visnu.[31]

Paradoxically, some of the very factors which had influenced Hinduism were also seen as abhorrent. Buddhism's denial of the importance of the caste system was eventually deemed to be irreconcilable with the fabric of Indian society, while the Buddha's failure to recognize the authority of the *Vedas* cast him in the eyes of some Hindus as an enemy of the people. For the "man-in-the-street" there must have been times when, as in Nepal today, Buddhism seemed to be a branch of Hinduism, and others when it was viewed as a real threat to Hindu society.

The Muslim invasions sounded the death-knell for Buddhism. Buddhism had never enjoyed the benefit of having a military wing as did Hinduism and, later, Sikhism. Consequently, Buddhism was put to the sword with little opposition. An easily recognizable *Sangha* was immediately identified and readily despatched; in any case, with crops already destroyed by the invasions the laity lacked surplus raw materials to offer alms with which to give the support essential to the monks. Buddhism was all but dead:

> Between the alien Muslims, with their doctrinal justification of a "holy war" to spread the faith, and Hindus, closely identified with Indian culture and with a more entrenched social dimension, the Buddhists were squeezed out of existence. Lay Buddhists were left with a folk form of Buddhism, and gradually merged into Hinduism, or converted to Islam. Buddhism therefore died out in all but the fringes of its homeland, though it had long since spread beyond it.[32]

Statistics collated by the famous Chinese pilgrim and traveller, Hsuan-tsang, who visited India in the seventh century, attest to the fact that on Indian soil the Hinayana and the Mahayana existed contemporaneously and harmoniously. A head-count showed 115,000 Hinayana monks living alongside 120,000 Mahayana monks, with half of the Mahayanists studying Hinayana scriptures.[33]

Although Hinayana Buddhism did spread its wings beyond its country of birth, it was the Mahayana which had the greater missionary success. With its more liberal attitude towards the *Vinaya*, it was possible for Mahayana missionaries to condone the eating of fish by the Japanese, for example, which would never have been tolerated by early Buddhism. Nor would the *Vinaya* accept that monks could practise medicine, an edict which the Mahayanists readily overlooked since these acts of healing, which they saw as *mahakaruna*, were found to win the hearts of many grateful listeners at home and abroad.

The adaptability and tolerance of Mahayana were conspicuous in China as well as Japan. After reaching China in the closing centuries of the first millennium, it developed over the next five hundred years, becoming a major force and introducing to Chinese religion the concepts of reincarnation and Buddha-nature. Its success lay in the way in which it tolerated a syncretistic belief system of China, where to this day, Taoism, Confucianism and Buddhism remain comfortable bedfellows.

Nearer home, Mahayana ideas began to influence Tibet, where esoteric Tantric schools developed, as in Nepal and Kashmir. These schools, known as *Vajrayana*, advocated the attainment of enlightenment by means of personal instruction from one's personal *guru*, which remains a feature of *Vajrayana* to this day. Each Tantric school has its favourite *bodhisattvas* and divine forces which are manifold; each school also has its secret teachings and initiation ceremonies.

5

Nichiren

As we grapple with difficult Buddhist concepts, it is also important that
we have the inner richness to be able to look up at the stars or the moon
and compose a poem once in a while . . . When we open wide our minds
and fix our gaze on the universe, we fix our gaze at our own life.

Conversations on the Lotus Sutra, no. 28

The Life of Nichiren

On 16 February 1222, a baby boy was born in the south-eastern corner
of Japan to two poor fisherfolk, Mikuni no Tayu and Umegiku-nyo.
The name of the small fishing village was Kominato in the province of
Awa, the name of the baby boy was Zennichimaro, which means
"Splendid Sun". At the age of twelve (in Japanese chronology a child is
deemed to be one year old at birth) the boy was sent to Seicho-ji, the
local temple on Mount Kiyosumi. In those times it was commonplace
to send teenage boys to monasteries and no exceptional circumstances
are attributed to Zennichimaro's departure.

Throughout the days of his novitiate, Zennichimaro was an ernest
seeker of the truth who directed his mind towards becoming a Buddha
with a dedication which won the admiration of the temple's master,
Dozen-bo. The boy became an ordained monk at the age of sixteen (in
Japanese chronology) and was given the name Zesho-bo Rencho.
Rencho means "Lotus Growth". In his quest for enlightenment,
Zennichimaro became confused by the diversity of beliefs and practices
of the various Buddhist sects in Japan, and he resolved to study them all
fastidiously in order to reach his goal, a resolve which he later regretted
deeply:

In his early days at Seicho-ji, Zennichimaro embraced the practice of the

Jodo sect of chanting Namu Amida-butsu, which in later years he termed
a slander . . . In his "Letter from Sado," dated 1272, he wrote: "Since
Nichiren himself committed slander in the past, he became a Nembutsu
priest in this lifetime, and for several years he also laughed at those who
practiced the Lotus Sutra, saying, "Not a single person has ever attained
Buddhahood through that sutra," or "Not one person in a thousand can
reach enlightenment through its teachings."[1]

Several years of praying to the *Bodhisattva* Kokuzo, whose statue was
enshrined at Seicho-ji temple, gave Zennichimaro what he later termed
a "jewel of wisdom", an appropriate term since his prayers to Kokuzo
were that he should become "the wisest man in Japan". With increasing
confidence, the young priest, still only eighteen, left for Kamakura and
the Kyoto-Nara area to study Buddhism for three years, determined to
find the truth.

The truth for Rencho (as Zennichimaro was now known), was to be
found in the *sutras*, and he scoured the libraries of the temples which
proliferated these great centres of learning, ever-searching for documentary evidence of what could justifiably be called "the true
Buddhism". His constant concerns were, "Which of the Buddhist
schools is the true one? What are its beliefs and practices? and, How do
these relate to my own enlightenment?" Initially, he believed that the
truth was to be found in the teachings of both the Tendai Hokke and
Shingon sects, an opinion he committed to writing during a brief return
to Seicho-ji. However, after considerable deliberation and further
reading, Rencho concluded that not only were Tendai Hokke and
Shingon far removed from the truth of Buddhism, but so was every
other Buddhist sect!

The more he studied, the more Rencho became convinced of the
truth that he had first realized before the *Bodhisattva* Kokuzo – that
among the vast libraries which comprise the Theravada and the
Mahayana *sutras*, the *Lotus Sutra* and the *Lotus Sutra* alone contains the
true teachings of the Buddha. In due course, the now thirty-two year
old priest returned to Seicho-ji and, after a week's meditation, it was
with great anticipation that the assembled company at Kasagamori,
awaited his revelations. Thirteenth-century Japan was a particularly
poignant time and place to await declarations on how to achieve enlightenment, for at this time the attainment of enlightenment through one's
own efforts was considered to be well-nigh impossible. It was generally
considered that this was an age of despair, an evil period called *mappo*,
"the end of the *dharma*", or "Latter day of the Law", a time so decadent

that the Buddha's teachings were considered to be in their death throes. This was the political backdrop to the revelations at Kasagamori.

With growing expectancy, the crowd assembled in the priests' lodging at Seicho-ji temple, waiting for the return of Rencho, not from Kamakura but a nearby hilltop. There, Rencho had proclaimed to the heavens, but not within human earshot, that the supreme law of life is *Nam-myoho-renge-kyo*; this he chanted at sunrise on 28 April 1253. A stunned audience listened as Rencho first proclaimed this chant (which they had never heard of) to be the true essence of Buddhism, and then proceeded to denounce those very forms of Buddhism which the assembled audience had cherished since childhood. He castigated the very foundations of Zen, and reviled the proponents of *Nembutsu*[2] (Pure Land Buddhists) for encouraging belief in a Western Paradise, which (claimed Rencho) does nothing to encourage people to establish peace in their present lives. These were not the revelations the assembled audience wanted to hear:

> Reciters of the nembutsu (Pure Land Believers), he declared, would go to hell; advocates of Zen were devils; Shingon, with its dependence on esoteric rituals, would destroy the nation; proponents of the Vinaya rules for ordination were enemies of the state; the Tendai sect, founded by Saicho, was outdated.[3]

Were this not enough, Rencho next attributed the decadence of the times to those very heresies which he had just castigated. Forsake these and accept *Nam-myoho-renge-kyo* as the supreme law of life, and not only will the age of decadence come to an end, but Japan will become a Buddha Land. This was the message he gave first to the assembled company and, later, the Japanese government.

Rencho reached his conclusions through researching the *sutras*. For him, there was unequivocal evidence that all teaching prior to that contained in the *Lotus Sutra* was simply provisional and should be discarded. The reason it was there at all was because of *upaya*, the Buddha's "skill-in-means", whereby the Buddha, the Great Physician, would prescribe only the medicine appropriate to the level of response of the patients, or in Buddhist terms, the *dharma* the audience was ready to receive in terms of their levels of consciousness. Interestingly, if Watanabe Hoyo is correct, this could well be true of Nichiren:

> An integral aspect of his method of conversion (*shakubuku*) was the condemnation of the popular sects of Buddhism. Nichiren held that by deliberately provoking people and raising their anger he would cause

them to evaluate their beliefs. Anger and hatred, in Nichiren's system, were productive and creative emotional states.[4]

Furthermore, Rencho then informed the startled assembly that in future he was to be called not Rencho, but Nichiren, "Sun Lotus", reflecting the fact that there is no light in existence brighter than the sun and the moon, and there is nothing purer than the lotus flower, "Giving myself the name Nichiren signifies that I attained enlightenment by myself."[5] His words were later interpreted by the Nikko school to mean that Nichiren was claiming to be the original Buddha. The new *sutra* which revealed the eternal truth was the Japanese title of the *Lotus Sutra*, *Myoho-renge-kyo*. The chanting of this title of the *Lotus Sutra*, with the addition of the prefix *nam* ("devotion" or "homage to"), was the direct path to enlightenment which would reveal the Buddhahood inherent within every human being. However, the level of consciousness of his audience was unprepared for this panacea, for though Nichiren certainly raised their anger this did nothing to cause them to evaluate their beliefs and Nichiren was fortunate to escape with his life.

Undaunted, he soon converted both his parents, and then a stream of disciples; nothing could shake the conviction of Nichiren in the efficacy of the *Lotus Sutra*. In his treatise, *On Attaining Buddhahood*, Nichiren echoed the theoretical analyses evident in the writings of T'ien-t'ai, but he went much further than this; his was a practical application to the teachings of the *Lotus Sutra*, a point fervently believed by devotees today.

Convinced that the *Lotus Sutra* was *the Sutra* for the age of *mappo*, and that the Buddha's teachings therein were the universal remedy for this evil and decadent period in Japan's history, Nichiren next turned his attention to the Japanese Government. He pointed to the aforementioned Buddhist sects which he had earlier castigated as "heretical", and laid the blame for the demise of the nation firmly on their doorsteps. Searching for documentary evidence to support his claims, Nichiren concluded that various *sutras* attest to the fact that the slandering of the Mystic Law of Cause and Effect, as exemplified in the *Lotus Sutra*, would bring a series of disasters upon the nation, and these were already in evidence, in thirteenth-century Japan.

The seven disasters differ according to the sutras. The *Yakushi Sutra* defines them as pestilence, foreign invasion, internal strife, extraordinary changes in the heavens, solar and lunar eclipses, unseasonable storms and typhoons, and unseaonable droughts.[6]

Internal strife and foreign invasion were yet to come; as for the others, not only were these calamities self-evident, they were also self-inflicted – those who were slandering the teachings of the *Lotus Sutra* had only themselves to blame.

In one of his most famous writings, *Rissho Ankoku Ron*, "The Establishment of Righteousness and the Security of the Country", Nichiren associates True Buddhism with national peace. This treatise, written in 1260, reminds the Kamakura officials of the dire state of the nation, extols the efficacy of the *Lotus Sutra*, and berates other Buddhist sects, particularly proponents of the *Nembutsu* (Pure Land) belief in Amida Buddha, all of whom Nichiren believed to be responsible for the nation's downfall. The treatise, written in the form of a dialogue, ends with a traveller forsaking his previous convictions and resorting to the one True Buddhism, following the teachings of the *Lotus Sutra*. This ideal ending did not materialize in actuality, however, and for the second time, Nichiren narrowly escaped with his life.

The next year, the full fury of the *Nembutsu* priesthood descended upon him and, in collusion with the government, these priests and adherents had Nichiren banished to the Izu Peninsular, where they held the ascendency. A determined Nichiren, far from being downcast, once again resorted to studying the *Lotus Sutra*, where, to his immense solace, he found that he was living out its predictions. Nichiren saw his life unfolding before him in the thirteenth *(Kanji)* chapter of the *Lotus Sutra*. There, the *bodhisattvas* are found reassuring the Buddha that all will be well after his death, for they will disseminate the *dharma* far and wide, despite the attentions of an ignorant laity, a presumptuous priesthood, and priests with friends in high places, all of whom will revile the votary of the *Lotus Sutra*:

> For more than two hundred and forty days, from the twelfth day of the fifth month of last year through the sixteenth day of the first month this year . . . I have been living the sutra all twenty-four hours, both day and night. It is for the sake of the Lotus Sutra that I am undergoing this exile.[7]

Throughout the Izu exile Nichiren was attended by one Nikko Shonin, a sixteen-year-old priest, who would become Chief of Doctrine and succeed the Daishonin[8] twenty years later. In 1263 the forty-two year old Nichiren was pardoned by Hojo Tokiyori and returned to Kamakura.

His exile had done nothing to cool his fervour, however, and he continued to denounce both the government and all other sects of Buddhism, particularly Pure Land, with the same energy that he had shown both before and throughout his exile in Izu. Incurring the fury of the Japanese court, the *Nembutsu* priesthood, and the nation at large, in 1271 Nichiren was summoned to explain himself in court. Undaunted, Nichiren repeated his accusations against all rival forms of Buddhism and delivered to one of his chief accusers and Amida devotee, the major-domo Hei no Saemon, his treatise *Rissho Ankoko Ron*. At the same time he reminded the government of the impeding Mongol invasion in the light of his previous warnings.

His declaration "The Pillar of Japan is now falling" was the last straw, and Nichiren was brought before the Supreme Court and charged with high treason. Sentenced to exile on Sado Island, Nichiren was placed in the charge of Hei no Saemon, who had other plans for the Daishonin. Escorted to the execution ground at the behest of Hei no Saemon, Nichiren paused at the Hachiman shrine at Tsurugaoka. Before his startled bodyguard he prayed:

> Bodhisattva Hachiman, are you truly a god? . . . I, Nichiren, am the greatest votary of the Lotus Sutra in Japan, and entirely without guilt . . . the Lord Buddha urged each Buddhist god to pledge to protect the votary of the Lotus Sutra at all times. Each and every one of you Buddhist gods made this pledge . . . If I am executed tonight and go to the pure land of Eagle Peak, I shall report at once to Shakyamuni Buddha that Tensho Daijin and Hachiman have broken their oath to him. If you feel this will go hard on you, you had better do something about it right away.[9]

The escort party continued its mission of death, and eventually arrived at the Dragon's Mouth on Tatsunokuchi beach, the place of execution. Seated on a straw mat before the executioner and the official witness, Hei no Saemon, Nichiren uttered the invocation of the *Lotus Sutra* – *Nam-myoho-renge-kyo* – for what should have been the last time. Then he stretched out his neck for the blow that would never come:

> a brilliant orb as bright as the moon burst forth from the direction of Enoshima, shooting across the sky from southeast to northwest. It was shortly before dawn and still too dark to see anyone's face, but the radiant object clearly illuminated everyone like bright moonlight.[10]

With a now-blind executioner and a panic-stricken bodyguard both incapacitated, the execution was terminated before it had begun, and

Nichiren Daishonin walked out of the Dragon's Mouth and into history. The incident at Tatsunokuchi was a turning point in Nichiren's life, but not in the way Hei no Saemon and his fellow conspirators intended.

When, in his writing *The Opening of the Eyes*, the Daishonin later claimed that he had died on Tatsunokuchi beach, he was not echoing the claims of Christianity for the events at Calvary, nor those which occurred on the road to Damascus. His message was that the prisoner escorted to the place of execution was one whose sole function was to teach the true Buddhism by disseminating the message of the *Lotus Sutra*, one who functioned in the role of the *Bodhisattva* Jogyo, the votary predicted in the *Lotus Sutra*. For the Nikko school, however, it was not Jogyo who emerged from the miraculous intervention at Tatsunokuchi, but the Eternal Buddha whose existence has been, and always will be, just that; this is what Nichiren meant when he said he had died at Tatsunokuchi. Furthermore, in *The True Object of Worship* the Daishonin claimed that the Eternal Buddha and the eternal law expressed in the invocation *Nam-myoho-renge-kyo* were identical.

In exile on Sado Island, where he somehow survived in a bleak hut, a half-starved Nichiren crystallized his philosophical and spiritual beliefs in what was to become a period of great creativity.[11] Convinced of his incarnation as Visistacarita, protector of the truth of the *Lotus Sutra*, Nichiren never waivered from his position that in the true Buddhist life, metaphysics and actuality are inseparable; they should become one. Nor did he shift from his conviction that within every human being, no matter how low the level of consciousness, there exists Buddha-nature. Time and again, his writings stress that this is no elitist dogma, for every being has it within:

The true Buddha is a common mortal, a common mortal the true Buddha

The problem is not that only certain, favoured people have Buddha-nature, but that everyone has it but not everyone realizes it (at least not very often), largely due to the fact that we don't know *how* to realize it. It was to this problem that Nichiren turned his attention on Sado Island. Accordingly, he designed an object of worship in the form of a *mandala*, known as a *Gohonzon*, which, in keeping with his conviction that metaphysics and actuality are inseparable, encompassed his philosophical beliefs in graphic form. It is before a copy of this *Gohonzon* that followers of the Buddhism of Nichiren Daishonin chant *Nam-myoho-renge-kyo* to this day, convinced of its efficacy to realize Buddhahood.

After two and a half years on Sado, Nichiren was mysteriously pardoned, perhaps as the result of events at home and abroad. With an impeding Mongol invasion and internal strive in the form of a failed coup very much in people's minds, it may have been that Nichiren's earlier predictions were recalled. Any thoughts of advising the Japanese people to turn to the Buddhism of Nichiren Daishonin was far from governmental minds, however, for they looked to the Shingon priests to help with first a drought and then the Mongol invaders. A saddened Nichiren sought solace in retirement at Minobu, near Mount Fuji, having failed to convert the nation to his form of Buddhism. There he was attended by Nikko Shonin, the young priest who spread Nichiren's message at every opportunity.

On 12 October 1279, three years before his death, Nichiren fulfilled what he considered to be the purpose of his appearance in this world, by inscribing not individual *Gohonzons*, as he had done hitherto, but the Great or *Dai-Gohonzon*. Housed to this day in the Main Temple at the foot of Mount Fuji, the *Dai-Gohonzon* is the very embodiment of the Daishonin, the efficacy of the *Lotus Sutra*, and Nichiren's legacy to mankind:

> A sword will be useless in the hands of a coward. The mighty sword of the Lotus Sutra must be wielded by one courageous in faith. Then he will be as strong as a demon armed with an iron staff. I, Nichiren, have inscribed my life in *sumi* [black Chinese ink], so believe in the Gohonzon with your whole heart. The Buddha's will is the Lotus Sutra, but the soul of Nichiren is nothing other than Nam-myoho-renge-kyo.[12]

Nichiren devoted his remaining years to the training of young priests and the writing of letters to lay followers. The profusion of writing which had been the hallmark of his life began to diminish as death approached, and his energies became focused on words of encouragement in times of political turmoil, rather than innovation. On 8 September 1282 Nichiren wrote the *Document for Entrusting the Law which Nichiren Propagated throughout his Life*, in which Byakuren Ajari Nikko (Nikko Shonin) was named as his successor. One month to the day later, Nichiren appointed six priests as elders – Nissho, Nichiro, Nikko, Niko, Nitcho and Nichiji. Five days afterwards he died. H. Byron Earhart concluded, "Nichiren . . . is one of the most forceful personalities in Japanese history. By his opponents he was despised; by his followers he was emulated."[13]

With the notable exception of Nikko Shonin and his immediate disciples, these elders proved a disappointment. Separated from the Daishonin in his closing years, they entirely missed the kernel of his message as his embodiment in the *Gohonzon* and *Nam-myoho-renge-kyo*. Ignoring both the object of worship and the invocation, they interpreted his teaching as a form of Tendai Buddhism, dispatching their disciples to the headquarters of that sect on Mount Hiei. Others forsook the Buddhism of Nichiren Daishonin for Shinto and *Nembutsu*, as well as setting up a statue of Sakyamuni, to the chagrin of Nikko Shonin.

Utterly frustrated with the events which followed his master's death, Nikko departed from Minobu, taking with him his loved one's ashes, letters, and the *Dai-Gohonzon*, before establishing a small temple, called *Dai-bo*, near the foot of Mount Fuji. It is this site which today houses the temple complex of Taiseki-ji to which millions of pilgrims flock every year to worship the *Dai-Gohonzon*. Such is the legacy of Nichiren Daishonin.

The *Lotus Sutra*, or *Lotus of the True Law* (*Saddharma-pundarika Sutra*)

Of unknown origin and authorship, the *Lotus Sutra* is unquestionably one of the most influential of all Mahayana scriptures, being revered over the centuries by Mahayana Buddhists throughout eastern Asia, particularly in China, Korea and Japan. It is likely that it originated in some form in India or central Asia, probably compiled in a local dialect, before translation into Sanskrit enhanced its credibility and authority. The first Chinese translation, from the Sanskrit, occurred in 255 CE; other Chinese translations followed in 286, 290, 335, 406 and 601, but it is the 406 CE translation of Kumarajiva which has won universal acclaim and is generally accepted as the most authoritative text. Other early translations were made in Tibetan, Mongol, Manchu, Korean and Japanese, while recent translations into English and other European languages have rendered the *Lotus Sutra* accessible to the western reader. The scripture today is regarded as one of the most influential religious books in the world.

The establishment of the supremacy of the *Lotus Sutra* amongst all Sakyamuni's teachings is directly attributable to the work of the sixth-century Chinese Buddhist, T'ien-t'ai, whose school of thought addressed itself to synthesizing a unified system of belief for many of the different teachings of Buddhism. The Buddhism of Nichiren

Daishonin considers T'ien-t'ai to be the Buddha of the Middle Day of the Law, The T'ien-t'ai school proposed that the teachings of Sakyamuni can be classified into five periods and eight teachings, a synthesis which, at least for T'ien-t'ai, demonstrated beyond cavil that the words of the Buddha were carefully chosen to suit the level of consciousness of his audience, and that his teaching was evolutionary in nature, being directly proportional to the increased consciousness of his listeners. On this view, not only does the *Lotus Sutra* represent the culmination of the Buddha's thoughts, but all of Sakyamuni's earlier teachings are regarded as provisional, merely a "skilful means", entirely appropriate to the unevolved levels of consciousness of his audience at any given time, but never intended to be regarded as ultimate truth. According to T'ien-t'ai, it is the *Lotus Sutra* alone which contains the ultimate truth of Sakyamuni's teaching, a truth which at one and the same time transcends all his earlier teachings, and yet unites them. Moreover, this scripture presents the nature of Sakyamuni as ongoing.

The decline of Buddhism in China and the consequent demise of the *Lotus Sutra* saw the sixth T'ien-t'ai high priest, Miao-lo (538–597), reaffirm the efficacy of the *Lotus Sutra*, and it was returned to pre-eminence. Its similar standing in Japan was the direct result of the efforts of Dengyo (767–782), a student of one of the disciples of Miao-lo, under whom he studied T'ien-t'ai's teachings. Dengyo founded the Tendai school of Buddhism in Japan, where he refuted the teachings of the other Buddhist schools.

Objections against the *Lotus Sutra* that, "Mahayanists have not a shred of real evidence to show that the Buddha ever delivered any of the addresses attributed by them to him . . . the unprejudiced cannot doubt that they are the invention of a later period", and "We may say, then, that the Lotus never had any direct connexion with Sakyamuni",[14] have done nothing to quell the fervour for study of the *Lotus Sutra*. Indeed, not only has this Buddhist scripture attracted more commentary than any other, but its legacy has left its mark on the classical literature of both China and Japan. Its appeal undoubtedly lies in its unequivocal affirmation that Buddhahood is universally accessible to everyone; it is not reserved for the chosen few – "elitism" is not in its vocabulary.

In typical *Prajnaparamita* imagery, the cosmic drama unfolds against a backdrop which transcends time and space, depicts philosophical concepts in concrete terms, but above all affirms the true ideal of the Mahayana – the way of the *bodhisattva* – to be the one and only vehicle to enlightenment. At first, the reader could be forgiven for mistaking the *Sutra* for an historical record, but this was never the author's intention.

In the first chapter, Sakyamuni's close disciple, Ananda, is depicted recalling events which occurred at Eagle Peak on the outskirts of Rajagriha in northern India. Mount Gridhrakuta finds the Buddha in a plausibly historical setting preaching the *Lotus Sutra* before his audience. As Ananda begins to describe the form and number of the assembled company, however, the reader finds himself lifted from the stage of world history and elevated to the stage of cosmic drama. The assembly comprises earthly and heavenly beings, and descriptions of their multifarious forms are surpassed only by the mind-shattering numbers which are cited at every juncture:

> Again and again we are told of events that took place countless, indescribable numbers of kalpas or eons in the past, or of beings or worlds that are as numerous as the sands of millions and billions of Ganges rivers. Such "numbers" are in fact no more than pseudo-numbers or non-numbers, intended to impress on us the impossibility of measuring the immeasurable. They are not meant to convey any statistical data but simply to boggle the mind and jar it loose from its conventional concepts of time and space.[15]

The second chapter of the *Lotus Sutra* (entitled *Hoben* in Japanese) continues by affirming that whereas Sakyamuni's earlier teachings had accepted unequivocally that there are no less than three vehicles to salvation, including that of the *shravaka* or voice-hearer, who attains enlightenment by eventually becoming an *arahant*; the *pratyekabuddha*, who reaches that goal of life unaided; and the way of the *bodhisattva*; Sakyamuni now contends that only the last of these three vehicles is the true path to enlightenment. His explanation for this apparent change of heart is that his earlier teachings, prior to their culmination in the *Lotus Sutra*, were provisional, an example of his "skill-in-means", and only given because they were appropriate to the level of consciousness of his audience at that time. The Eternal Buddha – for this is how Sakyamuni is later presented in the *Lotus* – now recognizes that the assembled company is eminently capable of receiving the true message, and delivers it accordingly, with no longer the need to resort to any "skilful means" as a matter of expediency. To demonstrate the necessity for employing his earlier strategy, there follows, in chapter three, the famous parable of the burning house, wherein a father entices his children from danger with gifts entirely appropriate to their level of consciousness.

This need not detain us here, however, for followers of the Buddhism of Nichiren Daishonin focus their attention on chapters two and sixteen (entitled *Juryo*). It is in this sixteenth chapter, in fact, that Sakyamuni reveals himself as the Eternal Buddha who transcends time. He is not, as was previously thought, a historical personality, but one who is both omniscient and omnipresent in the world, helping others in their quest for enlightenment. His apparent disappearance and reappearance at various points in time is merely another example of his skilful means (*upaya*) by which he prevents the taking of his presence for granted, and the consequent diminishing of effort on the part of those seeking enlightenment. He then illustrates his point in the parable of the good physician, whose sons refuse any antidote for the poison they have consumed until their father's temporary departure.

The *Lotus Sutra* has a venerated place in Mahayana scripture, and the chanting of the whole of *Juryo* and part of *Hoben* (a thirty minute assiduous practice called *gongyo*) is a twice-daily occurrence for followers of the Buddhism of Nichiren Daishonin. Along with the chanting of *Nam-myoho-renge-kyo* (known as *daimoku*), it forms the religious ritual observed by these schools.

For Nichiren Buddhists, the *Lotus Sutra* both encapsulates and surpasses the teachings of Sakyamuni, but familiarity with the text is of no avail unless its power is translated into practical living. Again and again these schools make this self-same point; again and again it is the practice of *daimoku* which translates the dynamism of the *Lotus Sutra* into the dynamism of life:

> No matter how many words and phrases of the text one has committed to memory, no matter how eloquently and aptly one may be able to interpret them, if one cannot apply the teachings of the text in one's daily life and translate them into practical and concrete terms of action, then one's understanding of the sutra is valueless.[16]

Nam-myoho-renge-kyo[17]

Nichiren Daishonin declared the invocation publically for the first time on 28 April 1253 at the Seicho-ji temple at Kasagamori. His intention was to introduce a simple mode of practice which would make supreme enlightenment available to everyone. In Buddhist teaching, the title or *daimoku* of a *sutra* encompasses the essence of the whole teaching, so that anyone who merely chants the seven characters of *Nam-myoho-renge-kyo* has recited the *Lotus Sutra* in its entirety.[18] This is best explained by the analogy of someone who happens to glance at the spine

of a book entitled *Wales*. Without so much as turning a page, images of
sheep on rolling hills, coalmines, choirs, chapels, Saint David's Day,
harps, love-spoons, Welsh costumes, Tom Jones, rugby union, and
Welsh bards at eisteddfoddau, not to mention the sound of the Welsh
language, come flooding to mind – and the reader has only read one
word.

The *Lotus Sutra*, or to be precise, "The Sutra of the Lotus Blossom
of the Wonderful Law", is a translation of the Sanskrit title, *Saddharma-
pundarika-sutra*. As we have seen, no less than six Chinese translations
have been published, the definitive version being that of the renowned
scholar Kumarajiva in 406 CE. The Chinese title is *Miao-fa-lien-hua-
ching*, which in Japanese reads *Myoho-renge-kyo*. For Nichiren, those
who chant the title of the *Lotus Sutra*, even without understanding its
meaning, realize the very heart of the *Lotus Sutra*, as well as the essence
of all the Buddha's teachings.

Let us now examine the meaning of each of the individual characters
of the invocation:

Nam

While the actual title or *daimoku* of the *Lotus Sutra* comes from the
Chinese, *nam* derives from Sanskrit *namas*, meaning "devotion". Since
the object of worship (Jap. *honzon*) in the Buddhism of Nichiren
Daishonin is the *Gohonzon* (*Go* is an honorific prefix), the first word of
the invocation indicates devotion to the *Gohonzon*. For Nichiren, this
devotion had a twofold application, for embodied in the *mandala* which
he inscribed is the Law or the Ultimate Truth, *Nam-myoho-renge-kyo*,
as well as the Daishonin himself, in whom the Law became manifest. So
the Daishonin and the Law are fundamentally one.

Myoho

Myoho means "the Mystic Law". *Myo* (mystic) is the word used to
describe the Law of life (*ho*) in its manifest form. Drawing on the well-
known Mahayana concepts of existence and non-existence, Nichiren
likened life to the mind. Any attempt to seek empirical proof of the presence of the mind leads one to the inevitable conviction of its
non-existence, a conviction which is instantly negated by one's thought
processes which furnish proof of its existence. Similarly, life is neither

existence nor non-existence, although it displays the qualities of both. When one reveals one's own Buddha-nature, one becomes co-extensive with the Universe, and *myo*, the essential nature of the Law, is the enlightenment which removes the darkness and delusion *(ho)*. Enlightenment is accompanied by recognition that as surely as the planets and all of nature are subject to the Law of life, so too are we.

Renge

Renge literally means "lotus blossom". Contrary to popular belief, the lotus is found in India only in the region of the Himalayas, an area well-trodden by Sakyamuni. Nevertheless, the symbol of the lotus is conspicuous throughout India's long history, and it is prominent in both sacred and profane literature. The writings of T'ien-t'ai, however, denied the lotus has any intended symbolism in the *Lotus Sutra*, rather the appearance of the word in the *Sutra's* title should be understood as both a metaphor for the Mystic Law and the Law itself. Nichiren Daishonin made the point that of the countless plants on earth, it is the lotus alone which flowers and seeds at one and the same time. By the same token, the accrual of *karma* occurs at the same instant as the action. Accordingly, the devotee who takes up the *Lotus Sutra* receives immediate enlightenment, while instant Buddhahood is accorded those who chant it – other *sutras* state that good causes must first be made, then *some time later* Buddhahood may be achieved. The Daishonin affirmed that whoever practises *Myo-renge*, the lotus of the Mystic Law, "will simultaneously obtain both the cause and the effect of Buddhahood."[19]

Kyo

Kyo is the Japanese word for *sutra* or "thread", the teachings of the buddhas. Both T'ien-t'ai and Nichiren drew attention to the fact that this teaching was originally given orally, and the Daishonin equated *kyo* with the sounds emitted by all living creatures, thereby affirming that Buddhahood exists within every living creature. The unfathomable, unmanifest subtlety within the cosmos known as *myo*, which can be drawn upon to achieve enlightenment, pervades all of manifest existence, and it is the *kyo* which threads all manifest phenomena together and unites with the unmanifest as the eternal and unchanging truth. The fact that the Chinese character for *kyo* originally meant the warp of a length of cloth, indicates the continuity, indeed the eternity of the teaching of the *Lotus Sutra.*

The true object of worship – the *Gohonzon*

Faith in chanting is the indispensable element of commitment. It is time-taking, in itself highly repetitive, and an exacting routine. Members have to believe that it is effective or they would have little reason to remain Nichiren Buddhists.[20]

The chanting of the Mystic Law, as the phrase *Nam-myoho-renge-kyo* exemplifies, may be undertaken at any time in any place, but it is the *Gohonzon* which is said to reflect the Buddhahood within every individual. Appropriately, when Nichiren claimed he saw his life reflected in a pond at Seicho-ji temple, he termed it "the great *mandala*". Consequently, the *mandala*, which is seen as the true object of worship for Nichiren followers, is more like a mirror than a god.

In the Sado exile, Nichiren formulated the philosophical and doctrinal basis for the establishment of the *Dai-Gohonzon*. This Great *Gohonzon* was to become the true object of worship for the present age. Enshrined in the Grand Main Temple *(Sho-Hondo)* at Taiseki-ji, at the foot of Mount Fuji, the *Dai-Gohonzon* is a plank of camphor wood bearing a carved inscription written in black *sumi* ink. *Honzon* means "object of fundamental respect" and *go* means "worthy of honour". The object of fundamental respect takes the form of a *mandala*. The inscription which runs down the centre of the *mandala* reads *Nam-myoho-renge-kyo, Nichiren,* fusing in a stroke the mystical law of cause and effect with the very Buddha whom the Nikko school believes to be the original Buddha, Nichiren Daishonin. Nichiren followers believe in ten worlds or life-conditions ranging from Hell to Buddhahood, which we experience with alarming regularity; these are to be found either side of the inscription. The point being made by this graphic representation is that as surely as these life-conditions are, by definition, conditions for life, so can they be brought under control in each individual by chanting the supreme law, thus making us authors of our own destinies.

We do not have to "work through" our negative karma, acquiring virtue, in order to attain enlightenment at some point in the future. At the moment of chanting to the Gohonzon we are able – if we wish – to observe our own mind and find Buddhahood within it.[21]

Graphic representations at the bottom of the inscription attest that the *Dai Gohonzon* is not the preserve of esoteric worshippers, but *ichiembudai soyo* – "bestowed upon the entire world", the point being that the Buddhahood of the Daishonin is embodied within the *Dai-Gohonzon* . . . this was his eternal legacy. Today, believers have their individual *Gohonzons* which are transcriptions of the original. These usually take the form of Chinese and Sanskrit characters written in black *sumi* ink on a paper scroll.

Fundamental to the Buddhism of Nichiren Daishonin are the three aspects of faith, practice and study. Study involves not only reading the writings of Nichiren, but their daily application also; practice is the assiduous practice of *daimoku* and *gongyo* twice daily and encouraging others to the practice; faith is belief in the *Gohonzon*. The teaching of Nichiren is that faith in the *Gohonzon* and the chanting of *daimoku* before it, together with the encouragement of others to do the same, will evoke the same life-condition of Buddhahood found embodied within the *Dai-Gohonzon*. The teaching of the Buddhism of Nichiren Daishonin to others, known as *kosen-rufu*, is believed to lead ultimately to world peace.

The nine consciousnesses

Nichiren Buddhism teaches that all sentient beings have nine levels of perception. The first five levels of perception are dependent upon the five senses which, by means of their corresponding sense organs, inform the mind of external stimuli. The sixth consciousness interprets the received information and draws conclusions about the physical world – that is a Wendy House: it is hard, that is a Teddy Bear: it is soft, etc. The seventh consciousness makes moral and value judgements – adultery is wrong; Pavarotti is the world's greatest tenor; children should not be allowed to watch late-night television; and so on.

The eighth consciousness operates at the level of the subconscious, the level at which accrued past *karma* is stored. Thus, although below the level of conscious thought, this level, or more correctly the *karma* which is stored at this level, is directly responsible for all our aversions and desires and their concomitant behaviour traits; in short, our every action.

The ninth and deepest level of all is Buddha consciousness, wherein clarity of thought and deed become the norm, and negative and impure thoughts have no place. This, then, is pure consciousness, which is equatable with pure life-force, *Nam-myoho-renge-kyo*. Since the ninth level of consciousness and pure life-force are identifiable, pure consciousness can be realized by chanting *Nam-myoho-renge-kyo* which will permeate our entire beings and purify all the other levels of consciousness. Nichiren Buddhism teaches that Buddha consciousness is impervious to *karma*.

The ten worlds

Each and every individual is believed to have ten life-conditions which he or she encounters from moment to moment in everyday existence. These life-conditions are known as the ten worlds, and most people are believed to spend the best part of their lives in what are known as the six lower worlds which are hell, hunger, animality, anger, tranquillity and rapture. Hell is what is experienced by the sufferer trapped in a frustrating job or relationship where the only escape often seems to be self-destruction or the annihilation of others. This festers self-doubt, loss of self-esteem and the wishing of ill upon others. Hunger is the insatiable craving for food, success, power, sex, wealth and much more, none of which gratifies; this is the *tanha* which Sakyamuni identified. Animality completes what are known as the three evil paths and is the amoral instinctive world of self-preservation and survival with no consideration for others. The four evil paths include anger, temporary madness, when our ego has been affronted, our reputation has been tarnished, our position challenged, our importance sullied. Tranquillity and rapture are certainly more harmonious; equally certainly they are just as transient and just as dependent upon environmental circumstances,

Nichiren Buddhism calls the four higher worlds, learning, realization, *bodhisattva* and Buddhahood, *the noble paths*, but these are paths which can be journeyed only with considerable effort. Learning and realization or absorption are similarly concerned with the meaning of life, and similarly threatened by delusions of grandeur which these states may induce. *Bodhisattva* has its own pitfalls, for the altruistic dedication to helping others through life's trials and tribulations can lead to loss of self-respect and its resulting effects. The highest state of all is Buddhahood, "the state of true indestructible happiness, a condition of perfect and absolute freedom, characterized by boundless wisdom, courage, compassion and life-force."[22] Although this happiness is impervious to environmental circumstances and is in this sense indestructible, it is nevertheless transient, just like the other nine worlds. In the state of Buddhahood, moreover, the negative aspects of the lower worlds become transformed into positive ones so that we become angry against injustice, hunger for world peace and so on.

These are the life-conditions through which we regularly move, and in the teaching of Nichiren Buddhism they apply to everyone: there can be no exceptions.

Ichinen sanzen

An immense philosophical system which incorporates the ten worlds was propounded by T'ien-t'ai. Known as *ichinen sanzen*, and based upon the *Lotus Sutra*, this doctrine is central to the Buddhism of Nichiren Daishonin; it is basically an explanation of the unity and inter-connectedness of the universe.

> *Ichinen sanzen* literally means "a single life-moment possesses three thousand realms", and explains the relationship between the Ultimate Truth, Nam-myoho-renge-kyo, and the everyday world. With this principle, T'ien t'ai demonstrated that everything in life – mind and body; self and the environment; the living and the non-living; cause and effect – are all integrated in the life-moment of the ordinary person.[23]

T'ien-t'ai formulated his theory by adding ten factors related to physical and spiritual activities of life in each of the ten worlds and the three realms of existence. Accordingly, he arrived at the conclusion that in each and every life-moment, three thousand categories are formed, only to change in the next moment. In other words, every thought, word and deed in every moment of every individual's life is inextricably bound to the whole of the cosmos.

These ideas are very much an elaboration of the general Buddhist doctrines of impermanence, and the concept of the constant flux and state of becoming of everything in existence. All is interdependent and relative to something else; what T'ien-t'ai did was to quantify this process. But the theory of *ichinen sanzen* goes further than this in seeing each life-moment as being inseparably bound to all the phenomena in the universe, making the whole universe condensed into just one life-moment of any individual. Conversely, each life-moment of a person will have an effect on the whole of the universe to which it is so inextricably bound and thus can affect the universe positively, negatively or neutrally. Thus, this is a theory of the unity of the universe, suggesting that the macrocosm of the cosmos is held within one moment of life but, at the same time, the essence of each individual pervades the whole universe. T'ien-t'ai believed that this was the knowledge which the Buddha awakened to at his Enlightenment – knowledge of the fusion and mutual relation of all things, knowledge of the mystic realm of life.

The interface between each life-moment and the rest of the cosmos may be likened to the surface of a frothy stream upon which conglomerations of bubbles no sooner form than break off to form new patterns which immediately disintegrate to reform new ones, a process which continues *ad infinitum*. Similarly, to the Nichiren Buddhist, there is no end to the *samsaric* cycle, no final *nirvana*, no escape from the continuous round of birth and death, redeath and rebirth.

As surely as the theory of *ichinen sanzen* holds that every life-moment is inextricably linked to the whole of the cosmos, so is each of the ten worlds inextricably bound to the others, for without any one of the ten worlds there can be no others. This is not, then, a theory of progression, whereby one ascends from the lowest hell-state over a period of time, gradually evolving over the years (or even lifetimes) through each of the ten worlds, leaving the previous life-condition behind forever until one reaches Buddhahood, where one remains until death, but a teaching of realization, the realization that in each and every world, even in the life-condition of hell, the potential for Buddhahood is always present, realizable through the chanting of *Nam-myoho-renge-kyo*. Just as surely, the potential of the other nine worlds is always present, even in the tenth world.

Acceptance of the theory of *ichinen sanzen* places a much wider interpretation on the law of *karma*, an interpretation which holds that the actions of each and every individual have repercussions not only for the individual concerned but for the whole cosmos. Since each action must, of necessity, arise in a cosmic moment, it must have its effect on the universe in that moment. Every action, therefore, will accrue its reaction instantly, though often in a latent form which will not manifest itself until some time later. In this light, the chanting of *Nam-myoho-renge-kyo* exemplifies the *ichinen sanzen* view that results inhere in their causes, for the words both embody yet ultimately transcend Buddhahood, and their invocation is believed to generate immediately the good *karma* which must later come to fruition. Hence the results (the accrual of good *karma*) inhere in their causes (the action of chanting itself). For followers of the Buddhism of Nichiren Daishonin, therefore, the theory of *ichinen sanzen* makes it *inevitable* that the very act of chanting will reap benefit not only for the individual concerned, but for the universe at large.

At this juncture, Nichiren philosophy parts company with the teachings of early Buddhism, for nowhere is there to be found the injunction of the Second Noble Truth that all desire is wrong. Nor is there a move towards an ego-less state and its attendant non-fruitive *karma* brought about by ego-less action (where there is no thought of "Look what *I* have done!"); rather, the energy to be found in desire is seen as the fuel which fires the drive towards positive action and the consequent acquisition of good *karma*; this is the path to spiritual fulfilment, not denial of the self or negation of desire. Accordingly, in the state of Buddhahood it is not desire itself which is condemned, but the base desires inherent within the other ten worlds; yet even these lower desires are not to be discarded, simply transformed into higher desires which have wisdom rather than ignorance as their base. In fact, for followers of Nichiren, it is the earlier teachings of Sakyamuni which should be discarded, for his condemnation of desire as set forth in the Second Noble Truth is seen as yet another example of his skill-in-means, appropriate only to the level of consciousness of his audience at that moment in time.

Soka Gakkai International

The teachings of Nichiren Daishonin gave rise to a large number of Nichiren sects, many of which revolved around a priesthood. Although Nichiren Shu, which has Kuon-ji as its head temple in Minobu, is often found used as a generic term for the many sects which regard Nichiren Daishonin as their founder, the issue is much more complicated than this and to pursue it here would inevitably misrepresent the position.[24] Nichiren Shoshu, the "Orthodox Nichiren sect", which has Taiseki-ji in Shizuoka Prefecture as its head temple, regards Nichiren Daishonin as its founder and Nikko Shonin as his immediate successor. The oldest major modern Nichiren sect is the Reiyukai, a lay organization from which many new Nichiren movements arose, notably the Rissho Koseikai.[25] The movement, which is larger than the sum of all other Nichiren sects, is a lay organization known as Soka Gakkai International, which has received surprisingly little attention from western academics:

> The Soka Gakkai International (SGI) is a worldwide association of 76 constituent organizations with membership in 128 countries and territo-

ries. In the service of its members and of society at large, SGI centers its activities on developing the positive human potentialities for individual happiness and for global peace and prosperity.[26]

In 1930, the educational system of Japan focused upon *training* individuals, using rote learning methods, rather than *educating* them by developing their critical analytical thought processes. This methodology was anathema to one educational thinker and author, Tsunesaburo Makiguchi. Together with a young teacher, Josei Toda, Makiguchi founded the Soka Kyoiku Gakkai (Value Creating Education Society) in that same year, with a view to enabling each and every individual to realize his or her full potential; his conviction was that the very essence of all humanity is its ability to create value. The determination of this educational reformer to understand the meaning of human life had unsurprisingly brought him and Toda into contact with Nichiren's teachings, in particular the Daishonin's view that all individuals have the potential to achieve enlightenment by their own efforts. This gave Makiguchi's quest a spiritual dimension germane to the foundation of the Soka Kyoiku Gakkai.

However, 1943 Japan and the demise of confidence in Second World War victory, was neither the time nor the place for reform thinkers who opposed the war effort and its attendant horrors. Makiguchi, Toda, and other free-thinkers were imprisoned as "thought criminals". Despite the brutality and hardships of imprisonment, Makiguchi never waivered from his convictions, and he died in the Tokyo Detention House the following year aged 73. Six months later a ravaged Toda was released from prison, and he immediately began to rebuild the organization which he now renamed the Soka Gakkai (Value Creating Society). No longer was the vision to be the sole preserve of education, for the abilty of humanity to create value should surely benefit the whole of society. By 1958, the year Toda died, more than three quarter of a million homes in Japan contained members of the Soka Gakkai; at the time it was hailed as "the fastest growing religion in the world".[27]

Toda's vision of world peace was continued by the third president, Daisaku Ikeda, who came to office in 1960. Having the ear of such notables as Mikhail Gorbachev and Nelson Mandela, Ikeda has worked unceasingly to this end, and the SGI's official associations with the United Nations have magnified the peace effort. Research centres have been set up with a view to assimilating the collective wisdom of international peace reformers and associations, often through active and rigorous debate. The breadth of the vision becomes immediately apparent when it is found manifest in the conviction that, "music, art and other cultural expressions enhance the richness of human life and can inspire mutual respect and understanding in our diverse world".[28] Concert associations, art museums and entire educational systems have been founded to this end, as well as a related political party, the Komeito (clean government party).

From May 1960 onwards, Ikeda worked tirelessly to expand oversees membership, and in January 1975 he resigned the presidency, becoming honorary president, in order to increase his efforts. He was given the United Nations Peace award in 1983. The SGI has recently dissociated itself from the priesthood of Nichiren Shoshu Buddhism and now presents itself as the organization which practices the Buddhism of Nichiren Daishonin.[29] One of the most rapidly expanding of all Buddhist schools, its undoubted appeal lies in the fact that its beliefs and practices are easily understood and readily accessible to the lay person. All that is required is faith in the *Gohonzon*, the time to chant twice daily with the teaching of others to do likewise, and time for study.

> Among these three, faith is the most fundamental for the attainment of Buddhahood. Faith gives rise to practice and study; practice and study serve to deepen one's faith.[30]

Its philosophy is very simple and is centred upon the title of the *Lotus Sutra*, yet this simple philosophy is considered by believers to be the catalyst which ensures the manifestation of Buddhahood in the individual and its consequent benefit to all mankind.

6

Tibet: The Land of Snow

The Land of Tibet is a phenomenon which, in a stroke, brings breath-taking imagery to the artist's brush, and concepts of mystery to the writer's mind. Snow-clad mountain ranges with tranquil monasteries, splendid in their isolation, unique in their setting, pay tribute to the country Tibetans call "The Land of Snow." Isolated in a geographical setting surrounded by mountains, its people have developed a spiritual culture which tends to look inwards rather than out at the world around them. Some of the highest mountains in the world have challenged man to ascend the peaks physically; some of the highest teachings have inspired man's aspirations spiritually.

If the snow-clad mountain ranges in question remain to this day the preserve of The Land of Snow, equally certainly Tibetan Buddhism does not. Neighbouring Himalayan countries such as Bhutan, Sikkim and Nepal were soon influenced, an influence which later spread to Mongolia and, later still, China. More recently, the tragic events which occurred as a result of the Chinese overthrow of Tibetan rule in 1959, and the consequent exodus of the Dalai Lama and many learned scholars to the safety of India and the West, far from heralding the demise of Tibetan Buddhism, has bequeathed a legacy of accessibilty to western scholarship which was never foretold:

By now, tens of thousands of Westerners have had direct exposure to the teachings of the lamas. Thousands have done some Tantric practice and hundreds have undertaken traditional three-year retreats or been ordained within the Tibetan traditions. The numbers involved are growing steadily, if with little publicity, and the eventual consequences for what is increasingly a world cultural system may be significant. It is evident, however, that any survival of Tibetan forms of Buddhism outside the Tibetan community will again involve their radical transformation.[1]

In its turn, Tibetan Buddhism has been bequeathed not one legacy, but three. The legacy of early Buddhism, which for want of a more suitable word I shall continue to call Hinayana, with its emphasis on monastic life, is self-evident. Indeed, the reader might well be forgiven for wondering why Tibetan Buddhism, with its commitment to the monastic tradition, does not belong to the Theravadin school. This question is answered immediately by the second legacy, however, for the Mahayana belief in *bodhisattvas* and emphasis on "great compassion", *mahakaruna*, which are the hallmark of Tibetan Buddhism, place this school firmly within the parameters of the Mahayana. It is the third vehicle, the final *yana* which gives Tibetan Buddhism its distinctiveness, however, for it is Vajrayana which bestows its legacy of esoteric beliefs and practices.

In Tibetan Buddhism, the three *yanas* are seen as the necessary vehicles to salvation for respective audiences of the Buddha. The Buddha's teachings are therefore classified under three rubrics appertaining to the differing spiritual needs of his listeners: the Hinayana would undoubtedly appeal to those who sought personal salvation (from the *samsaric* cycle); the Mahayana appeal was to those to whom compassion for others was just as important as personal salvation, and who sought the latter in order to inform the former; while Vajrayana adherents embrace both positions and are prepared to endure the hardships of Tantric practice for the sake of a swift enlightenment. Within the eclectic philosophical systems and meditative practices of all four Tibetan orders are found not only elements from the three vehicles, but also the four main schools of Indian Buddhism.[2]

Rather late beginnings

The aforementioned geographical isolation and a distinct culture of its own belie the proximity of Tibet to Buddhism's Indian birthplace. This may account for the fact that Buddhism arrived in Tibet rather late, in the seventh century CE and did not become established under royal patronage until the eighth century. Tibet was in need of a state religion and by the eleventh century Buddhism had become the dominant religion. Though modern scholarship has recognized China's contribution to the early history of Tibetan Buddhism, the diversity one normally associates with Mahayana Buddhism is conspicuous by its absence in Tibet, and David Snellgrove attributes this to the unquestioning acceptance of the monastic rule of just one Indian Buddhist order, that of the Mulasarvastivadins.[3] As surely as Tibet looked to seventh-century India for its alphabet, so did the Buddha's homeland furnish Tibet with its sacred texts, philosophical ideas and rituals. Snellgrove also points to the fact that the concept of religious lineage, whereby the beliefs and practices of a particular religious tradition are handed down in succession from master to pupil, is absolutely fundamental to the Tibetan mind.[4]

There is no shortage of historical figures whom tradition has associated with the beginnings of Buddhism in Tibet. These include the seventh-century Tibetan King, Song-tsen-gam-po, who is believed to have been an incarnation of the patron *bodhisattva* of Tibet, no less than Avalokitesvara himself, and the King's two wives who are both considered to be manifestations of the *bodhisattva* Tara. A century later the name of the great Indian scholar and monk, Santaraksita, is similarly associated, as is that of Padmasambhava, the Tantric esotericist whom all Tibetan schools revere to this day. The arrival upon the scene of the Indian Buddhist monk and exorcist Padmasambhava attests to the initial opposition to Buddhism in Tibet, for Padmasambhava was specifically invited to Tibet in order to overcome local enmity which was thought to have manifested itself in the form of indigenous demons. Although the native Bon religion is sometimes identified with those indigenous forces which proved hostile to the appearance of Buddhism in Tibet, this is an oversimplification of a very complex problem which should not detain us here.

Nor is there unaminity of opinion on the outcome of what has become known as the debate at Sam-ye. Padmasambhava's remit was given to him by the Tibetan king Trhi-song-de-tsen, successor to Song-tsen-gam-po, and involved employing his exorcistic talents to overcome native demonic forces that were considered to be a stumbling block to what should have been building blocks for the foundation of the Buddhist monastery at Sam-ye. The subsequent overthrow of these indigenous forces and the eventual establishment of the monastery at Sam-ye, however, did not herald common agreement on all matters Buddhist. The delayed appearance of Indian Buddhism in Tibet was followed by the arrival of a Chinese influence which did not always see eye to eye with its Indian counterpart:

> Some years later (about 792 CE), a great debate was held at the same monastery of Sam-ye, under the auspices of the Tibetan king. A Chinese monk, known in our source as Hwa-shang, represented the Ch'an school and argued that Buddhist realization was a matter of "sudden enlightenment," which was not the result of a long practice of good works and progressive meditations but an instantaneous awakening to one's innately

enlightened nature. The Indian master Kamalasila ... represented the view of the "gradual path," which argued not only for the systematic practice of compassion but also that wisdom was to be approached progressively through study, logical investigation, and meditative contemplation.[5]

This was a debate which was in no way confined by the monastery walls of Sam-ye, for this issue was considered by Buddhists to have sufficient import to be discussed in China and elsewhere, with far-reaching consequences. However, these consequences did not extend to the establishment of a vast galaxy of Buddhist sects either in China or Tibet, though in China the Southern and Northern Ch'an (Japanese Zen) schools became recognizable, as did the four major orders in Tibet.[6]

To affirm that Tibetan Buddhism today is informed by four quite distinct traditions – the Nying-ma-pa, the Ka-gyu-pa, the Sa-kya-pa, and the Ge-luk-pa – is at one and the same time to represent and to misrepresent the position. It is true that each has its own beliefs and practices, yet any suggestion that these are in fact diverse sects with little or no common ground is misleading. John Strong likens them to several currents following the same course in the same stream; they may diverge but they always remerge to feed one another.[7] In fact, differences are restricted to certain beliefs and practices which include the interpretation of common doctrines and the lineages of certain gurus.

In all four orders, the denial of attachment to cyclic existence and the prerequisite for sincere renunciation share common ground, a ground which has the *Vinaya* of the Mulasarvastivada school as its bedrock. John Powers observes that these rules of monastic discipline have:

> been the standard in Tibetan monasteries since the founding of the first monastic institution at Samye. In addition, they also share the same corpus of philosophical and liturgical texts imported from India, and all four orders present a path to enlightenment that incorporates practices of sutra and tantra systems.[8]

The Dalai Lama himself has noted that there is common agreement also that Tibetan Buddhism has the Middle Way of Nagarjuna, who founded the *Madhyamika* school in the second century of the common era, as its philosophical cornerstone, a point well made by Professor Murti when he wrote, "The Madhyamika remains to this day the official philosophy of the Tibetan Church."[9]

Commonality of beliefs and practices amongst all four Tibetan schools includes the acceptance of the views of Nagarjuna as the pinnacle of philosophical thought, and the viewing of the mind as being of the nature of pure light and emptiness. The indisciplined mind is open to delusion and, having deluded itself, will begin to think negatively. Negative behaviour will inevitably follow, repeat itself again and again, invite negative responses from others and ensure bondage to cyclic existence.

Tibetan Buddhism, with its distinctive practices of Highest Yoga Tantra, acknowledges the role of the mind in the bondage to *samsara*. Meditational practices which train the mind to centre upon love and compassion are far more likely to evoke loving compassionate responses than those from the deluded mind. Accordingly, all four schools agree on generation of the mind of enlightenment as the starting point along the path to liberation from the *samsaric* cycle, and the subsequent cultivation of the six perfections, as practitioners progress through the *bodhisattva* levels. This commonality extends to regarding Tantric practice as the ultimate Buddhist path, though each school has its favourite Tantras and lineages:

> The Nyingma school, for instance, emphasizes the practices of the "great perfection" (*rdzogs chen*; pronounced "dzogchen"), and its tantric practices are mainly based on the so-called "Old Tantras" (such as the *Secret Basic Essence Tantra*) and on practices derived from "hidden treasures" (*gter ma*; pronounced "terma"). The Kagyu school emphasizes the mahamudra system inherited from the Indian master Tilopa, and its tantric practices are mainly derived from the *Guhyasamaja Tantra* and the *Cakrasamvara Tantra*. The Gelukpa system of tantric theory and practice is based on the *Guhyasamaja Tantra*, the *Cakrasamvara Tantra*, and the *Kalacakra Tantra*. The Sakyapas favor the *Hevajra Tantra*, which is the basis of their "path and fruit" (*lam 'bras*; pronounced "lamdre") system.[10]

Each of the four schools also favours practices associated with particular deities; Geluk, for instance, features Tantric practices associated with Avalokitesvara, Manjusri, Vajrapani, Green and White Tara, Bhaisajyaguru, Guhyasamaja, Yamantaka, Heruka Cakrasamvara, Vajrayogini, and Kalacakra.

> The different Taras are considered to be individual emanations of the same buddha, each of which is manifested with a particular skin color.[11]

Known as "the ancients", the Nyingma trace their lineage back to

Padmasambhava, though the so-called "Old Tantras" upon which their Tantric practices are mainly based often contain elements of the Bon religion which was indigenous to Tibet but not always acceptable to the other schools. The Kagyu school is generally believed to be a continuation of the line of Indian *siddhas*, with Milarepa, one of the best known Tibetan monks, being a disciple of Marpa, who was in turn the disciple of the Indian master Naropa. Marpa lived in the eleventh century and is considered to be the school's founder. The yogic practices of the Kagyu school include the generation of inner bodily heat induced through meditation, known as *tum-no*, and the school emphasizes the short route to enlightenment.

The Sakyapas, as the name suggests, hail from the Sakya region in the province of Tsang in south central Tibet. The Sakya tradition emerged with the establishment of a monastery therein. The *Hevajra Tantra* upon which their system is based recognizes a universal consciousness within all sentient beings. Its distictive teaching, called the "path and fruit", advocates that pursuing the Buddhist path *guarantees* the fruit of Buddhahood since pursuit (the path) and Buddhahood (the fruit) are one and the same thing.

The last and latest of the four Tibetan schools, the Gelukpa, was founded by Je Tsong-kha-pa (1357–1419). His emphasis on discipline and scholarship (as well as celibacy) added an academic dimension to Tibetan Buddhism which manifested itself in a portfolio of written degree and other examinations, as well as rigorous debates held before critical audiences in the monastic universities of Tibet. In the Geluk tradition, Tantras are not for the uninitiated, rather they are the preserve of the most advanced scholars, for Buddhahood is not considered to be something which anyone can simply reveal, but something which can be realized only gradually through discipline. Known as the Yellow Hats, the Gelukpa reform movement gained political credence because of its associations with the Dalai Lamas.[12] In fact, the rise of Buddhism in Tibet has witnessed considerable political and economic activity in the monastic orders.

It is worth noting that religions tend to reflect the cultures in which they grow up and, notwithstanding everything that has been said, it would be high-handed to deny the presence of any syncretistic ideas in Tibetan Buddhism. Traditional non-Buddhist beliefs and practices, some of which come from the indigenous Bon religion, others from a popular non-monastic tradition of townsfolk and villagers, all of which remain deeply embedded within the religious culture of the people, have found their way into Tibetan Buddhism and are still evident to this day:

while the study of the Mahayana philosophical systems and the performance of elaborate Tantric rites take place within the confines of the monasteries, monks actively participate in a wide range of ritual activities outside the monasteries, and beliefs that do not derive from Buddhism are shared by monks and laypeople alike.[13]

Tibetan monks and *lamas*

The term *lama* is a standard Tibetan translation of *guru*, a spiritual teacher, and is a title given to the religious leaders of the monastic traditions in Tibetan Buddhism. A unique feature, peculiar to Tibetan Buddhism, is the concept of the reincarnation of a high *lama*. Though common to most Indian religious thought, of all Buddhist schools Tibetan Buddhism alone has a belief in reincarnation. There has been only one reincarnated female *lama* in the history of Tibetan Buddhism, though doctrinally women can become *bodhisattvas*; it is unclear textually whether a woman can become a buddha, though Tara is a fully enlightened buddha in the Tibetan tradition. The acceptance of this doctrine (by all the monastic schools of Tibet) gives each individual order a sense of security and stability, for it presupposes the succession by reincarnation of its spiritual head, time and again; sometimes the spiritual leader is considered to be the manifestation of a deity, sometimes (as in the case of the fifth Dalai Lama, 1617–1682) he is believed to be both. The Grand *Lama* of Bkra-sis-Ihun-po is considered to be the reincarnation of the Buddha, Amitabha. The acceptance in Tibetan thought of *lamas* as incarnations of important buddhas and *bodhisattvas* is concomitant with their acceptance as divine beings; accordingly, their right to political rule is unquestioned, though to take the equation further and accord the Dalai Lama the title "God-King" is a western convention which offends eastern ears.

The Dalai Lama is the spiritual head of Tibetan Buddhism. His depth of knowledge on all matters spiritual is attested in the term Dalai, which means "ocean" (of knowledge). The fifth Dalai Lama established himself as head of state, as well as the religious leader, and set up residence in Potala Palace in Lhasa, the ancient capital:

> situated on a hill, it symbolically reestablished the pre-Buddhist connection between the divine king and the sacred mountain.[14]

This reflects the Bon concept of a divine ruler who has descended to earth. For over three hundred years the Dalai Lama remained the spiritual and political ruler of Tibet. The present Dalai Lama is considered to be the fourteenth reincarnation of the original, though acceptance of the concept of the reincarnation of a high *lama* did not gain favour until the fourteenth century.

As he feels death approaching, a high *lama* will usually advise his followers of the time or place of his rebirth; sometimes he will have a vision of the birth itself. Within nine months of the demise of a high *lama* reports of an unusual infant will be expected at the monastery, though sometimes the wait is much longer; the search for the reincarnation of Khensur Rinpoche, the former abbot of Drepung monastery in Tibet, who died on the thirtieth of June 1985, took over four years. In this particular instance the child's mother had a vision during the birth, and she later noticed his gentleness and how fond he was of monks. The child also displayed special signs, and his mother wrote to the monastery asking if he could be a reincarnated *lama*.[15]

Tibetan Buddhism is unique in its belief that high *lamas* may choose to be reincarnated in order to help others achieve spiritual enlightenment. The thinking is that although the body has changed, inside is the same consciousness of his former self. The name given to an reincarnate *lama* is *Rinpoche*, which means "the precious one". Before the Chinese occupation of Tibet there were believed to be three thousand reincarnate *lamas* living in the Land of Snow; today there are some five hundred, most of whom are in exile.

There is no prescribed method of recognizing a reincarnated *lama*, though gentleness of nature and similar qualities, as well as being at ease with the monks he had known in his previous embodiment would be expected. Dreams and omens as well as divinations by high *lamas* would be considered and the State Oracle would be consulted. Divination is treated with great solemnity in Tibet, and in 1959 the decision for the Dalai Lama to forsake his homeland before the Chinese advance was made upon divination by the State Oracle. In the case of Khensur Rinpoche, the advice of the Oracle (who is believed to be possessed by a god) and the Dalai Lama was sought. The child would also be subjected to a series of tests whereby he would be expected to identify objects from others which pertain to his former existence; additionally, the child may be familiar, or at least comfortable, with religious ritual. Once the monks are satisfied that the child is indeed the reincarnation in question, he will be taken to the monastery for a lengthy period of training and teaching.

The present Dalai Lama was enthroned at Lhasa in 1940, at the tender age of five, after passing all the necessary tests. The Chinese invasion of

Tibet in the 1950s and the enforcement of communism saw the subsequent end of Tibetan rule in 1959, after an unsuccessful revolt against Chinese oppression. The Dalai Lama escaped to India where he lives to this day.

Buddhas and *bodhisattvas*

The figure of the bodhisattva is central to Mahayana. The Sanskrit term literally means "enlightenment (*bodhi*) being (*sattva*)," and it indicates that a bodhisattva is someone who is progressing towards the state of enlightenment of a buddha . . . the bodhisattva is viewed by Tibetans as a noble and courageous figure. This reflects the fact that bodhisattvas are often depicted in Mahayana literature as mythic heroes, possessing supernatural powers and ceaselessly working for the benefit of others.[16]

Since the time of the fifth Dalai Lama, all who hold this position are considered to be the embodiment not only of the previous Dalai Lama, but the national *bodhisattva* of Tibet, Avalokitesvara, *bodhisattva* of compassion. Known in Tibetan Buddhism as Chenrezig and in China as Kuan-yin (where he is often found in female form), Avalokitesvara and a host of other buddhas and *bodhisattvas* attest to the presence of the second of the three ways to salvation conspicuous in Tibetan Buddhism – the Mahayana. The compound name Avalokitesvara means something approaching "Lord who looks down", the inference being that the unbounding compassion of the *bodhisattva* is not for a chosen few, but for all whom he surveys. His omnipresence is sometimes depicted by a thousand arms which manifest his universal compassion; often, eleven heads symbolize his ability to see all. His unbounding compassion is attested in his willingness to experience rebirth in any situation, even in one of the Buddhist Hells, and in any form in order to help sentient beings to enlightenment.

Another important *bodhisattva* capable of manifesting himself in any part of the universe is Manjusri, *bodhisattva* of wisdom. Believed to be the founder of Nepal, mythology holds that Manjusri drained a great lake to this end, carving a huge opening in the mountains in order to drain the valley of Katmandu. However, the sword which he holds in his right hand is not intended to symbolize his carving through mountains, but carving through ignorance to reveal the wisdom of truth, which is reinforced by the *Prajnaparamita Sutra*, the Scripture of Supreme Wisdom, which he holds in his left hand. He is represented sitting in perpetual meditation, sometimes on the back of a lion, whose roar symbolizes the sound of truth. A crown adorns the head of this prince-like *bodhisattva* of youthful, golden complexion who represents the purity of the truth and of Buddhist teaching. His name, which is associated with teaching, learning, and wisdom means "Gentle Glory".

An emphasis on female, as well as male, aspects of the divine has always been a feature of the third *yana* which informs Tibetan Buddhism – Tantra, and Tara, the *sakti* of the Buddha Amoghasiddhi, has much in common with the *sakti* forces of Hinduism; Tara and the Hindu Brahmanic goddess Durga share several personal names, and iconographically are sometimes similar in form. Though scholarship has yet to determine exactly when and how the cult of Tara emerged,[17] this female counterpart of Avalokitesvara is immensely popular in Tibetan Buddhism, where meditation on Tara invariably features prominently in ritual *puja*.

The essence of loving devotion, her great popularity as Saviour of the World is due in no small part to her unwillingness to prejudge the worthiness of the recipients – everyone in distress is worthy of her loving care, regardless of their states of mind. Tara may emanate in twenty-one different forms, with Green Tara representing prosperity, and White Tara helpfulness. The sexual relationships between male and female aspects of the divine which one tends to associate with Tantric Buddhism are not a prominent feature of the relationship between Tara and Avalokitesvara, however.

Tibetan scriptures

These naturally form a twofold division – teachings which are held to be the words of the Buddha, and those which are not. The former are termed *Kanjur* and include both Mahayana and non-Mahayana texts as well as the *Vinaya* and Tantras. Tantras are not for the uninitiated, and their meanings are deliberately obscure and mystical. Their words were never intended to be taken literally, and their hidden messages need the erudition and enlightenment of scholastic monks for interpretation. The second group is known as *Tenjur*, which comprise philosophical and erudite commentaries.

A characteristic feature of Tibetan scriptures is the disclosure of previously hidden texts by oracles in a state of trance. Oracles (male and female) are prolific in popular (non-monastic) religion. These texts are known as *termas (gter ma)* and they are deemed to come to light when the time is right for their hidden meanings to bring benefit to the community.

Tibetan ritual

Pre-Buddhist Tibet was a land preoccupied with spirit possession and the acquisition of power. The appearance in the country of a Buddhism containing elements of Tantric ritual which featured both these factors must have appealed greatly to the Tibetan mind. Since both early Buddhism and Tantra itself are variants of shamanism, and since shamanism in Tibet today is still concerned with spirit possession and the acquisition of power by inducing a variety of altered states of consciousness, it is small wonder that Tantric ritual lies at the heart of Tibetan religious beliefs and practices.

Shamanism is conspicuous in Tibetan religion; it is associated with the many different planes of existence within which a profusion of spirits, gods and demons abound, yet who are still bound to the *samsaric* cycle in the same way as everyone else; it continues in folk traditions; and it is part of the official cult. Mediums are termed *Iha-pa* (god-possessed) or *dpa' bo* (heroes), and at the New Year festival before the Dalai Lama, the Oracle, while in a state of trance, will first deliver an arrow to the heart of a flour and butter statue, symbolizing the destruction of the forces of evil of the old year, and then Avalokitesvara will bless the people and State through the Oracle.

Although Tantric ritual lies at the heart of Tibetan religious beliefs and practices, there will inevitably be practitioners who have not yet mastered the art. For those who have failed in this lifetime, and have deceased, guidance is at hand as they enter the intermediate state known as *bardo*. The chanting for forty-nine days of the *Bardo T'odrol*, more popularly known as the *Tibetan Book of the Dead*, has the aim of enabling the deceased to escape the aimless wandering of *samsara*, and the objective of ensuring a better rebirth. Lamps remain alight throughout this period of time to light the way to the next life. In the Land of Snow, the Himalayan ranges support neither soil nor trees and so the body of the deceased is dismembered and exposed to the elements as a matter of exigency.

Conspicuous in a Tibetan shrineroom decorated in strikingly bright and highly symbolic colours are the many buddhas and *bodhisattvas* before whom devotees prostrate themselves three times before commencing *puja*; this symbolizes the Three Refuges. *Puja* will vary at different centres, although chanting is both traditional and usual. Traditionally, the chanting of the *mantras* promoted the awakening of *bodhicitta*, the contemplation of emptiness and, later, the dedication of merit. With the twin pillars of Mahayana Buddhism, wisdom and compassion, underpinning the ritual, the practitioner would develop a highly-tuned adeptness in the powers of the body, speech and mind. Speed of speech and thought would manifest themselves in the swift and accurate recitation of the *mantras*, as well as developed visualization and contemplation techniques, while co-ordination would be demonstrated in the precise hand-positions known as *mudras*, which are a distinct feature of both Buddhism and Hinduism. Circumambulation is important and conspicuous in Tibetan Buddhism, particularly when effectuated entirely by prostrations.

A profusion of deities permeates every aspect of Tibetan religion and culture. They are recognized as manifestations of the forces in life; they are also recognized to be empty of "own-being", *svabhava*, and therefore empty of reality. In this light, it is not difficult to appreciate that there is ultimately no difference between a deity and a mortal, since both are without *svabhava*. Accordingly, there is no reason why the monk who focuses on a particular buddha or *bodhisattva* in yogic meditation, employing techniques known as the "Highest Yoga Tantras" in order to transcend normal perception, should not *become* that deity. To this end, the devotee is normally assigned a divine being commensurate with his or her personality, upon which to meditate. Visualization and conceptualization techniques aim at the full assumption of the divine being by the meditator; on this view, meditation on Avalokitesvara could evoke the great compassion and wisdom of the *bodhisattva* manifesting itself as the meditator's whole being.

> The ritual proper was the process of generation, which involved three steps: visualization of the deity's mandala, abandonment of one's own world and identity so as to assume the deity's identity through the power of the mantra, and recollection of purity ... The assumption of the deity's identity, or "pride," was crucial in that one could not expect to control the deity's power unless one "became" the deity. The recollection of purity – another reference to emptiness – was essential for returning to the emptiness from which the deity had sprung so that one could make contact with the source from which all things come, and thus be able to exercise power over them.[18]

Although the misuse of Tantric powers was not unknown in Tibetan villages, it was expressly condemned in Tibetan folklore as well as in texts such as the *Hevajra Tantra*. This is why the practitioner is reminded at every juncture that compassion and wisdom should lie at the heart of his exercise of ritual power.

Traditionally, communal *puja* is accompanied by the sound of bells, gongs, drums and trumpets. Praise is chanted to particular buddhas and *bodhisattvas*, in a very deep base chant, adding a further dimension to the importance of sound. For their part, the laity make pilgrimages to the monastery, and offerings of incense, flowers, food and water are given in sacrifice to the images of the various buddhas and *bodhisattvas*, who are also adorned in white scarves. In return, the lay people are afforded education, expert religious ritual and protection from super-natural forces.

Tradition also has it that in Tibetan Buddhism the two paths to enlightenment are signposted by the attainment of wisdom, and merit. Normally, the lay person has neither the time nor the inclination for rigorous textual study, and resorts to the accumulation of good merit in order to reach his goal. Studies of female religious imagery have concluded that in the case of Tibetan Buddhism the low position of women in Tibet has done nothing to promote profound and positive religious imagery.[19] In fact, a standard Tibetan expression (though one not found in books) is the abusive term for women, *saydman* (pronounced *kaymen*), which means "inferior birth". The Pali Canon clearly has women becoming enlightened as women, but attitudes to women worsened. As in Theravada Buddhism, one important means of accumulating good *karma* would be for the laity to support the monks; pilgrimage to important shrines such as the Potala Palace in Lhasa would be another. Personal *karma* in Tibetan Buddhism can also be developed by appealing for help or advice to local oracles. These mediums serve as mouthpieces for the various buddhas and *bodhisattvas* and may even reveal new sacred literature. Their appeal lies in the need of an ancient people to access a host of spiritual forces who can improve individual *karma*.

This need is also conspicuous in the earth, the house, and the sea, which are home to a host of gods, goddesses and spirits, all of whom are subject to *karma* and bound to the same "aimless wandering" through *samsara* as humankind. All are to be appeased, for they are considered to be easily offended, and could bring disease and distress if disturbed by animals or annoyed by people; such are the *klu* spirits who reside beneath the ground and under the sea. In the home are to be found guardian house deities, who must also be appeased and can also be upset. This is particularly the case with the god of the fireplace *(thab lla)*, whose hearth must be unpolluted. Tutelage of the male and female household residents is considered to be the role of the "male god" and "female god" respectively. Per Kvaerne also notes that, despite its name, it is the so-called "enemy god" who protects the entire household.[20] The "enemy god" is represented by a banner on the flat roofs where both he and the other guardian deities are worshipped at their altars in memory of the times when they were revered on mountaintops.

The good and bad *karma* one has accrued throughout life is carefully weighed at death on the scales of justice. Each individual is accompanied throughout life by a white god and a black demon, who respectively record one's good and bad thoughts and deeds, weighing the former with white pebbles and the latter with black. This is a dualistic concept of good and evil not unfamiliar to Muslims, and Islam as well as Tibetan Buddhism may have the dualistic teaching of Zoroastrianism or the *yin* and *yang* theories of Taoism to thank.

Tibetan ceremonies and life-cycle rites

The richness and complexity one associates with Tibetan scriptures and Tibet itself is conspicuous also in the tradition of a people who rejoice in very elaborate ceremony and festivals. In Tibetan Buddhism initiation into the monastic tradition is an important feature and may take place for small boys as young as four years. At a tender age this may involve no more than a very brief stay with friendly local monks well-known to both the boy and his family, though from the age of eleven a boy may elect to spend the rest of his days in a Tibetan monastery. Ordination is based upon the *bodhisattva* ideal – the attainment of enlightenment with a view to saving all humankind, the overthrow of delusion, and immersion in the Buddha's *dharma*.

Religions tend to reflect the cultures in which they grow up, and this is very true of Tibetan Buddhism in general and Tibetan festivals in particular. Far from being the preserve of monastic life, Tibetan (as indeed other) festivals invite the laity to share and participate in the religious and historical traditions of their faith and culture. The Tibetan New Year begins in February and the end of the old year is marked by the festival called *Gutor*, wherein the victory of good over evil is enacted in ritual dance by monks in grotesque masks chasing away the evil spirits of the past year. Householders join in the ritual and parade through homes, which have been meticulously cleaned and whitewashed, brandishing guns, fireworks and lighted torches. Good luck charms and decorations adorn the houses, and a special dish called *guthok* is prepared.

The New Year opens on the first day with the festival of *Losar*. On this and the following day the family takes precedence, before neighbours are welcomed on the next two days. An early morning wash at a local stream or well is followed by celebrating the coming of the New Year. *Kapse* "cakes" are consumed, as is a traditional alcoholic drink called *chang*. Of special interest to the laity is the festival of *Monlam Chenmo*, arguably the most important Tibetan festival. This is celebrated on the fourth day of *Losar*, and participation in *Monlam Chenmo* is considered to ensure not only the overthrow of evil but also the generation of both individual and collective *karma* throughout the community. This great prayer festival, which commemorates the miracles of Sakyamuni, dates back to the fifteenth century and has associations with the Gelukpa school. Its name means "Great Aspiration", and it is fitting that traditionally, when Buddhism was the religion of Tibet, this is the day when monks would aspire to higher degrees, such as the highest award of *geshe* (the equivalent to the title of Doctor of Philosophy) by sitting their examinations on *Monlam Chenmo*.

The opening month of the Tibetan New Year is dedicated to the expulsion of the forces of evil which are hanging on from the old year, and on the fourteenth day the monks perform a spectacular sacred dance to this end, adorned in elaborate costumes and masks. "Hanging on" is no more a feature of Tibetan Buddhism than any other form of Buddhism, a point well made in the Butter Sculpture Festival which took place in Buddhist Tibet the following day; the folly of attachment to what can only be impermanent was exemplified by the total destruction of mammoth statues of butter and flour which took months to make. The colour and ritual which permeates Tibetan Buddhism manifests itself in festivals, where all manner of customs find expression in the home and in the community. The richness of a tradition which is informed by elements found in pre-Buddhist as well as Buddhist Tibet firmly places Tibetan among the most fascinating of festivals of Mahayana Buddhism.

Many modern Buddhist festivals have their origins in pre-Buddhist celebrations, but have become overlaid with Buddhist symbols. Although they retain some of their original characteristics, they have become so infused with Buddhist imagery and significance that most are thoroughly Buddhist in character, despite the fact that some external aspects hearken back to pre-Buddhist practices.[21]

Tantra

Although the origins of Tantra are lost in the mists of time, Tibetan records attest that its presence predates the advent of Buddhism in ninth-century Tibet. Indeed, scholarship accepts that, "Tibet became an extraordinary center for Tantrism as well as the major storehouse of Tantric literature".[22] Great store has also been placed in the observation that the writings of the Chinese pilgrim Hsuan-tsang, who visited India between 629 and 645 CE, are bereft of any mention of Tantric teachings or practices, the suggestion being that Tantra had not yet arrived. We will do well to remember that absence of evidence is not evidence of absence, however, and it is generally accepted that, despite the pilgrim's scrupulous attention to detail, he simply may have been unaware of or unmoved by what he saw; in other words, he may well have witnessed Tantric ritual without making the connection with Buddhism or, if he did associate the two, what he saw left him singularly unimpressed.

Be this as it may, the magical and supernatural elements of an indigenous popular religion in pre-Buddhist Tibet acted as a ready catalyst for those systems of practice and meditation which have become known as *tantra*, and which today give Tibetan Buddhism its definitive character:

> The term *tantra* (Tibetan: *rgyud*; pronounced "gyu") refers to systems of practice and meditation derived from esoteric texts emphasizing cognitive transformation through visualization, symbols, and ritual. These in turn gave rise to a vast commentorial literature, as well as oral traditions, and tantric practices, ideas, and images today permeate all aspects of Tibetan Buddhism.[23]

The Tantric aspect of Tibetan Buddhism is known as *Vajrayana*, and Tantric texts are readily discernible from their content, though not always from their titles, as David Snellgrove has noted.[24] The term *tantra* has a variety of meanings,[25] with "loom" being a meaning preferred by Herbert Guenther, who adds the nuance "living one's possibilities".[26] On this view, far from having one's potential impeded by an ego-bound self-awareness and self-centredness, the individual is given the means to realize his or her full potential through mystical and esoteric practices, and so access the truth of reality.

Different Tantric practices are peculiar to each of the four schools of Tibetan Buddhism, though most Tantras are believed by Tibetan scholars to be the recorded words of Sakyamuni or, sometimes, other buddhas. The fact that these utterances were unheard of for over a

millennium has not won this claim universal support, though proponents insist that this was intentional since, such was the potency of these
secret texts, their revelation was intended to be neither universal nor
untimely. Rather, the intention was for the potency of the Tantras, when
the time was right, to show the initiated follower how to become a practitioner of the "Highest Yoga Tantra", and realize Buddhahood in just
one lifetime, as opposed to the Mahayana *sutras* which taught that this
would take "countless aeons". Then, *as now*, practitioners were warned
that the slower way of the *sutras* was still the recommended path for
most people. Tantra is only for those with quite exceptional compassion, intelligence, and compulsion to attain enlightenment in order to
help others; *to ignore this is extremely dangerous and could court
disaster.*

This promise of a faster route to Buddhahood, by following Tantric
practices which emphasized the path of the *bodhisattva* alongside great
compassion, was not without its appeal, an appeal which was magnified
by the obvious associations with the Mahayana teaching, and diminished by objections that ritual sex, demonic phenomena and horrific
deities have no place in Tibetan Buddhism. At one and the same time,
Tantra was viewed as the final degeneration of Indian Buddhism, and
the ultimate in all Buddhist teaching. Tibetan scholars are proponents of
the latter viewpoint, but their formulation of the Tibetan Canon in the
thirteenth century, far from accepting all Tantric literature unre-
servedly, sought verification of authenticity in the form of Sanskrit
originals. Further objections that Tantric practices are without mention
in biographical details of Sakyamuni are countered by the claim that
Sakyamuni's apparent attainment of enlightenment was simply a *display*
for an audience which was not yet ready to receive the supreme teaching,
the ultimate example of Sakyamuni's *upaya*, his "skilful means"; he had,
in fact, as all buddhas, become Enlightened in the distant past as a practitioner of "Highest Yoga Tantra".

An interesting teaching of *Vajrayana* is another example of "skill-in-
means". Whereas the orthodox Buddhist position, in keeping with the
Second Noble Truth, is that the cause of *dukkha* (suffering) is *tanha*
(desire), Tantric Buddhism advocates employing the great energies and
power of desire in order to overcome desire. Rather than harnessing and
suppressing, or even ignoring, misdirected desire towards power, sex,
fame, wealth, and material possessions in general (which in itself
requires an enormous amount of energy), these energies should be
tapped into and utilized in the desire to help others; on this view, it is
not desire itself which is wrong but the direction desire takes. Nor is it

wrong to desire happiness and be averse to suffering; again, it is the
direction which is usually wrong, not desire itself, as Lama Thubten
Yeshe illumines:

> Contrary to what some people might believe, there is nothing wrong with
> having pleasures and enjoyments. What *is* wrong is the confused way we
> grasp onto these pleasures, turning them from a souce of happiness into
> a source of pain and dissatisfaction. It is such grasping and attachment that
> is the problem, not the pleasures themselves.[27]

As surely as Buddhism is a mind-culture so, in the Tantric view,
happiness is to be cultivated as a blissful state of mind; the seeking of and
grasping at pleasure purely to gratify our selfish ends, brings a happiness which will surely be ephemeral, with suffering in its wake. The
direction this takes is also wrong, because such happiness is inevitably
sought externally, rather than developing a blissful state of mind. Far
from removing all pleasures from life, and regarding those who openly
seek pleasure as being, at best, "misguided" and, at worst, "sinners",
which unfortunately is the case in some religious circles, Tantra advocates directing those energies released in this quest towards the
development of an enlightened mind, having a blissful awareness of the
nature of reality.

On this view, the powerful energies of desire are not to be suppressed
or harnessed, but utilized as an "indispensable resource for the spiritual
path".[28] If this spiritual path is to lead to an enlightenment free from all
dualities, free from aversions and desires, then the path itself must be
similarly unencumbered. Accordingly, there should be no distinction
drawn between what is normally considered to be "religious" and what
is not, and walking and sleeping are just as much a part of the path as so-
called religious ritual. In the same light, there should be no distinction
drawn between sex and no-sex and pure food and polluted food; the
monk who abstains from sex only to develop an aversion to it, and the
classification of food into acceptable and unacceptable categories, illustrate the point – a point which is enforced in some Tantric circles by the
deliberate contamination of Tantric meals.

Tantric symbols

Mandalas

As a rule a mandala (*dkyil 'khor*) is a strongly symmetrical diagram, concentrated about a centre and generally divided into four quadrants of equal size; it is built up of concentric circles ('*khor*) and squares possessing the same centre (*dkyil*). Indeed, a great many mandalas are also aids to meditation, visualization and initiation.[29]

Although the Sanskrit term *mandala* literally means "circle", any simple definition of this sacred circle of Tibetan Buddhism is bound to mislead. Martin Brauen warns that not all *mandalas* are immediately recognizable as such; sometimes the term may be used for other structures and beings, such as palaces and even deities; sometimes the term is applied to the whole cosmos.

The Potala Palace in Lhasa, formerly the religious centre of Tibet, is an example *par excellence* of a ritualistic *mandala*. Built in the seventeenth century as a palace, a monastery and a temple, it served as the Tibetan religious and political centre until the Chinese overthrow. It was also built as a three-dimensional *mandala*, at the centre of which is the divine realm of the *bodhisattva* Avalokitesvara. Pilgrimage to Lhasa is a highly desirable feature of Tibetan Buddhism, as is circumambulation, and pilgrims circumambulate the Palace many times in order to increase their good *karma*. Circumambulation is punctuated by frequent, sometimes continuous successive, prostrations. Another highly significant feature of Tantric practice, associated with prostration, is visualization; in this case the visualization of the divine realm of Avalokitesvara, upon whom the mind is focused.

Many *mandalas* are highly symbolic and complex, an awesome and arresting spectacle even to the casual observer, but the *mandalas* that adorn the walls of Tibetan shrines (most Tibetan shrines would have a pictorial representation of the Potala Palace) are not intended to be symbols of pride; rather they are vehicles which aid the mind on its journey to enlightenment. These important features of Tantric Buddhism were visualized by former high *lamas*, who transposed their meditational visions into figurative forms upon which devotees could meditate on the path to enlightenment.

Usually associated with a particular buddha or *bodhisattva*, the *mandala* symbolizes an enlightened mind freed from the impediments which obstruct the path to liberation. Its precise architecture is representative of the order of an enlightened mind, and the nature of reality which the ordered mind alone is capable of realizing. This realization is effectuated as the meditator is drawn into the very heart of the *mandala* through a series of concentric circles which welcome the Buddhist into a whole buddha-world.

Mantras

Another means of stimulating the cognitive potential for enlightenment is the *mantra*, spoken sounds made by the meditator which are invocations to buddhas. Most *mantras* are secret, passed down from master to pupil only when the master feels that the time is right and the pupil is spiritually ready for the appropriate *mantra*. Other *mantras* are omnipresent, *Om mani padme hum* (Hail to the jewel in the lotus) being the most well known. This is the *mantra* of Avalokitesvara, which is embedded in the hearts of Tibetans who wish to develop greater compassion by invoking the *bodhisattva* who personifies this quality. His *mantra* is ubiquitous throughout Tibet, being conspicuous on prayer flags which bedeck temples and shrines, prayer wheels, temples themselves and other buildings, flagstones and even rooftops. The recitation of Avalokitesvara's *mantra* over and over again attunes the meditator's mind to the nature of the *bodhisattva* who is the very embodiment of compassion. The *mantra* is such an important vehicle in the visualization of and summoning of buddhas and *bodhisattvas* during meditation, that Tantric practice is often called the "Mantra vehicle".

The Vajra

Vajras are generally five-pronged scepters which are usually made from bone or metal. Edward Conze noted that, "In later Buddhist philosophy the word is used to denote a kind of supernatural substance which is as hard as a diamond, as clear as empty space, as irresistible as a thunderbolt."[30] This supreme symbol of Tantric Buddhism represents the enlightened mind of a buddha, manifest in wisdom and compassion. It is found in association with a bell, indicating a buddha's direct perception of emptiness. Originally the weapon of the *Vedic* god Indra, the *vajra* represents the irresistible active force in the union between method and wisdom, while the bell, appropriately, represents the Void, *sunyata*, and the Perfection of Wisdom. The final aspiration of Tantric practitioners is to develop an enlightened mind unsullied by ignorance, replete with wisdom and compassion; to this end practitioners direct their aspirations, with enlightenment in their sights and *vajras* in their hands.

The Tantric practitioner

Tantra is not for everyone, and the decision as to whether a candidate has the necessary spiritual and intellectual aptitude is the responsibility of the *guru*. Even where the mind has been sufficiently tuned previously by appropriate Mahayana practices, Tibetan meditation literature makes the point time and again that the way of Tantra is not to be made without a personal *guru* (Tibetan *bla ma*; pronounced *lama*). Indeed, the obligatory initiations are seen as the means by which a unique bond between the student, the *guru* and the meditational deity is formed. Careful screening of candidates by the *lamas* ascertain whether motives are noble, and succesful initiates are enjoined to secrecy. Initiation is not only an initial experience, for experienced Tantric practitioners appreciate the regenerative powers that repeated re-enactment of Tantric initiation can bring:

> Tantric initiation is often a complex ritual involving detailed visualizations, prayers and supplications, offerings, special ritual implements and substances. The purpose is to establish the initiate in the proper frame of mind, forge a karmic bond with the lama and meditational deity, purify defilements, grant permisssion to practice a particular tantra, and to give instruction concerning how this should be done.[31]

The goal of the Tantric practitioner is to become a fully enlightened buddha, and deity yoga is followed assiduously to this end. Indeed, the Dalai Lama has gone so far as to assert that the way of Tantra is impossible without deity yoga. If the mantra path is the swiftest, most effective means to enlightenment, then it is deity yoga which makes this possible. The practice involves the visualization of a meditational deity and oneself as the embodiment of this fully enlightened buddha. The buddha in question will manifest the self-same qualities which are latent within the meditator, and repeated practice will align the thoughts of the meditator to the enlightened mind of the buddha, until they are both one; indeed, the simultaneous accrual of wisdom and merit, which the mantra path alone offers, results in the practitioner having not only the body, speech and mind of a buddha, but his very actions also. Adepts of the Tantra path are believed to have enlightened minds which, because they perceive the reality of emptiness, are able to actualize the embodiment of compassion as form bodies of the buddha. At the same time, the enlightened mind, replete with wisdom, has the capacity to actualize the truth body, "and thus both bodies are complete in one consciousness".[32]

Preliminary practices

All *lamas* teach of the folly of embarking upon the Tantric path without first preparing the mind to forsake its selfishness, and develop concern for others. To this end, five preliminary practices are advocated:

Taking refuge

In meditative practice, refuge is to be sought in a fully enlightened Buddha, for only one who has overcome ignorance and its attendant afflictive emotions is capable of assisting the initiate to do the same. In the words of the Dalai Lama:

> Therefore, one should mentally go for refuge to a Buddha, praise him with speech, and respect him physically. One should enter the teaching of such a being.[33]

Time and again, Tantric texts make the self-same point – that enlightenment is attainable only by those who have total commitment to their *guru*, their practice and the Three Jewels. Time and again, intending initiates recite the refuge prayer, at least 100,000 times as a rule. The affirmation that one is dissatisfied with one's life circumstances is not considered to be sufficient grounds to conclude that one is therefore ready to embark upon the Tantric path, for the cause of this dissatisfaction and its attendant misery should first be analysed. The overcoming of ignorance, the root cause of suffering, and the appreciation that the Buddhist path is the way to true happiness, rather than any promises of a heaven or practices of self-abnegation, which other traditions propose, is to be realized through meditation with the expert help of a spiritual guide. Indeed, Tantric initiates would take refuge in their guru before taking refuge in the Three Jewels. The objects of refuge of initiates of Highest Yoga Tantra are *dakinis*, wisdom beings who feature strongly in their Tantric practice.

Prostration

Another means of negating afflictive emotions, particularly false pride, is the act of prostration, either partially or fully, before images or symbols of buddhas and *bodhisattvas*. The cumulative effects of prostration are considered to be so powerful that this practice is continued throughout the duration of the Tantric path, often as a feature of the daily practices of advanced meditators.

Prostration begins in a standing position. The practitioner's hands are in the "gem holding position," in which the base of the palm and the tips of the fingers are touching, with a space between the middle of the palms. The thumbs are tucked in. The folded hands are raised above the head, and with them the practitioner touches either three or four points on the body. In the first method, one touches the crown of the head, throat and heart, and in the second, the crown, forehead, throat, and heart are touched. Touching the crown symbolizes one's wish to attain the body of a buddha; touching the throat symbolizes one's goal of attaining the speech of a buddha; touching the heart symbolizes the aim of actualizing the mind of a buddha.[34]

Prostration is a part of Tibetan culture, and a common sight in Tibet is that of Tibetans fully prostrate before religious sites and religious people. Sometimes sacred sites are circumambulated entirely by a continuous series of full prostrations which may well take weeks to complete. With the proximate goal of overcoming false pride through physical abasement, and the ultimate goal of enlightenment firmly in mind, prostration becomes far more than a series of physical actions. On the contrary, Tantric visualization techniques should enable practitioners to visualize divine realms before them, attended by *gurus* and innumerable deities. Hundreds of thousands of prostrations may be made along the Tantric path and the inhabitants of the divine realms listen to the transgressions of the practitioners. Confessional prayers are chanted at the same time and pledges are made to avoid negative thoughts and deeds.

Vajrasattva meditation

Buddhist meditation texts make clear that the surest way to overcome negativity is to engage in mental purification techniques, with Vajrasattva firmly in mind. This buddha embodies the perfections of fully enlightened buddhas and is identified with the initiate's root *lama*. After confession, a contrite meditator visualizes Vajrasattva as his or her *guru*, at the crown of his head. The buddha sits in the half-lotus position and holds a golden *vajra* in his right hand and a bell in his left, the symbols of wisdom and compassion. This powerful visualization technique has Vajrasattva transform from the syllable *hum*, which emanates light of such intensity through the universe that the very obstacles which prevent clarity of thought and enable the mind to become a breeding ground for negativity are purified. Importantly, clarity of thought identifies the vision itself as being precisely that, empty of inherent existence and not an object of attachment, *any more than one's negativity is a permanent entity which cannot be overcome by mental purification techniques.*

The visualization has the wisdom and compassion of Vajrasattva permeating the meditator's body in the form of ambrosia, displacing all that is negative and leaving the meditator with the understanding that he or she *has become* Vajrasattva. This mental purification process is cultivated by the recitation of two Vajrasattva *mantras*, ideally hundreds of thousands of times. Wisdom and compassion are rightly conspicuous at the end of the meditation, when all that has been gained is offered for the benefit of others.

Mandala offering

This is another practice performed at least one hundred thousand times, wherein the practitioner combines physical effort with visualization techniques in order to remove the obscurations of his or her Buddha-nature which are present in the three defilements of desire, hatred and ignorance. Visualization is directed towards the creation of a *mandala* which represents the entire universe and all its attributes, thereby symbolizing the practitioner's forsaking of everything he or she owns for the benefit of others; in so doing, *mandala* offering is seen to be an effective means of accumulating merit. Since the Objects of Refuge, the buddhas themselves, are devoid of impurities, it is the wish of the practitioner to cultivate the self-same qualities of body, speech and mind as those of the buddhas.

Guru yoga

Tibetan meditation literature is unequivocal that the path of Tantra and a spiritual teacher are inseparable; this is a point stressed by all four schools of Tibetan Buddhism. The personal relationship that exists between *guru* and practitioner is something which even surpasses that between practitioner and buddha. The *guru* not only sets forth the teachings and practices of the established lineage to which he belongs (an extremely important aspect of Tibetan Buddhism), but suits the action to the word and applies them. As the name implies, the root *guru* is someone so deeply rooted in an established lineage of teaching that he is eminently capable of drawing upon a rich source of oral tradition in order to expound the hidden meaning of Tantric texts.

Since the *guru* is held as a mirror to one's mind, visualizion of the *guru* as a buddha will embody the meditator with the mind of enlightenment; should the practitioner find fault with the *guru*, however, these can only be the self-same faults inherent within the perceiver. Pre-eminent in the practitioner's mind at all times should be the wisdom and compassion of the *guru*, so much so that the *guru* and the buddha are seen as one. Visualization techniques include the visualization of the lineage from one's own *guru* back through a continuous tradition of *gurus* to the meditational deity, and the request for blessings and assistance with one's practice:

> It is important that the meditator believes that this actually occurs. At this point in the visualization, the deities and gurus merge into one another, then they enter into one's body through the aperture at the crown of the head and descend into the central channel. They dissolve into the energy center, or cakra, at the heart. At this point, all conventional dualistic appearances dissolve into emptiness. Through this practice, one should develop a feeling of close connection with the guru, who is perceived as being identical with the meditational deity and with one's own consciousness.[35]

Shingon

The Japanese expression of Tantric Buddhism is to be found in the only surviving Tantric sect in east Asia, Shingon. Still fairly popular in Japan today, Shingon was founded by the monk Kukai (774–835). *Shingon* is the Japanese translation of the Sanskrit *mantra* ("true word") and the esoteric nature of its teaching is immediately apparent when we consider that the "true word" received by its adherents is held to be the teachings of the cosmic Buddha rather than those of the Buddha who walked the earth. The centre of attention, therefore, is not Sakyamuni Buddha in *Nirmanakaya* form, but the cosmic *Dharmakaya* which pervades the whole of the cosmos; the word of the former is manifest in the teachings of the *sutras*, including the *Lotus Sutra*, but the "true word" of the cosmic Buddha, Mahavairocana (as the *Dharmakaya* is called), finds expression in Yoga Tantra.

As surely as the sun is the great illuminator and centre of our universe, so its namesake, Mahavairocana, is the centre of the whole cosmos, its source and the sustainer of all life:

> And just as the rays of the sun are manifest in the universe and shine on rich and poor alike, on old and young and good and evil, so the essence

of Mahavairocana is within everything in the cosmos. However, although the essence of Mahavairocana is in all things, Mahavairocana is *greater than everything* in the cosmos in a panentheistic sense. He is the creator and sustainer of the universe but is also its originator. All buddhas and *bodhisattvas* are merely expressions, or manifest aspects, of this great cosmic Buddha, and every individual is a microcosmic replica of Mahavairocana; every individual has within him or her part of the cosmic Buddha, the seed of enlightenment, *bodhicitta* or *buddha-nature*. So human consciousness is, in its *real state*, identical with the cosmic consciousness of Mahavairocana and the human body is identified with the cosmic body of Mahavairocana.[36]

Kukai proposed a system (or, more accurately, drew up a map) whereby the realization of the profound nature of one's body and mind is achievable only after following a series of practices which gradually reveal this insight, an insight which culminates in total revelation of the nature of the mind through Shingon Tantric practice. Since every individual is a microcosmic replica of Mahavairocana, and since every single aspect of Mahavairocana in body, speech, mind and action is in perfect union with every other on the macrocosmic level, the secret is to realize that this harmony and the wisdom which enables the practitioner to see this harmony are one and the same thing. Accordingly, the adherent will utilize the precepts of the *Vinaya*, along with *mudras*, employing both the sound and colour of *mantras* and complex *mandalas*, to bring about harmony of action, body and speech on both the microcosmic and macrocosmic levels.

Kukai taught that Mahavairocana is the essence of the entire cosmos itself, represented in Shingon Tantric ritual by *mandalas* taking the form of cosmograms depicting the cosmos in symbolic form. Of the two *mandalas* central to Shingon ritual, the *Womb Mandala* depicts the transcendent cosmic Buddha in manifest form, resplendent amidst four hundred and fourteen attendant buddhas and *bodhisattvas* in the outer courts, attended by another four in the innermost of twelve courts. A heightened awareness in the level of consciousness of the meditator brings about the realization that there is no sense of duality between manifest and unmanifest divinity and that the microcosm and the macrocosm are really one; accordingly, there is no reason why the meditator and a chosen divine being should not *become one*. The *Diamond Mandala*, meanwhile, depicts Mahavairocana as the Ultimate Reality, who, together with eight levels of human consciousness, is represented by nine halls. These two *mandalas* of Shingon Buddhism serve as maps to enlightenment, but not maps to be read by the casual traveller, for their complex routes have to be explained by a guide. Unsurprisingly, both these *mandalas* feature strongly in daily ritualistic practice, as do the so-called "Three Mysteries" – *mudras*, *mantras*, and yoga – all of which inform the practitioner in the quest for enlightenment, and the subsequent attainment of super-human power. This power becomes manifest not in egoistic assertion, but in compassion for others as Buddha-nature is realized. Faith in the power of the Three Mysteries (as well as faith-in-action in the world) is therefore a prerequisite to the realization of Buddha-nature, for it is repetition of the *mantra* (each divine being has its own) which will raise the consciousness of the meditator to a level where the mind becomes a living embodiment of the Ultimate Reality, and the practitioner and the *Dharmakaya* become one.

Zen

_____

> A special transmission outside the scriptures;
> No dependence upon words and letters;
> Direct pointing to the mind;
> Seeing into one's own nature and realizing Buddhahood.[1]

"Zen" is a word which has a familiar ring to western ears, and most westerners feel they have at least some familiarity with the Way of Zen. Popular images of Zen gardens, martial arts, monks, meditation, and even Japanese Tea Ceremonies spring readily to mind, and if associations with Buddhism are not always immediately apparent then perhaps this is because Zen is not really Buddhism at all, but simply "pure experience" unbridled by culture or religion.[2] Paradoxically, when the much-maligned "man-in-the-street" is asked to name but one school of Buddhism, he invariably answers "Zen", while other schools remain quite unknown to him. He even may have heard of "koans", nonsensical riddles, with no rhyme nor reason, which is what one would expect of Zen, which has neither time nor place for logical thought. If this is the common notion of Zen then it is as far removed from truth as The Land of the Rising Sun is from The Land of Snow.

Zen Buddhism is arguably the least understood of all the Mahayana schools. The problem of understanding Zen correctly has not been helped by the uncritical acceptance by western scholars of the high-minded words of Japanese apologists, such as Soen Roshi, D. T. Suzuki and Nyogen Sensaki, steeped in nationalistic tendencies yet fascinated with western culture, who brought Zen to the West. Romanticists of the nineteenth century, particularly Schelling and Carus, whose interest in the transcendental made them so receptive to the Oriental mind, paved the way for Suzuki, whose determination to make Zen comprehensible to the western reader tempted him to introduce Zen within a formula propounded by William James of the American School of the Psychology of Religion. Accordingly, a popular misconception of Zen has grown up which sees Zen as "pure experience" beyond religion, beyond philosophy, beyond doctrine, no more Buddhist than any other religion; it is a misconception which curries little favour with most moderns today and one strongly refuted by Robert Sharf:

> Classical Zen ranks among the most ritualistic forms of Buddhist monasticism. Zen "enlightenment," far from being a transcultural and transhistorical subjective experience, is constituted in elaborately choreographed and eminently public ritual performances. The koan genre, far from serving as a means to obviate reason, is a highly sophisticated form of scriptural exergesis: the manipulation or "solution" of a particular koan traditionally demanded an extensive knowledge of canonical Buddhist doctrine and classical Zen literature.[3]

Indeed, Heinrich Dumoulin, widely held to be an authority on Zen, wrote:

> The roots of Zen, however, are to be found more immediately in the soil of the great Mahayana sutras ... Another essential trait of Zen in its historical form is its total embeddedness in Buddhist religion. Zen sprouts from the Buddhist mother soil, and remains piously rooted in it. The great Zen masters are without exception spiritual men who are indebted for their best qualities to the Buddhist religion.[4]

So what is the Way of Zen? It is already clear that Zen is a subject extremely easy to misunderstand and, at the risk of doing precisely that, it could be said at the outset that there is no *way*. Man's inherent desire to identify and follow *the correct path* stems from his overwhelming conviction that all is not well within his being; having reached this conclusion, obviously the first step on the right path is to recognize what is wrong and then *do* something about it. In so doing man is transformed into some egotistical actor, playing out a part for which no words have been written, yet one in which he is the author of his own destiny. Far from alleviating suffering, however, this conviction has quite the opposite effect, as noted by Reverend Master Daishin Morgan, abbot of Throssel Hole Priory in Northumberland:

> What is a feature of probably everyone who comes to Buddhism ... is the fact that they experience suffering on some level or another, and as far as

Buddhism is concerned the cause of that suffering is ignorance, in that because we don't understand what it is that we do, we create consequences that produce suffering for ourselves and for others.[5]

Since we know ourselves better than anyone else (so the argument goes), clearly we are the best persons to identify the problem and rectify it. The teaching of Zen is that suffering is not caused by the fact that each individual has something inherently wrong within, but because we are quite unaware that there is nothing *wrong*, which needs to be put *right*. In the words of the French psychologist, Hubert Benoit:

> In short everything appears to be wrong in me because the fundamental idea that everything is perfectly, eternally and totally positive, is asleep in the centre of my being, because it is not awakened, living and active therein.[6]

On his awakening, Sakyamuni made the self-same point: "How wonderful, how miraculous – all beings are fully endowed with the Tathagata's wisdom and power but sadly, because of their attachments, human beings are not aware of this." Appropriately, after his Enlightenment, the Buddha was asked, "Are you a God?" Sakyamuni said he was not. "Are you a saint?" Again the answer was in the negative. "Then what are you?" persisted his questioner. And he answered, "I am awake."

Though I shall continue to use the term for the sake of convenience, on this view there is no Way of Zen, because there is nowhere to go. It is not a question of going somewhere or doing something but simply becoming awake, an awakening which Zen calls *satori*. As surely as mankind deludes itself that all is not well, so does it suffer from the illusion that, in order to achieve liberation, it needs to free itself from the chains which keep it in shackles. Ironically, as long as man feels duty-bound to achieve his own salvation, he will remain precisely that, bound and as far from liberation as ever:

> Since realisation signifies liberation one arrives at the absurd paradox that man is subjected to the coercive duty to be free.[7]

The thrust of Zen thought teaches that it is not chains which have to be thrown off, for there are no chains, only the illusion of chains which keep one bound, thus preventing liberation. What has to be discarded is the illusion that there is the *need* to free oneself and the attendant duty of salvation. Mankind will be free as soon as it is awakened to the fact that it is free already – there are no shackles.

In Zen thought, mankind lacks nothing other than the need to awaken to the fact. It is like a block of ice in man which has all the properties of water and needs only the generation of heat in order for these properties to become manifest. Zen masters over the centuries have addressed the question of how best to awaken their students, sometimes subtly, sometimes not so subtly, to this awareness. The master—pupil relationship is an important one in Zen, but since its abiding teaching is that mankind lacks nothing other than awakening, it is the pupil who is often expected to provide the answers to the problem.

A lay Buddhist, recently locked into a seemingly imponderable problem, reluctantly concluded after much deliberation that the realization of its solution was beyond his competence. He therefore determined to visit his abbot, a drive which took many hours. Although he was expected, the abbot seemed in no great hurry to see his pupil and could be seen occupying himself with seemingly unimportant tasks for what seemed an eternity, while the pupil waited in anguish. At long last, he was summoned to the abbot, who listened patiently to the "insurmountable" problem. Having poured out his heart, the pupil waited expectantly for the words of wisdom which would ease his pain. He was prepared for a detailed analysis of the problem and its attendant solution, but as soon as he finished speaking was dumbfounded to find the abbot simply indicating the pupil's bench (a "bench" is what Soto Zen Buddhists call their meditation stool), and the abbot walked away. A thunderstruck pupil was left trying to cope with a flood of emotion, before reconciling himself to the fact that there was nothing he could do but heed the advice given, such as it was. The answer to his "insurmountable" problem came to him instantly! This is a true but common story.

Now this illustrates several key characteristics fundamental and peculiar to Zen. First and foremost is the so-called "mind-to-mind transmission" between master and pupil, wherein enlightenment is directly transmitted outside of orthodox teachings; this is said to be the strength of Zen. The second feature is that Zen has no *dependence* on scriptures or other sacred writings, at least in as much as the master did not quote chapter and verse to the pupil as is common in other religious traditions, though it is important to note that it always operates within the framework of the Buddhist Precepts. And finally, Zen points directly at the human heart. D. T. Suzuki was probably the greatest single influence in bringing Zen Buddhism to the West. He was once

said to have given the West nine-tenths of all it knows on the subject.[8]
This is what he had to say about Zen teaching:

> If I am asked, then, what Zen teaches, I would answer Zen teaches
> nothing. Whatever teachings there are in Zen, they come out of one's own
> mind. We teach ourselves; Zen merely points the way.[9]

Suzuki further observed that:

> Zen claims to be Buddhism, but all the Buddhist teachings as propounded
> in the sutras and the sastras are treated by Zen as mere waste paper whose
> utility consists in wiping off the dirt of intellect and nothing more.[10]

But we have seen that the uncritical acceptance by western scholars of
the teachings of Suzuki has long been recognized as a sign of the times:

> In short order, "direct experience" was being touted as the characteristic
> feature of Eastern spirituality in general, and Zen in particular. Given the
> importance placed on "religious experience" in the works of Friedrich
> Schleiermacher, Rudolph Otto, Joachim Wach, William James, and other
> leading Western scholars of religion around the turn of the century, it is
> no wonder that Western enthusiasts, seeking alternatives to their own
> seemingly moribund religious institutions, would find the emphasis on
> personal, unmediated, veridical experience the single most attractive
> feature of Zen.[11]

Suzuki presented Zen to the West as pure mysticism, beyond history
and metaphysics and outside the remit of any religious framework, a
presentation which Rudolf Otto has long since shown to have no
warrant:

> No mysticism is merely a heavenly vault. Rather it rests on a foundation
> which it denies as far as it can, but from which it continuously receives its
> peculiar character, never identical with forms of mysticism developed
> elsewhere.

Suzuki himself refuted his own position that Zen is beyond metaphysics
by repeatedly stressing in his writings the close association between Zen
and the *Prajnaparamita Sutras* and the doctrine of *sunyata*. Indeed, the
basic metaphysical tenets of the Mahayana *sutras* have been echoed by
both Chinese and Japanese Zen masters throughout the ages. It was Hui-

neng (638–713), the illiterate Sixth Patriarch of Chinese Zen, who once said, "Do not let yourself be bowled over by the *sutra*, you must instead bowl over the *sutra* yourself." Though unable to browse through the *sutras* himself, his understanding of them was complete, and he was able to expound them to anyone who cared to read to him. In fact, Otto made the point that the Buddhist scriptures "which 'must be burned' to come to knowledge" should be studied first; only then will Zen be properly understood.

Suzuki went so far as to say that, "the spirit of Zen abhors all forms of intellectualism",[12] but although it is certainly true to say that it is the practice and not the scriptures which is the author of the insights, it is equally true that a scriptural framework is necessary:

> I would like to clear up a common misunderstanding which is that the Zen tradition is in some way anti-intellectual, and that it disregards the sutras. The first patriarch Bodhidharma brought the *Lankavatara-sutra* (Consciousness Only Sutra) with him from India. In the Zen tradition, as in all Buddhist traditions, insights that arise from practice are always matched with the teachings of the Buddha or the Patriarchs. If there is a discrepancy, then that discrepancy has to be investigated a little more deeply. This is how study and practice are matched up, one against the other.[13]

Venerable Myokyo-ni is also unequivocal – very strongly so!

> Nowhere is it stated or implied that the Scriptures can be dispensed with; yet just this has been affirmed by the "rice-bags" of all ages who failed to make the grade, or has been misunderstood by outsiders too lazy to inform themselves.[14]

Nevertheless, Reverend Master Daishin Morgan, incumbent abbot at Throssel Hole Priory, observes that Zen Buddhism is less dependent than some other traditions upon the written form. A student once needed to know the textual source of the Four Noble Truths in the *Sutta Pitaka*, and when he was invited by a Zen friend to the Festival of Wesak, which celebrates the birth, Enlightenment, and death of the Buddha, he saw this as a golden opportunity to attain this knowledge. During lunch he determined to ask those present, and was surprised to learn that the first Buddhists he asked didn't know. After asking more and more Buddhists and receiving a negative response each time, he realized he would have to ask the monks (in Soto Zen men and women are called "monks"). To his complete astonishment, he gradually came to realize that no one in the entire *sangha* could answer his question, nor did anyone consider it to be a particularly interesting question.

Personal experience is everything in Zen. A writer once told his Zen Buddhist friend that he had been commissioned to write about Zen. His friend congratulated him and invited him to spend a weekend in retreat at a monastery. Thanking him for his kindness, the writer objected, "But it's not experience I want; it's information." His friend then told him something he should have already known, "But they go together." The writer was being offered first-hand experiential knowledge, which is the only way to understand Zen, but he failed to recognize this. Being a writer, words were all-important to him, for his brief was to write about Zen Buddhism. In his view, his approach should be intellectual, but such an approach can only be made from a position of unreality since there is always a breach between abstract knowledge and actuality. This is not to deride intellect, but to affirm that the approach must be an experiential one by which means a framework may be constructed from which intellect may be employed. Suzuki went so far as to say, "to study Zen means to have Zen experience, for without the experience there is no Zen one can study".[15]

The Way of Zen is all about *experiencing* reality, not describing it, for such an experience of reality is beyond description, beyond words, beyond direct teaching. On this view, it could be said that throughout forty-five years of tireless ministry, replete with discourses and dialogues, communicating with countless disciples, forever teaching about reality, the Buddha actually *said* nothing, for there is nothing which words can express about reality. Far from being revelations of truth, words were used by Sakyamuni to show the way to reality, as mere pointers and nothing more. Perhaps the following incident illustrates the point.

Tradition has it that once the Buddha was seated before a typical assembly of earthly and celestial beings, who waited expectantly in silence for his words of wisdom. This silence was not peculiar to his audience, however, for on this occasion the Buddha, too, remained silent. Instead, he held aloft a golden flower without comment. Amidst the entire assembly, Mahakasyapa alone understood the meaning of the action and a smile dawned:

> At that the Buddha proclaimed, "I have the Jewel of the Dharma-Eye and now hand it to Mahakasyapa". This transmission is said to have continued unbroken from "heart to heart", to this day. What did the Buddha show?

What was transmitted? What is the Jewel? The Buddha raising the flower?
Mahakasyapa's smile? Endless speculations will not reveal it – it is to be
discovered each for him or herself, in the course of Zen training.[16]

To presume to comment at this point in order to expound the true
meaning of what went on between the two spiritually enlightened beings
is as vacuous as a casual observer trying to interpret a glance between
two lovers. As Ashvaghosha once said, "We use words to get free from
words until we reach the pure wordless Essence."

Suzuki claimed that the human tongue is inadequate to express the
deepest truths of Zen, but if this is the case, how can such profundities
be realized? The wordless transmission which began with Sakyamuni
when he conveyed his teaching to his chief disciple, Mahakasyapa,
continued from generation to generation until it was brought to sixth-
century China by an Indian monk called Bodhidharma. Bodhidharma
taught that the practice of meditation is the means by which to access
the direct transmission of the Truth, and that this wordless transmission
is available to everyone. This tradition became known as Ch'an in
China, since *ch'an* is Chinese for "meditation"; for the same reason
when it was introduced to thirteenth-century Japan it became *"Zen"*.
Since the essence of meditational practice is self-realization, perhaps we
should remind ourselves of the words of the *Dhammapada* which
emphasize that self-conquest is the greatest victory of all; the *Tao Te
Ching* is also emphatic on this point: "He who knows others is wise; he
who knows himself is enlightened." In order to effectuate this knowledge, the practitioner is enjoined to depend on the mind, rather than
words and letters, which can only offer what has been termed a "second-
hand knowledge of Reality".[17] The advice to look within rather than at
the outside world is no stranger to Buddhism, of course, but how is this
to be achieved and what precisely is it that is achievable?

Zen, therefore, most strongly and persistently insists on an inner spiritual
experience. It does not attach any intrinsic importance to the sacred sutras
or to their exegesis by the wise and learned. Personal experience is
strongly set against authority and objective revelation, and as the most
practical method of obtaining spiritual enlightenment the followers of
Zen propose the practice of Dhyana, known as *zazen* in Japanese.[18]

Zazen

More than any other person, Zen master Dogen, who introduced Soto

Zen to Japan from China, may be described as "the master of *zazen*." For Dogen, the practice of *zazen* and the realization of Buddhahood are synonymous, and Dogen's impact on *zazen* continues to this day. Correct posture and breathing are all important, and much has been written on these issues, both then and now.[19] Among all the Zen schools, each with its own ideas on spiritual training, meditation in the posture in which Sakyamuni "awakened" remains to this day the chief path to enlightenment (Jap. *satori*). *Zazen* may be taken to mean "to sit in meditation", and meditation in Zen Buddhism is essentially concerned with addressing the questions, "Who am I? What am I? and Why am I the way I am?" This is the essence of meditation. The answers to these questions are not to be found by examining theories of the self, or theories of human nature, however, but by personal encounter, an encounter which is made difficult by an ego which constantly demands attention and directs our thoughts away from that which is real. With the best will in the world, the meditator has to contend with an attention-seeking ego, filled with self-importance, false-pride and the like which demands attention through constant chatter like the inhabitant of some monkey-temple. When we still the mind and the chattering ceases, however, although the ego doesn't go away, it is no longer attention-seeking, it is simply there, like a sleeping child, and we come face to face with reality, for in the words of Reverend Master Daishin Morgan:

> If one learns how to be still, then that which underlies the sense of ego, the sense of "me", the sense of self-importance and so on is simply there, it doesn't demand acknowledgement, it is simply there of itself . . . so when we turn to look we can begin to see it, and this is what we call Buddha-nature.

At this juncture, it is important to recognize that attachment and fixation have no place in Zen, for the way of Zen is a way of freedom, as Suzuki noted:

> If there is anything Zen strongly emphasizes it is the attainment of freedom; that is, freedom from all unnatural encumbrances. Meditation is something artificially put on; it does not belong to the natural activity of the mind. Upon what do the fowl of the air meditate? Upon what do the fish in the water meditate? They fly; they swim. Is not that enough? . . . there is no object in Zen upon which to fix the thought. Zen is a wafting cloud in the sky. No screw fastens it, no string holds it; it moves as it lists. *No amount of meditation will keep Zen in one place.* Meditation is not Zen.[20]

Indeed, Dogen himself recognized the dangers of consciously using meditation as a means to strive for Buddhahood. Meditation in Zen is not a question of striving or holding on, but of letting go of thought patterns which separate us from reality. A thought pattern is sometimes called "a train of thought", which is an apt metaphor indeed. As surely as the engine pulls the first coach which, in turn, pulls the second coach, and so on, so does one thought lead to another, but, unlike the diesel, our train tends to lose direction. Formal meditation, *zazen*, starts the day for the Zen Buddhist with the express purpose of grounding oneself. Accordingly, as thoughts arise naturally in *zazen* so are they allowed to go as easily and quickly as they come; we do not allow our thoughts to develop by going from one thought to another. The sound of heavy rain on a window should be interpreted as just that, and left at that, without worrying that the grass should have been cut last week, the lawn mower should have been repaired last season and may not start even if I have remembered to buy some petrol, and I'm not sure that I have, the strimmer doesn't run well when it's damp ... and so on. With thoughts from external stimuli not allowed to come to fruition, rather than looking out at the world around us, we tend to look inwards, *directly pointing to the mind, directly pointing to the human heart*, and in so doing we gain direct experience of our Buddha-nature.

The master–pupil relationship

Tradition has it that the smile of realization that dawned on the face of Mahakasyapa when the Buddha first raised the flower all those years ago, also heralded the dawn of Zen Buddhism; this was the first wordless transmission which is only possible in an unbroken line when insight matches insight, and the beginning of the master—pupil relationship so central to Zen:

> This transmission is said to have continued unbroken from "heart to heart" to this day ... From then on the tradition cites twenty-seven Indian patriarchs who handed on the Dharma to a successor, from Mahakasyapa to Ananda and so on, each with a "Transmission Verse", and bestowing the Buddha's own begging bowl and robe as visible proof. The twenty-eighth patriarch, Bodhidharma, then brought it to China and is thus also the first Chinese patriarch and considered to be the founder of the Zen School.[21]

The fact that historical attestation of the Zen school prior to the generation after the Sixth Patriarch is without textual support has tempted some to dismiss the historicity of the tradition as myth. This temptation misses the point of the wealth of profound truths in a tradition which embraces the teachings of both early and Mahayana Buddhism and is expressed through metaphorical insight rather than literal interpretation.[22]

The origin of the tradition which began with Sakyamuni and is transmitted through the lineage via the master—disciple relationship is of fundamental importance to Zen, and finds expression in the chanting of the ancestral line, which spans twenty-five centuries, each morning in all Soto Zen monasteries. It is important to remember the source, for Zen has to find expression within the culture which it finds itself; the singing of the scriptures in English to a plainsong chant would be but one of many such forms of expression within the Soto Zen tradition's adaptation to Western form. Until her death on 6 November 1996, the UK and USA head and source of the Soto Zen Order known as the Order of Buddhist Contemplatives was Reverend Master Jiyu-Kennett. Invited to Japan in 1962 to train as a disciple by the chief abbot of one of Japan's principal monasteries, she was ordained as a Buddhist monk in Malaysia on route, where she was given the Chinese equivalent of her name, Sumitra (Jap. Jiyu: True Friend). The eventual death of the chief abbot saw her return to the West in 1969 as a *roshi*, a Zen master, where she founded not only Throssel Hole Priory in Northumberland but also Shasta Abbey in California, where she lived out her life.[23]

The master is held in deep respect as the incumbent representative of Sakyamuni, and his or her purpose is not to introduce a new teaching but to point the way towards one's Buddha-nature, which is something which we all have. It is most important to follow one's master's teaching, which is *always* given within the framework of the Buddhist Precepts.

Monks and monasteries

> I wish to find the truth. I wish to become one with the eternal, and so sitting down in meditation is a statement of that.
>
> Reverend Master Daishin Morgan

Monasteries are for those wishing to dedicate themselves to the spiritual life. The true monastery is the heart, and the monastic life is not mandatory for all Zen Buddhists since, on this view, the monastery is anywhere and everywhere; nor is there any suggestion that the monk is in some

way superior to the lay Buddhist, nor that he or she has a deeper awareness of Buddha-nature. Some simply feel that practice within the
monastic tradition is the right way for them while others don't. Both
monastic and lay traditions have long and successful histories, and have
proved good bedfellows.

Despite Suzuki's affirmations to the contrary, and his preoccupation
with the paradoxical and irrational, meditation is the heart of Zen. Both
within and without the monastery walls the intention is to enable meditational practice to embrace each and every action in order to become
grounded in yourself, totally at one with what you are doing at the time,
and not frantically trying to keep pace with a mind which is forever
racing ahead. Friends who come to my home and express an interest in
milking my goats for the first time, always speak of a deep satisfaction
in "being at one with myself", or "being close to the earth". The emotion
they are voicing is their being mindful of what they are doing at the time,
living in the moment (as do small children) rather than fretting about
what they have to do next.

Inside the monastery, the day begins with *zazen*, formal meditation,
with the intention of grounding oneself, a grounding which is reinforced
throughout the day by work, meditation and ceremonies, which give the
day a contemplative feel. The term "grounding" is an apt one, for it is
not a question of the monk trying to get somewhere, rather the opposite is true. Appropriately, in the West the Soto Zen school is called
Serene Reflection Meditation, a meditative practice wherein the meditator simply *lets go* of any thoughts which arise without allowing them
to develop. The outcome of this extremely simple and straightforward
practice is the realization that everyone has the Buddha-nature to which
we are inseparably connected, and the act of bowing which permeates
monastic life is a recognition of this. Bowing is also an expression of
gratitude in as much as through meditation we are able to find the source
of Truth. This recognition of the importance of bowing is expressed in
a saying found in the Soto Zen school:

As long as bowing lasts Buddhism will last.

Letting go is the essence of monastic life. As surely as the monk lets
go of arising thoughts, so must the world itself be renounced. But this
is a gradual process which cannot be achieved in one fell swoop; the
physical move from urban culture to monastic retreat is the easy part,
renouncing emotions, fixed-views, opinions and prejudices which are in
the very depths of one's being is far more difficult. Perhaps the weekly

shaving of the head is a reminder that the act of renunciation is a gentle, gradual, but ongoing thing. Nor must it be assumed that because the Buddhist's aim is to go beyond suffering, and the monk is aware of how he or she should respond to internal and social causes, monks are spared the mental anguish that torments us all; indeed, the more one becomes aware of and compassionate towards others' pain, the more one suffers for them.

It is a common mistake to see meditation as some form of escapism, with the meditator who stares at the wall intentionally facing in that direction so as to turn his or her back on the world and all its problems. But there is nowhere to hide in the monastery, nor, indeed, in meditation, for with extraneous thoughts not allowed to come to fruition, one comes face-to-face with oneself and all one's personality problems . . . a sobering thought indeed:

> So the way through that inner landscape entails penetrating and dissolving all the encrustrations on that human heart that is smothered by my lusts, greed, fears, hatreds, my stubbornness, opinions, notions, assumptions, passionate beliefs and assertions, my longings and aversions which together make up my dissatisfaction with what is.[24]

As surely as meditation is said to be the heart of Zen, so the monastery itself has a pulse, a heartbeat which pumps its lifeblood away from the heart and returns it to the source, the heart of meditation. In a monastery which is functioning perfectly, with every action of every meditator performed as an act of meditation, then the monastery itself becomes an expression of the mind of meditation.

Lay Buddhists

The novice monk has a six foot by three foot area on a raised platform on which novitiate monks meditate and sleep in the meditation hall or *zendo*. But Soto Zen extends far beyond the *zendo*, indeed far beyond the monastery walls. Lay Buddhists may support the monastery financially but Throssel Hole Priory supports the lay Buddhists spiritually, for it is also a training centre. Some thirty groups throughout the country meet regularly and follow the teachings of Throssel Hole. The advice given to lay Buddhists is to establish a regular twice-daily pattern of meditation, with regularity being far more important than duration. Whenever possible, meditation within a group situation is encouraged.

As with the monks, the emphasis is on being mindful, mindful of the task in hand rather than fretting over what also needs doing. The power of this practice is not diminished by location, for you can be just as mindful of walking the dog in the park as working for the monastery within its confines.

The Soto school (Chn. *Tsao-tung*) is the oldest surviving school of the Zen tradition. Its emphasis is that all beings have the Buddha-nature and that training and enlightenment are indivisible. The teaching operates within the framework of the Buddhist Precepts and encourages the Buddhist to cease from doing evil, to do only good, and to do good for others as the heart of compassion is awakened. At the same time, it is necessary to examine what it is that we do which causes suffering and to cease from this; when suffering is caused by extraneous, such as social, pressures then how we respond to these is all-important.

Origins of Zen

Although Buddhism arrived in China in the first century CE, it did not really flower there until the sixth to ninth centuries. Western scholars, who were swift to recognize the affinities between Zen and Taoism, displayed a tendency to see the former as a variant of the latter. Although it would be churlish to deny a strong Taoist influence, this view of Zen is now considered untenable; indeed, Suzuki's emphasis on the place of Zen within the framework of the Mahayana *sutras* has influenced Japanese Zen scholars to rightly view Zen not as a tributary within a main stream of Taoist philosophy, but within the context of the expansion of Mahayana Buddhism throughout east Asia. Similar caution is needed when we consider that Zen was introduced into Japan during the Kamakura period (1185–1333) as "the religion of the samurai".

Tradition has it that in about 520 CE a Buddhist monk, Bodhidharma, arrived in China from India. Bodhidharma's emphasis was on meditation or *dhyana*, and once in China he founded the Ch'an school of Buddhism, *ch'an* being the Chinese for *dhyana*. It was a simple but tough and disciplined tradition and monasteries became self-sufficient, thanks to the manual efforts of the monks. Of some five Ch'an sects Lin chi (Jap. *Rinzai*) and Ts'ao tung (Jap. *Soto*) became the most well known. Soto Zen was introduced into Japan from China by Dogen (1200–1253), still revered today as one of the great Buddhist thinkers. Although Myoan Eisai (1141–1215) is generally credited with bringing Lin chi to Japan in the twelfth century and becoming the founder of the

Japanese Rinzai school, recent scholarship points to the previously
neglected contribution here of a predecessor of Eisai, one Dainichi
Nonin. Chinese Rinzai masters are also credited with bringing the third
Zen school, Obaku, to Japan near the end of the Ming period
(1138–1644):

> Preeminent among the Japanese monks was Tetsugen Doko (1630–1682),
> who prepared the canon of writings from all the Buddhist schools in 6,956
> Chinese wood-block printed volumes. The Obaku school took an open
> attitude toward Buddhism as presented in the *sutras*. It also cultivated the
> veneration of the Buddha Amida (Skt. Amitabha), which it interpreted in
> a Zen manner. The style of life in the monastery by and large followed
> Chinese ritual patterns.[25]

The koan

The koan (Chn. *kung-an*) is a Chinese invention which literally means
"public notice or notification", a meaning which has long been all but
ignored. These short paradoxical riddles, or slightly longer stories,
sometimes offer the listener a choice between two possible answers,
neither of which is acceptable. As surely as the meaning and purpose of
life cannot be resolved by use of the intellect, neither is it possible to
solve the riddle of the koan by this means. Since enlightenment cannot
be attained by conceptualized thought processes, the koan is employed
not to develop powers of conceptualization, but to disrupt the sequence
of logical thought and so bring about enlightenment by inducing an
altered state of consciousness.

Although the koan is an extremely efficacious device, long associated
with the essence of Zen, it must be said that it is not the only means of
attaining *satori*, nor is it the most important method, which remains to
this day the practice of meditation as exemplified by the Buddha
Sakyamuni. In *zazen*, attention is given at the outset to correct posture
and breathing, but concentration may be increased by the introduction
of a key word such as *mu* (meaning, "not" or "nothing") upon which to
meditate, and the practitioner who uses this technique transcends dualities in terms of subject—object differentiation and "becomes one with
nothing". Zen masters have likened the difficulties of transcending
conceptualized thought patterns and the subsequent realization of intuitive knowledge to the chick tapping away at the eggshell from which it
needs to escape.

The introduction of the koan in the form of a paradoxical riddle which forbids rational solution is designed to reveal intuitively, through a flash of insight, the Buddha-nature within. The first koan in a collection known as the *Mumonkan*, compiled by Wu-men Hui-k'ai (1183–1260), begs the question, "Has a dog also got Buddha-nature?", to which Master Chao-chou replies, "Mu". Clearly, the monk's question is one which could reasonably be expected to elicit a negative or positive response; equally clearly, this is not the way of the koan. Perhaps the most well-known koan asks, "What is the sound of one hand clapping?", while koans in the form of short stories include the tale of the goose that grew increasingly larger inside a bottle until it was too large to leave. The koan asks how the owner removed the goose from the bottle without harming either.

Normally associated with the house of Rinzai, the koan is not peculiar to this school; Dogen was introduced to the koan during his stay in China, and though less popular in Soto Zen, the use of koans is not unknown here. Conversely, some eminent Rinzai masters have ignored the use of koans in their teaching, though the efforts of Hakuin Ekaku (1685–1768), who introduced a systematized structure to the classification of koans, offered this method a rejuvenation which has been maintained to the present.

Heinrich Dumoulin observed that even today, the precise purpose and function of the koan remains unclear, and its use and abuse by both writers and sixties drop-outs such as hippies and beatniks, with their attendant drug problems, brought nothing but discredit to both Zen in general and the koan in particular. Nevertheless, amidst all the confusion and misunderstanding, some genuine, some deliberate, it is possible to discern a kernel of truth:

> The koan, as understood in Zen Buddhism, consciously or unconsciously includes a moment of questioning and doubt. The Zen practitioner is a seeker who turns for guidance and help to the master. The experienced, creative master is able to give the disciple the answer appropriate to him, which is imprinted indelibly on the questioner's memory. From this initial situation, we must suppose, the koan arose.[26]

The arresting, terse retorts of the esteemed Rinzai masters, designed to create a tension which in turn would bring about an altered state of consciousness, were soon in circulation amongst the disciples, and Suzuki went so far as to say, "To my mind it was the technique of the koan exercise that saved Zen as a unique heritage of Far eastern culture."[27] Sometimes, but not always, the "case" of some koans would take the form of a dialogue between master and pupil, engaged in with such rapidity that the sequence of logical thought patterns would be transcended and intuitive knowledge attained instantly – this is the characteristic *mondo* of Rinzai Zen.

Satori

When the normal flow of conscious thought is interrupted and the senses no longer inform the mind, a state of bliss is attained which has been described as being "outside one's self": this is enlightenment, the ultimate goal of Buddhism, which Zen calls *satori*. Beyond intellect and conceptual thought, this indescribable state, in which one awakens to the Buddha-nature within, is one where all dualities cease, and no subject—object differentiation exists, since the common notion that there is an "I" which has to be appeased and satiated no longer obtains. Once Sakyamuni's insight into the concept of "No-I" becomes internalized, the vista that lies before us is the realization that everything in the cosmos is the Buddha-nature. This is the Ultimate Reality and Truth. With this intuitive realization, this awakening to the Ultimate Truth, comes the dawning that, since the egoistic self is unreal, so the fears which become attached to that which is unreal are vacuous, as are all forms of attachment.

In theory, *satori* and enlightenment are identical, but in practice not all Zen Buddhists would credit *satori* with this distinction. There are those who would equate *satori* with the Indian *samadhi* which is achieved in deep meditation, without being considered to be enlightenment itself, believing that full Buddhahood lies beyond *satori*. Given the paradoxical nature of Zen, perhaps it is fitting that we leave Heinrich Dumoulin the last word on the subject:

> Therefore, without disparaging the significance of Zen enlightenment for earnest Zen disciples, we are driven to question its claim to be the norm of truth. Furthermore, as a mystical phenomenon, the *satori* experience is imperfect. No human effort to attain enlightenment, no matter how honest and self-sacrificing, can ever lead to the perfect truth.[28]

But if we accept this, we can only conclude, on Dumoulin's view, that Sakyamuni Buddha was either not human, not enlightened or neither! Zen is certainly a subject which is easy to misunderstand.

8

Pure Land

In order for the devotee to be saved by Amida and welcomed to the Pure Land through pronouncing the Name, NAMU-AMIDA-BUTSU, in all sincerity, the devotee cannot know what is good or bad for him. All is left to Amida. That is what I, Shinran, have learned.[1]

A first encounter with Devotional Buddhism is likely to leave the reader confused over whether he or she is reading about one of the main schools of the Mahayana, or an aspect of all schools in that tradition. There is good reason for this. It is perhaps a curious fact that the Buddhist schools in India which argued for the integrity of Devotional Buddhism, where faith in, and devotion to the Buddha took precedence, were the very schools which had historical associations with the *Madhyamikavada*, for whom Wisdom had always held pride of place. This close association with the upholders of Wisdom tradition meant that although there was always a place in Buddhism for simple faith in, and total devotion to the Buddha, this was, for centuries, very much a *second* place. Ever in the intellectual shadow, Devotional Buddhism in India and central Asia never gained recognition as an independent school. In east Asia, however, a characteristic form of popular Buddhism evolved, centred upon the cult of Amitabha, the Buddha of Infinite Light, which found expression in a variety of sects and movements known collectively as "Pure Land". The major sects in Japan are the Jodo, Jodo Shin, Ji, and Yuzu Nembutsu.

This said, the integrity of Devotional Buddhism was upheld, albeit in the Indian tradition outlined above, by no less a person than the founding father of the *Madhyamikas*, Nagarjuna. The debt owed to Nagarjuna is immense, for it was his spiritual insight which identified two possible paths which the would-be Buddhist could tread – the difficult path of self-reliance and the easy path of dependence. For Nagarjuna, the former comprised the practice of the Ten Perfections and the Four Abodes of Mindfulness, while the latter depended solely on the compassion of the two Buddhas, Amitabha, the Infinite Light, and Maitreya, the Loving One. Although both are held to be Buddhas, strictly speaking Maitreya is not a Buddha but a *bodhisattva*. Semantically, the word *bodhisattva* means one whose essence or being (*sattva*) is perfect Wisdom (*bodhi*), but the term took on the meaning of one who has delayed his *parinirvana* (the destiny of the Enlightened) in order to help mankind. In both Theravada and Mahayana traditions, Maitreya's domain is the Tusita Heaven, where he is on the brink of achieving Supreme Enlightenment. This will take place on earth beneath a tree, during his final rebirth, towards the end of the present world-period.

> Maitreya enjoys the distinction of being the only Bodhisattva worshipped today in Theravada countries, for which reason it has been suggested that devotion to the ideal of Bodhisattvahood as exemplified in the career of Maitreya, the Loving One, the future Buddha, could be a unifying and harmonizing factor in modern Buddhism.[2]

Maitreya is sometimes worshipped as a Buddha, and sometimes as a *bodhisattva*. In China, where he is widely popular, he is known as Mi-lo-Fo, the "Laughing Buddha", a recognized Zen "holy fool", identical with Pu-tai, a tenth-century Chinese monk.[3] The *bodhisattva par excellence*, however, is Avalokitesvara, the *Bodhisattva* of Compassion, for whom the *Karandavyuha* is our primary source material. In the Far East, only Amitabha is more popular, and the *Lotus Sutra* attests that Avalokitesvara can incarnate in any form. Since the tenth-century, China has depicted Avalokitesvara in female form as the goddess Kuan-Yin, known in Japan as Kwannon, "Regarder of the Cries of the World".

In many ways, it was inevitable that Devotion should find its way into the Mahayana tradition. The whole Doctrine had expanded to such epic proportion that its profound philosophy could no longer look to science for verification. Since empirical knowledge could no more verify this immense Doctrine, the scientific stage of this world became too small to portray the eternal and universal truth; accordingly, the Doctrine of the Mahayana looked to a backdrop of infinite proportions, where space and time have no bounds, where the heart can be unlimited in its compassion – the realm of the cosmic myth.

Ironically, it was this need to expand into the realm of cosmic dimension, where boundless compassion was enacted, through myth, upon the universal stage, which was one of the factors that brought about the demise of Buddhism in India. It became customary in Devotional Buddhism to worship the Buddhas. This took the form of praising him, paying homage to him, meditating on him and asking him if the worshipper could be born as a Buddha in the future. All such worship results in the accumulation of merit. In meditation, the name of the Buddha or *bodhisattva* is either repeated silently, or chanted; power has always been believed to be in the name of a person or deity. Sometimes longer formulae are recited, e.g, "I pay homage to (or take refuge in) Amida/Amitabha Buddha":

Namu Amida Butsu (Jap.) or

Om Namo Amitabhaya Buddhaya (Skt.)

In certain Buddhist traditions it is believed that just one such act or thought of devotion will bring salvation. To the eastern (non-Buddhist) mind, this was simply a form of Hindu *Bhakti* (Buddhism has even appropriated the term *Bhakti* to describe Devotional Buddhism), and it ceased to be regarded as anything different.

Amida

Amida is the Japanese form of the Sanskrit names for the supramundane ruler of Sukhavati, believed to be a paradisical Land of Bliss in the western part of the universe. Known in Mahayana Buddhism as Amitabha (infinite light) or Amitayus (infinite lifespan), the texts portray this saviour creating the Land of Bliss from the force generated by his "Original Vow"; to those who recognize him as saviour is given the assurance of rebirth therein, where they will remain until they reach *nirvana*. Without mention in the Pali Canon, Amitabha is a creation solely of Mahayana Buddhism, though nowhere does Indian Mahayana accord him special veneration. Indeed, the religious lore into which Amitabha and Sukhavati are woven is a familiar Mahayana backdrop, with "extraterrestial" Buddhas, of which Amitabha is only one, rejoicing in the legion of cosmic realms, of which Sukhavati is only one, that have been created by the generation of their past *karma*. The theme that believers may be reborn in these celestial regions is also a common Mahayana notion.

However, with the shift from the Indian Mahayana to the east Asian cults of China, Korea and Japan, where veneration of Amitabha gave rise

to a distinct sect in Mahayana Buddhism, the backcloth changes; so
much so that scholars have looked to Iran rather than India for the origin
of a number of features endemic to Pure Land Buddhism, yet inimical
to Indian Mahayana.[4] The rise of the common era, moreover, witnessed
widespread belief that, because of mankind's decadence, the end of the
world was imminent; salvation was quite beyond man's own efforts and
could only be brought about by devotion to and intervention by some
powerful saviour.

Amitabha is regarded by devotees as Buddhahood itself, the embodiment of Wisdom and Compassion *par excellence*. In India, Nepal, Tibet
and Mongolia, the Buddha of Infinite Light was worshipped at the
Sambhogakaya level as a purely transcendental figure. In China and
Japan, Amitabha achieved recognition as the Ultimate in Wisdom,
Compassion and Infinite Love, not even "marginalized" as one of the
Buddha's five principal *Sambhogakayas*, as Amitabha was in the countries mentioned above. In the Far East, Amithabha is, at one and the
same time, immanent and transcendent, the supreme personification of
the *Dharmakaya*.

Unmentioned in texts which list the Buddhas who walked the earth,
Amitabha is considered by eastern scholars to be a myth. Whether
Amitabha was ever an historical figure should not detain us here; it is
not the point at issue. Many sacred texts contain mythological elements
which are unlikely to be historically accurate, but that is not their function. The purpose of such literature is not to record an historical truth,
but to point the way to the truth.

> We must not forget that Amitabha is the main object not of any system
> of philosophy but of the Buddhism of Faith and Devotion. What we are
> therefore concerned with here is an attempt not to convince the head but
> to move the heart. Since the heart is moved much more powerfully by a
> myth than by an argument the Buddhism of Faith and Devotion is neces-
> sarily in form mythical rather than historical, akin more to poetry than to
> logic.[5]

Scriptures

The principal Scriptures of Devotional Buddhism are rather short and
fall into two broad types – those which extol the spiritual qualities of
Amitabha and the virtues of rebirth in his Land of Bliss, and those which
describe techniques which enable the practitioner to visualize Amitabha

in his transcendental domain. The principal scriptures are the Larger and the Smaller *Sukhavati Sutras*, or the "Array of the Happy Land" (both believed to have been compiled in north-west India around 100 CE) and the *Amitayurdhyana Sutra*, or *Sutra* of "Meditation on the Buddha of Infinite Life". The first Chinese translation of an Amitabha myth dates from the early third century CE.

The Larger *Sukhavati Sutra* opens in a geographical setting well known to the Indian reader. In the course of the Buddha Sakyamuni's conversation with his companion, Ananda, and as the Amitabha myth unfolds, the scene transcends the familiar Vulture's Peak in Rajagaha and moves to a stage of cosmic proportions. The kernel of the text and, indeed, the core of the teaching of the Pure Land school, are the forty-eight vows made by Dharmakara, once a powerful king who renounced his kingdom to become a monk, and who resolves to attain perfect knowledge as a condition of his entering Sukhavati, a Happy Land eighty-one times more immeasurable than the ideal Buddha-country he has had described to him by his teacher, the Buddha, Lokesvararaja. Ananda is told that Dharmakara not only fulfils all his vows and has achieved his goal of attaining Supreme Enlightenment, but is now the Buddha of Infinite Light, Amitabha. As such, he is preaching the *dharma* in Sukhavati, leading countless beings there, simply by their having entrusted their own salvation and enlightenment to his care, as Dharmakara's eighteenth, Primal, Vow attests:

> If, when I attain Buddhahood, sentient beings in the lands of the ten directions who sincerely and joyfully entrust themselves to me, desire to be born in my land, and call my Name even ten times, should not be born there, may I not attain perfect Enlightenment. Excluded, however, are those who commit the five gravest offences and abuse the right Dharma.[6]

An account of the career of Amitabha is followed in the *Sutra* by a description of the Happy Land itself, which ranks among the finest examples of descriptive writing anywhere to be found in world literature. Sukhavati is portrayed as an immense plain, "level as the palm of one's hand", inhabited solely by gods and men, with jewelled ponds and trees, exquisite flowers raining down from the sky, celestial music, surrounded by golden nets with lotus flowers made of jewels. The imagery is also a fine example of the Buddha's "skill-in-means" *(upaya)*, for this is not merely a literal description of some celestial realm to which devotees aspire, but a literary device for presenting the enlightenment of *nirvana* to ordinary people who think in imagery of our every-day world, and to whom metaphysical expositions of reality are unintelligible.

The *Sutra* goes on to extol the virtues of Amitabha, whereupon the names of his associates, the *bodhisattvas* Avalokitesvara and Mahasthamaprapta, appear for the first time. The cosmic myth next describes, in literary imagery of mind-blowing proportions how, through the grace of Amitabha, Sakyamuni's companion Ananda, as well as every living being, is allowed to view the Happy Land of Sukhavati. Rebirth in Sukhavati, the *Sutra* explains, is dependent upon the accumulation of good *karma*, though all but the gravest sinners may enter this Land of Bliss, where even the birds' songs echo the *dharma*.

The Smaller *Sukhavati Sutra*, on the other hand, emphatically denies that good *karma* is a necessary condition of rebirth in Sukhavati. This text describes Sukhavati in similar, if far less splendoured terms than the larger *Sutra* (which is eight times its length). Herein is found residing Amitabha, now rejoicing in his other name, Amitayus, the Infinite Life. Of the Happy Land, Sakyamuni tells his companion:

> Beings are not born in that Buddha-country of the Tathagata Amitayus as a reward and result of good works performed in this present life. No, whatever son or daughter of a family shall hear the name of the Blessed Amitayus, the Tathagata, and having heard it shall keep it in mind for one, two, three, four, five, six or seven nights . . . they will depart this life with tranquil minds. After their death they will be born in the world Sukhavati in the Buddha-country of the same Amitayus, the Tathagata.[7]

According to the Smaller *Sukhavati Sutra*, rebirth is assured those who have complete faith in Amitayus at the moment of death; this state of mind is rewarded by the appearance of the Buddha, and transportation of the soul (essentially a non-Buddhist concept!) to Sukhavati, where it is reborn from a lotus flower thanks to Amitabha's grace.[8]

The Larger and Smaller *Sukhavati Sutras*, together with the *Amitayurdhyana Sutra*, "the *Sutra* of the Contemplation of Amitabha Buddha", are the texts which form the heart of Far Eastern Devotional Buddhism. The last named Contemplation *Sutra* describes meditations employed in order to visualize Amitabha in the transcendent beauty of Sukhavati. All three texts feature the Buddha, Sakyamuni, but he is never portrayed as the main object of devotion: rather, his role is that of one who introduces Amitabha to an audience and illuminates his greatness. The highly developed Mahayana Doctrine, with its sophisticated belief in the *Trikaya*, rendered the direct worship of Sakyamuni out of the question. Other influential texts fall into two broad divisions – those which regard a Buddha as the central object of worship, and those which place a *bodhisattva* in that position.

Outside the *sutras*, the *Tannisho*[9] and the *Shoshinge*[10] are the two most quoted documents in Pure Land Buddhism, while the writings of Ippen Shonin (1239–89), founder of the Jishu (Time Sect) are also very popular.[11]

Pure Land

From the late fourth century onward, the cult of Amitabha, with its characteristic features (devotionalism; "visualization"; beatific visions at the moment of death; invocation of the Buddha's name), is attested in Chinese sources, but it is generally combined with other Buddhist beliefs and practices. It was only in the sixth century that Pure Land Buddhism became established as a distinct religious movement.[12]

By definition, a "Pure Land" in Mahayana Buddhism is a land which has been purified by *bodhisattvas* in preparation for their future appearance there as Buddhas. Said to be as "numberless as the sands of the River Ganges", these Pure Lands bear witness to the leading of all sentient beings to Buddhahood as part of the purification process. In contrast, the realms from which unenlightened sentient beings come are called "Impure Lands" in recognition of the blind passions of the three defilements – greed, anger and delusion – to which we are all subject. The concept of a "Pure Land" is not peculiar to Mahayana Buddhism, for early Buddhists recognized what they termed a *buddhaksetra* (Skt.) or *buddhakkheta* (Pali), a realm wherein the teachings of Sakyamuni Buddha predominate. For the Mahayana, however, with its *bodhisattva* ideal, these worthies, who will become Buddhas, must be accommodated in a veritable galaxy of Pure Lands, since each has accumulated sufficient merit from his past *karma* to generate his own Pure Land, more especially since no two Buddhas can preside over the same Buddha-field. Although Sukhavati is only one of many Pure Lands (others include Abhirati and Vaiduryanirbhasa, as well as Maitreya's Tusita Heaven and the Potalaka Mountain of Avalokitesvara), it is also the best-known, and is described in detail in the Larger and Smaller *Sukhavati Sutras* as well as in the *Kuan wu-liang-shou ching* of central Asian origin.[13]

The rise of Pure Land Buddhism in China, as founded by T'an-luan

(476–542) and developed by Tao-ch'o (562–645) and Shan-tao (613–681) owes much to the widely-held view in currency throughout the East at the beginning of the common era that, due to man's decadence, the downfall of the world was not only inevitable but imminent. Widespread persecution of Buddhism in sixth-century China leant its full weight to this feeling and created a situation where serious study of the Buddhist scriptures as a means to enlightenment became all but impossible. As a consequence of both these conditions a simpler solution was sought which answered the problem in a stroke. If salvation was quite beyond man's "own power" (Jap. *jiriki*), then clearly there was a need to look outside this to a powerful saviour, thus "relying on the strength of the Other One" (Jap. *tariki*).[14]

> By participating in and allowing oneself to be permeated by this power, one transcends the world of causal necessity (*karman*). Implicit in the Pure Land teachings concerning the power of the Original Vow is the belief that, even if the escape from this world of *samsara* (the round of birth and death of unenlightened existence) is possible through inspired insight alone, the ground of the possibility of that insight depends in turn on something higher or deeper than mere human insight: the divine power (Skt., *adhisthana*) of the Buddha.[15]

The simplicity of this appeal was immediate and widespread, and by the middle of the eighth century it was not only the common people who had made Amidism a powerful movement, but the upper classes too.

The attractiveness of the belief that *nirvana* was inevitable for those reborn in the Pure Land was great indeed, particularly when the said rebirth simply required devotion to Amitabha, though the mercy of the *bodhisattva* Kuan-yin later became just as important as the Buddha's saving grace. Consequently, contemplation of Amitabha to this end became widely popular amongst ordinary people, and the invocation of his Sacred Name (Jap. *Nembutsu*) as part of the formula

> *Homage to (or refuge in) the Buddha Amitabha*

constantly chanted in the vernacular, sometimes up to a hundred thousand times a day became the norm:

> However, in spite of its doctrinal simplicity, Amidism in China developed an elaborate and characteristic liturgy, with hymn singing, the chanting of spells, collective prayer, and penitential ceremonies that in many vari-

ations have continued until the present ... As may be expected, Pure Land devotionalism appealed to the lay public, and the collective activities of lay believers, both male and female, often in the form of pious societies or congregations organized for common prayer and the performance of good works, always have played an important role.[16]

External influences

There can be little doubt that indigenous Taoism played no small part in the development of Pure Land Buddhism in China. From the outset, Sukhavati was associated in the eastern mind with the K'un-lun mountain prominent in Taoist thought, and current Taoist religious practices were known to include visualization techniques and invocation recitals with supramundane beings in mind. Inevitably, as time passed, more philosophical Buddhist doctrines began to make incursions into the simplicity of Pure Land Buddhism. The "One Vehicle" doctrine of the *Lotus Sutra* began to appear, as did certain esoteric aspects of Tantric Buddhism. The influence of Ch'an, meanwhile, with its ideal of an inner Buddha-nature within each individual, led to the belief that the Pure Land to which Amitabha devotees aspired was not to be sought in some western paradise in a distant part of the universe, but within oneself. At the same time, Sukhavati came to be viewed as the embodiment of Mahayana Buddhism in general, and the Enlightenment of Sakyamuni Buddha in particular, in a stroke removing Sukhavati from the realm of the cosmic myth and transforming it into the most popular object of veneration in east Asia.[17] Ch'an also appropriated the Pure Land formula, "Homage to (or refuge in) the Buddha Amitabha" in meditation, and by late imperial times, most Chinese monasteries bore witness to Ch'an-Pure Land syncretism in some form or other.

Amidism in Japan

At the horrible time of the end, men will be malevolent, false, evil and obtuse and they will imagine that they have reached perfection when it will be nothing of the sort. *Lotus Sutra*

Seventh-century Japan was just as concerned about the impending end of the world and "the final phase of the Doctrine" (Jap. *mappo*) as China, and the arrival in that country, via Korea, of Pure Land Buddhism was welcomed first at the Japanese court, and then by the common people. As the days, as well as the charisma, of Sakyamuni

Buddha began to distance themselves in time from the memory of
Buddhist minds, the path to enlightenment became increasingly difficult, and certain texts espoused a declining view of history where *mappo*,
the age in which we currently live, marked the third and most degen-
erate stage of the Buddha's *dharma*, wherein no individual could attain
enlightenment in a single lifetime. Appropriately named "The Latter
Days of the Law", all that remained of the Buddha's memory were his
teachings; practices were a thing of the past and "enlightenment" a mere
word. With people becoming ever-aware that the attainment of enlightenment was now something beyond their power, the time was ripe for
the emergence of a Buddhist teaching which claimed to be tailor-made
for such disconsolate times, and the Pure Land tradition made its
appearance on the stage of Japanese history.[18]

Recognition of Japanese Amidism as a distinct sect was slow but
inevitable; its appeal was to members of all social classes. At first, the
emphasis was on *tariki* and *nembutsu*, the latter accompanied by the
visualization of Amida and the circumambulation of his image, but the
Buddhist monk, Honen (1133–1212), later taught that if *nembutsu* is
practised assiduously, then the saving grace of Amitabha is assured, and
nembutsu practice came to be regarded as the sole means to salvation.

> Constant repetition of the Nembutsu, he held, ensures the continual
> purification of one's mind and body and the dissolution of doubt.
> Moreover, it leads to a moment of awakening (*satori*) in this lifetime and,
> eventually, to rebirth in the Pure Land. To those detractors who argued
> that repeated recitations signified reliance on Self Power Honen answered
> that the necessary requisite of each invocation was the proper concentra-
> tion and sincerity of the mind that comes only from absolute faith in
> Amida's salvific power. However, he never fully explicated the relation
> between faith, the Nembutsu, and Other Power.[19]

Not all were convinced of this, however, and Honen's disciple,
Shinran (1173–1261), made the point that Amitabha's "Original Vow",
made aeons ago while still the *bodhisattva*, Dharmakara, affirmed that
the Buddha's grace was a gift for every genuine believer; *nembutsu*,
therefore, was not the means but the end, a way of expressing one's gratitude for Amida's salvation, not a device for invoking it. On Shinran's
view, what is all-important is faith in the Other Power, *not* in the
nembutsu; the practice of *nembutsu* is *not* a prerequisite for birth in the
Pure Land, but that which naturally arises spontaneously out of gratitude for the wonder of the vow, thus promoting the arising of *shinjin*.[20]
Accordingly, two main Japanese Buddhist sects evolved, both centred

upon the worship of Amida Buddha, the Jodoshu (Pure Land sect) founded by Honen, and that founded by Shinran, the Jodo Shinshu (True Pure Land sect) or, as it is often called, Shinshu. These were seen not as rivals, but as sister schools, for "Nembutsu practice and faith come to be two sides of the same coin, with Shinshu emphasizing the moment of salvation and Jodoshu stressing the process of arriving there".[21]

The term *namu-amida butsu* is the Japanese rendering of the original Sanskrit *nama amitabhuddhaya*, which means "Adoration of the Buddha of Infinite Light", the recitation of which is not only an expression of adoration by Amida's followers, but an affirmation of their total conviction that Amida has the power to grant them rebirth in his Land of Bliss. More than this, *nembutsu* is a metaphysical formula, representing a state of consciousness wherein all dualities cease and subject (the devotee) and object (of adoration, Amida) become one:[22]

> Amitabha's all-embracing grace erases all distinctions, including even the distinction between "own effort" (*jiriki*) and "relying upon the Other One" (*tariki*). Shinran also stressed the fact that Amitabha is the only Buddha who should be worshiped. All other Buddhist teachings and practices are secondary, or even irrelevant.[23]

Today, some twenty million Japanese Buddhists are to be found before the family altar in their daily worship of Amida, which incorporates recitation of *nembutsu*, the chanting of Pure Land scriptures and making offerings to Amida. But *nembutsu* is not confined to the home, nor even to funerals and religious services, for the constant invocation of the Sacred Name is to be heard on radio and television programmes as well as on the lips of devout believers as they perform their daily tasks.[24]

Shinjin

Shinjin literally means "Entrusting Mind", though as a religious concept it defies translation. It expresses itself in the familiar Buddhist resolve to "let go", to "abandon" or "cease attachment to" the egocentricity which impedes enlightenment, whose only Triple Treasure is "I, Me, and Myself"! Filled with false-pride, the ego deceives us into an inflated sense of self-importance. Instead of recognizing our true place in this world, and acknowledging the worth of others, we vindicate our own misdemeanours, at the same time as we revile the shortcomings of others, setting ourselves up as the centre and standard of the Universe, around which the whole world revolves. It is the ego which feeds the darkest depths of our hearts and minds, promoting our evil desires, overt and covert passions, our greed and delusion. It is the ego also which tolerates, even encourages the dark side of our nature, by justifying the need for power, wealth and fame, forever interpreting our selfishness as "good intentions"; not that we can see this, indeed we would be quite horrified to learn that we have any evil whatever within us, as we continue to feed the ego with deception, remaining blind to our failings as we embark upon yet another "ego-trip". The Infinite Light of Amida Buddha, however, because it is infinite, can see through the masquerade into our darkest depths, leaving us shorn of the tinsel which deceives us into thinking that we are, in some way or other, superior to our fellow human beings.

For the Pure Land Buddhist, the root of the problem lies not in trying to fathom how to eliminate the ego (which will always be there anyway, no matter how hard we try to negate it), but in releasing the stranglehold which the ego has on our lives, as it develops and encourages our blind passions, anxieties and egocentric tendencies. Once we loosen the ego's grip and see it for what it really is, it can no longer constitute a *karmic* impediment to enlightenment. But we cannot do this alone! Our ego convinces us that we have the "own-power" to overcome anything (which it would do, since it is hardly likely to promote its own demise!), but this is a contradiction in terms, since it would mean relying on the ego to overcome the self-same egoism. Dependence, therefore should not be upon the vicissitudes of a fickle ego using "own-power" (*jiriki*), but on the all-embracing Infinite Light of Amida by means of "Other-power" (*tariki*).

If our *karma* is favourable, our lives assume a pattern whereby we can accept the teaching which enables *shinjin* to arise in us. The arising of *shinjin* is, at one and the same time, the sole condition for rebirth in the Pure Land, and a guarantee of enlightenment in the life to come; it is not *nirvana* itself. Seen in this light, through the mind of the wisdom and compassion of Amida, it is clear that the arising of *shinjin* in an individual embraces not only recognition of the efficacy of Amida's vow to save all sentient beings, but realization that our ego can make no contribution whatever to our own enlightenment, let alone that of others.[25] After all, argue Shin Buddhists, this is simply a natural progression from the Theravada and Mahayana Buddhist concept of *anatta*, which contends that there is no such thing as a permanent, unchanging self, and if there were (as Hindu *Advaitists* hold) then this most certainly would not be the ego.

Shinjin and *nembutsu*

So how does one realize *shinjin*; what religious practices have to be followed to this end? In a word – none! Recitation of the *Nembutsu*, though considered by the Pure Land tradition to be a contemplative participation in the Buddha's Infinite Light, imbued with all the virtues and power of Amida himself, is no more a prerequisite to the arising of *shinjin* than traditional Buddhist meditative practices (which are considered by many Pure Land Buddhists to be too demanding anyway) and ethical prescriptions. This said, there are still Pure Land Buddhists today who employ meditative techniques involving statues, paintings or *mandalas*, as well as following at least some of the galaxy of visualization exercises found throughout the traditional Pure Land *sutras*. Originally, the purpose of meditation forms in the *sutras*, such as the *Amitabha-samadhi*, was to effectuate the visualization of Amida Buddha and his Pure Land, and they are said to have been successful to this end, but nowadays their function is seen as an expression of joyful gratitude to Amida Buddha and his *dharma*.

Shinjin and *Nembutsu* are inseparable,[26] which is why reciting the name cannot be termed a religious practice; "In Jodo-Shinshu there is no really religious practice."[27] This is not to say that any or all such practices cannot be undertaken as a spontaneous act(s) of gratitude to Amida, which is, of course, the purpose and function of *Nembutsu*, but any suggestion of their being used solely, or even partly, for self-aggrandizement can only be self-defeating; used in this manner, such practices are seen to resort once more to "own-power" and yet again the ego raises its ugly head. It remains for the devotee simply to trust in the wisdom and compassion of Amida Buddha and to reflect on Amida as the supreme reality embracing all things, though this cannot be achieved without a measure of contemplative mindfulness. In so doing, the Pure Land Buddhist's total acceptance of Amida and his *dharma* brings recognition of the distress of our human condition as well as our true place in this world of suffering. With this comes also the assurance of the salvific "Other Power" of Amida with the promise of enlightenment to come which, given human limitations, is beyond the power of humanity. "To be deeply imbued, in this way, by Amida's mind of compassionate wisdom is to live the life of shinjin."[28]

Jodoshu and Jodo Shinshu doctrine

Although there are a number of Pure Land traditions in east Asia, the two main schools are the Jodoshu and the Jodo Shinshu. Both have several sects; Jodo Shinshu alone having ten, of which the eastern and western Honganji are the largest. The essence of Pure Land Buddhism is that it parts company with earlier forms of Buddhism which follow the difficult path of wisdom *(prajna)*, meditation *(dhyana)*, and austerity *(sila)* as the means to salvation, and advocates what is termed "the easy path" total dependence upon the salvific power of Amida Buddha, with the hope of attaining rebirth in his Pure Land. In other words, all Pure Land Buddhists place *tariki* ("Other power") above *jiriki* ("own power"), which they consider to be not only difficult but, given the limitations of human capabilities, for most people, ineffectual.[29] Indeed, Shinran had such little confidence in human goodness and such faith in the salvific power of Amida that he reversed an earlier saying of Honen:

> "Even a bad man will be received in Buddha's Land, how much more a good man", to read "Even a good man will be received in Buddha's Land, how much more a bad man."[30]

Japanese festivals

The unusual events which marked the birth of Siddhartha are recalled in the festival of *Hana Matsuri*, an April festival which, understandably, is the most important of the many flower festivals for which Japan is renowned. The Lumbini gardens where Siddhartha was born are commemorated by the placing of model flower-gardens in temples and courtyards; sometimes the gardens are guarded by large papier-mache white elephants, which again recall details of the birth narratives. Siddhartha's very first bath was taken in perfumed water provided by the gods, an occasion which is not forgotten by Japanese Buddhists as they pour delicately perfumed tea over Buddha images in the temples.

The Enlightenment of the Buddha is remembered in the Japanese festival of *Jodo-e*, which occurs in December. Zen Buddhists recall the prolonged meditational period endured by Siddartha beneath the *bodhi* tree, when they undertake *rohatsu*, a period of intensive meditation which lasts throughout the day and the night. The Buddha's death is commemorated in the festival of *Nahan-e*, which occurs in February. Zen Buddhists meditate and chant in darkened temples, before the turning on of the lights symbolizes the hope that the light which

Siddhartha brought into the world is not gone out forever, but will continue as long as Buddhists follow his *dharma*.

A four-day festival which begins on 13 July is *Obon*. Also known as *Urabon* or simply *Bon*, the festival has many names, including The Festival of Lanterns or The Joyful Ceremony. It is a good example of where traditional aspects of pre-Buddhist customs have been appropriated into a Buddhist festival. Ancestor veneration is a feature of Far Eastern culture and Japan is no exception. Tradition has it that the Buddha's compassion released from suffering the deceased mother of one of his disciples, so *Obon* is a time for Japanese in the East to visit their mothers, as is the custom on Mothering Sunday here in the West. Although these homecomings are joyful occasions with family reunions marked by fêtes, side-shows, music and traditional dancing, the festival also has a serious side. Graves are attended and decorated, while offerings to Buddha images are accompanied by prayer for better rebirths for ancestors, whose spirits are invited to return home; incense is lit and burning hemp reeds guide the pathway home. The welcome accorded the ancestral spirits, for whom the family altar has been decorated, is both an oral and a material one, with the family actually talking to the spirits, who are then offered food. The Festival of Lanterns ends with the names of the deceased written on lanterns which float away on waterways, taking the spirits with them.

Ancestral graves (and temples too) are also visited during the festival of *Higan*, when water from wooden ladles is poured over tombstones in order to give merit to the deceased. *Higan* is celebrated not annually but twice a year, at the Spring and Autumn equinoxes when the harmony of nature is conspicuous, with no one element in the ascendency. Again pre-Buddhist (Chinese) influence is evident here, for the equinox is the time of the year when *yin* and *yang* are in perfect balance, before one begins to dominate the next six months. Harmony of life, then, is the central concern of *Higan*, and its aim of the realization of *nirvana* for all nature and every person finds expression in the six traditional *bodhisattva* "perfections" – generosity, non-violence, patience, effort, meditation and wisdom – which are remembered in order that this shore (the world of *samsara*) can be forsaken for the other shore (*nirvana*).

Springtime begins in February in Japan, and *Setsubon* is a festival which marks this event with the driving out of evil spirits from households. Finally, the old year is seen out on the last day of December when temple bells are struck one hundred and eight times on the festival of *Joya no Kane*, the Japanese "Evening Bells Ceremony".

Curiously, followers of the Buddhism of Nichiren Daishonin, which is one of the most popular forms of Japanese Buddhism, celebrate none of the above Japanese festivals, preferring to remember so-called "Commemorative Days" throughout the year, such as New Year's Gongyo (1 January), the inauguration of Daisaku Ikeda as the first president of the Soka Gakkai International (26 January), the Declaration of Invocation by Nichiren Daishonin (28 April) and the inscription of the *Dai-Gohonzon* by Nichiren in 1279 (12 October).

9

The State of the Art

___

"The transcultural character of the Buddha's path; the fact that such major strongholds of the faith as Japan and Tibet were opened late to extensive contact with Europeans; the tendency of Buddhism to syncretize with indigenous religions; and its puzzling disappearance from the land of its origin – all these factors combined to make that distant persuasion seem elusive to western eyes."[1]

A student new to the study of Hinduism, who was reading about the *Vedic* gods, once asked me why it was necessary to study the religion of a people who lived, "all those years ago". Clearly, he was quite oblivious to the fact that every time a Hindu lights a flame, that Hindu is worshipping Agni, the Hindu god of fire. But what of Buddhism? Interesting it may be, but is Buddhism not a religion more suited to people who lived "all those years ago", or at least live "all those miles away"? Perhaps the words of Jim Pym, writing in 1997, best answer this question: "Buddhism in the U.K. has grown tremendously in the last few years. New groups are springing up like lotus flowers on a hot day." In fact, the seventh (1997) edition of the Buddhist Society's Directory lists 340 Buddhist groups and centres throughout the UK alone. Instead of offering an apologia for the current popularity of Buddhism East and West, let us first see how this came about.

The Enlightenment of the eighteenth century was hallmarked by an emphasis on reason and individualism, rather than tradition, and long-cherished beliefs began to be called to question. Western scholarship's determination to uphold the "word of God", with its attendant anthropomorphic concept of deity, and maintain the integrity of the biblical record in the face of growing scientific knowledge, far from reassuring believers, had quite the opposite effect, and evoked charges of dogmatism, irrationality and even regression. Since the Enlightenment, science and secular liberalism have dominated cultural evolution in the West, challenging the inviolability of the biblical record's insistence upon a

Creator God, who made the world "one fine day", giving mankind dominion over the natural order, at the same time imposing edits upon mankind in a dogmatic moralizing tone often prefixed with the command, "Thou shalt not ... "

By contrast, with the introduction of Buddhism to the West came the realization that commitment to a religion and belief in a Creator God are not necessarily synonymous, nor are scientific advance and Buddhist teachings incompatible. On the contrary, in the light of recent scientific developments, Buddhist cosmology and modern science are shown to be converging rather than diverging; indeed, the former could almost be said to have anticipated the latter. Often, those westerners who found the dogma and moralizing tone of orthodox religion offensive, looked on the teachings of Buddhism, with a minimum of emphasis on credal formulae, as a breath of fresh air; in stark contrast to the edicts of established religion, which have often been written in blood, Buddhism advocates trying out its teachings, to see whether they are advantageous to the practitioner in question.

If the undogmatic, open-minded approach of Buddhism, which encouraged understanding and questioning, held an appeal for the rational western mind, so too did its teaching about rebirth. Since, in Christian thought, only mankind has an immortal soul, there is nothing wrong with the priest who rejoices in the torment of a bull in the ring, or a fox on the run, while experimentation on unwilling victims in laboratories in the name of vivisection is positively welcomed. But this is not in keeping with the holistic tenor increasingly evident today, and most certainly, this is not the way of Buddhism!

> Except in the sense in which all things are unique, Buddhism, unlike the Semitic faiths, does not regard man as an absolutely unique being brought into existence by means of a special creative act and endowed by his divine maker with an immortal soul the possession of which constitutes an unbridgeable difference between him and all other creatures and entitles him to exploit and torture them for his own benefit and amusement.[2]

In Buddhist terms, sentient beings are not considered as separate life-forms, each totally discrete from another, but as separate currents of psychical energy which can associate with any form. Viewed in this light, every sentient being is deserving of respect in its own right, while the Buddhist position that *results inhere in their causes*, with each and every cause accruing (though not manifesting) *karma* instantly, makes nonsense of the claim that "the end justifies the means since experimentation on animals can eventually only bring positive results!"

   In today's world, the middle way between workaholism and unemployment is an increasingly narrow one, and meditational practices have brought comfort to those suffering from stress (which has now become a condition of life) and other psychosomatic disorders. Buddhism, together with other meditative techniques, has been of help here, in coping with the trauma of life as we enter the twenty-first century. This is the age of computer technology, which advances so rapidly that almost every statement is obsolete before one finishes writing the sentence. *At the time of writing*, however, the latest advances include the linking by computer of a network of Buddhist groups in the USA, known as the *Cyber Sangha*, and the accessibilty via the Internet to journals such as the *Journal of Buddhist Ethics*. It was not the Internet which first brought Buddhism to the West, however, and we will now look at how this came about:

> it was not until the middle of the nineteenth century that serious interest in Buddhism developed and detailed knowledge of its teachings became available . . . through three main channels: the labour of Western scholars; the work of philosophers, intellectuals, writers, and artists; and the arrival of Asian immigrants who have brought various forms of Buddhism with them to America and Europe.[3]

Without doubt, these contributions to our knowledge of Buddhism have been enormous; equally doubtless, it would be a mistake to assume that all such knowledge should be accepted uncritically. On the campus recently I came across a foreign student introducing herself to another as a Buddhist. Excusing myself, I asked if I might enquire how long she had been a Buddhist. "All my life," came the reply. I then asked if she was a Theravada or a Mahayana Buddhist, to which she replied, "No. We call him Buddha." Glenn Mullin, furthermore, draws our attention to the fact that the errors of earlier writers are still perpetuated in authoritative works to this day, almost a century later, much to the annoyance and frustration of scholars:

> Western writers constantly repeat an historical error perpetrated by L. Austine Waddell, a Christian missionary who, writing at the turn of the last century, stated that the First Dalai Lama was a nephew of Tsongkhapa, founder of the Gelug school . . . He most certainly was not.[4]

The colonial period saw the posting to Asia of European officials, many of whom were proficient amateur scholars, who now, for the first time, had ready access to Buddhist scriptures. A British civil servant named B. H. Hodgson collected and studied Mahayana Sanskrit manuscripts in Nepal, but it was the British resident in Sri Lanka, T. W. Rhys Davids (1843–1922), who was to become the founder of the Pali Text Society in 1881 and, subsequently, a household name in Theravadin Buddhist studies. Translations of Theravadin and Mahayana texts were also made by professional scholars, notably the great French savant, Eugene Burnouf, whose publication of a Pali grammar and his translation of the *Lotus Sutra* in 1852, followed his 1844 *Introduction to the History of Indian Buddhism*. The American Henry Warren also translated selections from the Pali Canon, entitled *Buddhism in Translations*, which was published in 1896. At the first World Parliament of Religions held in 1893 Chicago, the practising Theravadin monk, Anagarika Dharmapala, addressed the assembly impressively. He later became the founder of the American branch of the Maha Bodhi Society, and the seeds of Buddhism in the United States were firmly sown.

Germany's Herman Oldenberg ensured that the Fatherland joined France (Burnouf) and the USA (Warren) in their desire to learn about Buddhism when he wrote *The Buddha, His Life, His Doctrine, His Community* in 1881. By the second half of the nineteenth century other famous names included Senart, Minaev and Fausboll. By the beginning of the twentieth century, Belgium, in the form of Louis de La Vallee Poussin and Etienne Lamotte, had walked onto a stage which now embraced the study of Tibetan and Chinese sources; Japan completed the picture in the form of D. T. Suzuki's quite enormous contribution to the study of Zen in the West.

Western philosophers, meanwhile, were introduced to Buddhism through the (somewhat imperfect) knowledge contained in the writings of the German philosopher Arthur Schopenhauer. The eclectic disposition of the Theosophical Society founded in New York in 1875 by Henry Olcott, an American attorney and journalist, and Madame Blavatsky, a Russian-born mystic, embraced the esoteric truths of eastern and western religions alike, and in 1880 the pair became possibly the first modern westerners formally to become Buddhists. Victorian England welcomed the epic poem on the life of the Buddha, *The Light of Asia*, penned in 1879 by the Christian poet, Sir Edwin Arnold. The reading of this poem persuaded an Englishman, Allen Bennett, to take the ochre robe in Burma in 1902 as Ananda Metteyya, thus becoming the first known Buddhist monk of occidental extraction. Towards the end of the nineteenth century, scholarship's "quest for origins" gained momentum, and the attraction of Theravada Buddhism, which was purported to be the earliest form of Buddhism, and the one closest to the Buddha's teachings, had obvious appeal.

The way for the visit of the now Ananda Metteyya from Burma was prepared by the foundation of the Buddhist Society of Great Britain and Ireland in 1907; its orientation was, unsurprisingly, Theravada; its publication, *The Buddhist Review*, later became *The Middle Way*. The onset of World War I signalled the dissolution of the Buddhist Society, which was reformed and renamed the Buddhist Lodge of the Theosophical Society in 1924 under the presidency of Toby Christmas Humphreys. Theosophy and Buddhism were not considered to be good bedfellows, however, and two years later the independent Buddhist Society was formed. The considerable influence which Judge Humphreys had on British Buddhism lasted for more than half a century, but not so the Theravada dominance. The prodigious writings of D. T. Suzuki in particular brought to the West an interest in the Mahayana in general, and Zen in particular, an interest which was perpetuated by the popular writings of the young Englishman, Alan Watts, who published *The Spirit of Zen* while still only twenty.

Buddhism also reached a wide audience through the universal appeal of Herman Hesse's 1922 novel *Siddhartha*, which was made into a film in the 1970s. I have already credited the excellent Everyman TV documentary, *Khensur Rinpoche*, and the Wessex Consortium video, *Soto Zen Buddhism*; more recent is the film, *The Little Buddha*. The novels of Jack Kerouac and Allen Ginsberg had previously attracted the attention of the "Beat" generation in the late 1950s and early 1960s, a movement with which Alan Watts, now living and writing in the United States, was associated. The sixties also heralded an interest in meditation, which was accelerated by a young set interested in psychedelics. The audience was widened further as it tried to view Zen by looking through the 1974 exhaust pipe of R. M. Persig's *Zen and the Art of Motorcycle Maintenance*, albeit with narrowing consequences.

It is with some embarrassment that tourists sometimes leave the Christian Quarter in the Old City of Jerusalem admitting they were expecting to find the market place manned by European Caucasians, not Palestinians. No doubt their unease is due to the fact that they were unable to distinguish the Christians from others; this is often the case with Buddhists, particularly lay Buddhists. Although immigration was undoubtedly the third avenue for Buddhism to enter the West, of the million or so Buddhists in Europe (200,000 of whom are estimated to live in the UK) the vast majority are European Caucasians from the middle classes who have converted to Buddhism and whose forebears never so much as set foot in a Buddhist country.

The demise of Buddhism in India has meant that among the profusion of immigrants to the United Kingdom from the Indian subcontinent there have been few Buddhists. This has not been the case in the United States, whose relative proximity and cultural history ensured that the Mahayana strongholds of east Asia gained a foothold on the American mainland. Accordingly, it is with no surprise that we learn that, unlike Britain, Buddhism in the United States first acquired visibility through the Mahayana. Chinese labourers began arriving in the States for the Californian Gold Rush just after the middle of the nineteenth century, setting to work in the gold mines and on the railroads, and establishing first typically Chinese syncretistic temples and, later, centres which were purely Buddhist orientated. Hawaii became home to both Chinese and Japanese immigrants some time before it became a US possession, while the end of the Vietnam war saw some half a million settlers arriving in the States from south-east Asia. Buddhism today is even more popular in the United States than it is in Europe, and it is estimated that between three and five million Buddhists are to be found across a thousand Buddhist groups. An examination of over a thousand Buddhist groups is far beyond the remit of this modest book, and even further beyond the writer's competence, but at least we can look at a few.

Soka Gakkai

Today, the Soka Gakkai International is committed to an expansion programme which exemplifies the vital spirit of a branch of Buddhism which, in the 1960s, was described as the "fastest growing religion in the world". Today, 25 per cent of the worldwide Christian community are Evangelical/Charismatics, and by the year 2000 it is anticipated that there will be 30 per cent.[5] Appropriately, the highly successful growth rates of Evangelical/Charismatics and the SGI are directly attributable to outreach programmes which emphasize the value of their belief systems in today's world; indeed, Soka Gakkai means "value-creation society".

The year 1963 saw the establishment of an American Soka Gakkai headquarters in Los Angeles, which in 1967 became the lay wing of Nichiren Shoshu, though a schism developed in 1991. Initially, and understandably, membership was largely Japanese, though its appeal to young Americans was immense, and by 1970 it was they, and not the Japanese, who comprised two-thirds of its members. Today, the SGI is a worldwide association of 76 constituent organizations which has membership in 128 countries and territories, including some six and a half thousand members in the UK.

Tibetan

In the 1960s, Tibetan Buddhism began to acquire visibility in both Europe and the United States through the arrival of refugee lamas. One of them, Tarthang Tulku, in 1969 established the Nyingmapa Center in Berkeley, California; the following year another lama, Chogyam Trungpa, founded a center in Vermont, later moving his headquarters to Boulder, Colorado, where among other works he directs the Naropa Institute as a sort of Buddhist University.[6]

The Chinese invasion of Tibet in the 1950s and the enforcement of communism saw the subsequent end of Tibetan rule in 1959, after an unsuccessful revolt against Chinese oppression. This proved to be the single most dramatic historical event which has shaped the course of Buddhism in the twentieth century. The opportunity afforded by the Tibetan diaspora to enter dialogue with native *lamas* and engage in esoteric ritual was not without appeal in the West. Chogyam Trungpa (1939–87) also took responsibility for the Samye Ling Tibetan Buddhist Centre in Dumfriesshire, Scotland, though he was not its founder, this distinction going to Ananda Bodhi and Dr Akong Tulku Rinpoche, the incumbent Abbot and administrator of Kagyu Samye-Ling. In Tibet itself, the eighteenth-century social reformer Gzan-phan-mtha'-yas held that monks had a responsibility to society, arguing that monastic rules and education were interdependent; today, however, although the monasteries in Tibet certainly bear witness to religious ritual and ceremony, they are bereft of political power, and no form of monastic study and its concomitant dissemination of knowledge is permitted.

The Dalai Lama escaped to Dharamsala in India where he lives to this day, establishing it as the religious and cultural centre of Tibetan Buddhism in India. Far from living the life of a recluse, however, the Dalai Lama is a figure of international stature, who travels the world, and Tibetan Buddhism has become widely disseminated. In May 1993 he visited the Lam Rim Buddhist Centre at Raglan in Monmouthshire, where so many of my own University students have been made welcome for more than a decade. The Centre was opened in 1978 by the Venerable Geshe Damcho Yonten two years after he had come to the West. Geshe Damcho Yonten studied for twenty-three years from the age of six at Drepung in Tibet and later Ladakh in India. A new shrineroom at Lam Rim was dedicated and blessed by the Dalai Lama on that auspicious day in May 1993. Today there are some 117 Tibetan monasteries world-wide, and the education of the children of Tibetan refugees in such countries as India, Nepal and Bhutan is enhanced by the establishment of some eighty-three schools around the world.

Pure Land

The True Pure Land School, Jodo Shinshu, was established in Honolulu in 1899. After World War II, missionaries became active in those countries which had opened their doors to large numbers of Japanese immigrants, and temples began to appear in Hawaii as well as North and South America and elsewhere. By 1983 Jodo Shinshu, of which there are ten sects, the largest being the eastern and western Honganji, boasted a worldwide membership of over thirteen million, with forty thousand priests and twenty-one thousand temples. Today, it is reputedly the largest Buddhist sect in Japan, though Nichiren Buddhism is also immensely popular.

Understandably, the UK membership is far more modest, but still active, and in 1997 Jim Pym spoke excitedly and enthusiastically of the opening of a Jodo Shinshu Temple and Meditation Garden in London.[7] Jodo Shinshu is non-sectarian and some members in Britain follow Chinese and Vietnamese traditions. In the 1980s, the other major Pure Land School today, the Pure Land or Jodoshu, had an estimated seven thousand temples and nunneries throughout the world, and offered visible support in the secondary and university sectors of education, as well as to those socially dependent.

Friends of the Western Buddhist Order

The FWBO was founded in 1967 by Ven. Sangharakshita, an English monk with no great love of Christianity, who lived twenty years of his life in India, where he was ordained into the Southern, Northern and Eastern traditions of Buddhism; unlike other Buddhist groups, the FWBO remains critical of Christianity to this day. The Order draws on the whole Buddhist tradition but, despite affirmations to the contrary in popular literature, it is not eclectic. Its mission is to find ways of developing Buddhism to meet the needs of the modern western world. Today, the FWBO has spread from Britain, which has a thriving community of several thousand Buddhists, to some twenty-three countries around the world, including continental Europe, New Zealand, Australia, the United States and India, where the Karuna Trust has raised several thousand pounds for Buddhists formerly designated "Untouchable". The 1997 edition of the Buddhist Society's Directory attests that there are seventy-eight FWBO centres worldwide, with thirty-one of them in the UK, including eight retreat centres.

The Western Buddhist Order itself has some 660 members, many following "right livelihood" businesses, though all sharing the common belief that "commitment (to Buddhist ideals) is primary, lifestyle is secondary". Order members are neither monks nor lay people but *Dharmacharis* or (*Dharma*-farers), commited followers of the *dharma*, the Buddhist path. They do not possess robes, but wear a stole or *kesa* on ceremonial occasions.

Soto Zen

Known in Britain as the Serene Reflection Meditation tradition, the Soto Zen school has Throssel Hole Priory in a quiet valley in Northumberland as its training monastery and retreat centre. It also has a small priory in Reading, Berkshire, with future plans for similar small priories. Founded in 1972 by the recently deceased (6 November 1996) Rev. Master Jiyu-Kennett, the Throssel Hole monastery has over thirty men and women ordained monks under the guidance of the incumbent Abbot, Rev. Master Daishin Morgan, a senior disciple of Rev. Master Jiyu-Kennett. The monastic order is celibate, though there are some thirty meditation groups affiliated to the monastery throughout the UK.

The spontaneous, simple and direct appeal of Zen was attractive indeed to post-war America, whose military personnel had gained personal experience of Zen in World War II Japan. The writings of D. T. Suzuki, the anti-authoritarian appeal of Zen to the "Beat" movement of the 1950s and the "Hippy" generation of the 1960s all increased the momentum, and large Zen centres were established in Los Angeles in 1956, San Francisco in 1959, and Rochester, New York in 1966. The Order of Buddhist Contemplatives has its headquarters in Shasta

Abbey, California, founded in 1970 by Rev. Master Jiyu Kennett as the headquarters of the Zen Mission Society.

Theravada

England has been a home for Theravada Buddhism for almost a century, and developing interest in Pali, enhanced by the recent accessibility of the Pali Canon electronically, has drawn added attention to this first form of Buddhism to appear in the West. In 1985 at Great Gaddesden, near Hemel Hempstead in Hertfordshire, the Amaravati monastery was founded by the American monk Ajahn Sumedho; under his direction is a resident community of monks, nuns and postulants. Overnight accommodation is offered to visitors free of charge and guests are expected to keep the Eight Precepts, observe morning and evening meditation and help with the chores in the monastery and its spacious grounds. The interested reader will be appreciative to learn that Amaravati is a distribution centre for the publications of Ajahn Sumedho and fellow Buddhist masters, requesting payment for postage alone; all books are free of charge. Ajahn Sumedo is a pupil of the Thai monk Ajahn Chah, and the monastery is related to Wat Pah Pong and Wat Pah Nanachat in north-east Thailand. In Thailand itself, a revival of interest has been activated by *dharma* education programmes, while here, as in Burma, meditation centres have sprung up, with Burma alone embracing more than two hundred since World War II. Other Theravadin monasteries in England include Cittaviveka Chithurst monastery in Sussex, Ratanagiri Harnham monastery in Northumberland and Devon Buddhist Vihara. Thanks to the energy and vitality of these centres, the low profile which long accompanied Theravada Buddhism in England has now begun to change.

The establishment of Theravada monasteries in Thailand began to blossom in the 1960s and '70s, and 1966 saw the founding of the first Theravada centre in the United States, in Washington D.C. There are now some twenty Theravada monasteries in the United States, populated by monks from countries which have been a home to Southern Buddhism for many years, as well as Americans themselves.

Towards Enlightenment

It will be clear by now that commonality of beliefs and practices is not a feature of Buddhism and that the approaches adopted by the different schools vary enormously; although Sakyamuni Buddha rejected ritual, regarding it as a hindrance to *nirvana*, some schools are rich in ritual while others are almost bereft of it. The traditional Theravadin rice-farmer, the Japanese devotee of Amida Buddha, and the UK member of Soka Gakkai International may well have no immediately identifiable common features, but all Buddhists everywhere are concerned with the realization of Enlightenment, for this is their common ground. Some Buddhists regard Enlightenment as permanent, pointing out that once Sakyamuni realized Enlightenment, he never regressed, but remained Enlightened for more than forty years until the day he died. Others regard Enlightenment as momentary, an instant of realization which, like a bubble on the surface of a frothy stream, is as transient as anything else in Buddhist thought.

We are now at the end of the journey through which Buddhism has led us and hopefully the reader will have found the journey fascinating and enthralling, and will be eager to learn more. But Buddhism is not about knowing more, or becoming more and more informed as we acquire information and assimilate knowledge; it is about *experience*. Time and again, the reader of Buddhist literature is enjoined to *practise*, not simply read, within a Buddhist tradition with which the voyager feels comfortable, for only by so doing will he or she get to know what it is to *be* Buddhist. A friend once went to a party and was enthralled to enter conversation with someone who began to explain to him the beliefs of a Buddhist tradition with which he (a non-Buddhist) could immediately identify. At the end of the evening, he was asked if he would like to practise. Dismissing the idea, he said he didn't think it would ever work for him, to which came the response, "Then why not practise for a hundred days? If nothing happens then you will have proved that it doesn't work, but if the quality of your life improves, you will have proved that it does work." Try as he might, my friend could think of no logical objection to this suggestion. He has been a Buddhist ever since.

The Cover Pictures

———

The front cover depicts Sakyamuni Buddha in meditation, displaying distinctive hand positions or *mudras* that are a feature of both Buddhism and Hinduism. The back cover shows an image of Manjusri. Manjusri is a youthful, golden-complexioned, prince-like *bodhisattva* usually depicted with a five-peaked crown. He holds a sword in his right hand which symbolizes the kind of discrimination which cuts through ignorance to reveal the truth, while in his left hand he often holds the *Prajnaparamita Sutra*, the Scripture of Supreme Wisdom. He is sometimes pictured sitting on a lion, the roar of the lion being symbolic of the sound of truth. He can become manifest in any part of the universe, though he sits in perpetual meditation. He is believed to have been the founder of Nepal, having cut a huge opening in the mountains in order to drain a great lake so that Nepal could rise up in the valley of Katmandu.

The traditional meditative position of the hands in Buddhism is to be seen on some Buddha images. Here, the hands are brought together in the lap with the fingers lined up with each other, back to back, and the thumbs gently touching on top of the fingers. This creates a kind of circuit and is the standard symbolic hand position for nearly all Buddhism, though the position of the fingers may vary. When in this position, the hands are showing the gesture of concentration and therefore symbolize the concentration needed in order to rid oneself of desire and ego, as the Buddha himself did. Another symbolic gesture of the hands is that of "turning the Wheel of the Law". Here, in the context of Buddhist iconography, it serves to represent the teaching, the *Dhamma* of the Buddha. To show this, the forefinger and thumb on each hand are brought together to form a circle or wheel and the two hands are brought together to touch just where the fingers and thumbs unite.

Notes

Note: M. Eliade (ed.), *Encyclopedia of Religion* (New York: Macmillan, 1987), 16 vols, is abbreviated throughout the notes to *ER*.

Preface

1 Venerable Myokyo-ni, "What is Buddhism?" in *The Middle Way* (the Journal of the Buddhist Society), vol. 73, no. 3 (November 1998), pp. 131–3.

Chapter 1   *Towards Enlightenment*

1 See M. D. Fowler, "Excavated Figurines: A Case for Identifying a Site as Sacred?" in *Zeitschrift für die alttestamentliche Wissenschaft*, Band 97, Heft 3 (Berlin: De Gruyter, 1985), pp. 333–44.

2 R. T. H. Griffith, *The Hymns of the Rg Veda* (Delhi: Motilal Banarsidass, 1991 reprint of new revised 1973 edn), p. 130.

3 A. L. Basham, *The Wonder that was India* (London: Sidgwick and Jackson, 1982 reprint of 3rd revised 1967 edn), p. 235.

4 Sangharakshita, *The Eternal Legacy* (London: Tharpa, 1985), p. 16, notes that the *canonical* Jataka stories of the previous lives of the Buddha depict him as a wise man of old. It is only the much later *non-canonical* stories of the Theravada Jataka Book which relate the Buddha's lives as an animal. See R. Chalmers, W. H. D. Rouse, *Jataka* (three vols) (Oxford: The Pali Text Society, 1995. First published by Cambridge University Press in 1895).

5 Sangharakshita, *The Eternal Legacy*, p. 2, warns that, strictly speaking, Pali is not the name of a language at all: "The word means literally, 'a line, a row [of letters]' and thus, by extension of its meaning, 'the [canonical] text'. Early Western students of Theravada literature, finding in the commentaries expressions such as *palinayena*, 'according to the [canonical] text', took the word for the name of the *language* of the texts and, through their writings, gave currency to this misunderstanding."

6 R. F. Gombrich, "Dating the Buddha: A Red Herring Revealed", in H. Bechert (ed.), *The Dating of the Historical Buddha* Part 2 (Gottingen, 1992), pp. 237–59. Cf. R. F. Gombrich, *How Buddhism Began: The Conditioned Genesis of the Early Teachings* (London: Athlone, 1996), p. 76, note 11.

7 M. Pye, *The Buddha* (London: Duckworth, 1979), p. 11.
8 M. Carrithers, *The Buddha* (Oxford: Oxford University Press, 1983), p. 13.
9 Book I: 34. Text in E. B. Cowell (trans.), *The Buddha Carita or the Life of the Buddha* (New Delhi: Cosmo, 1977). First published 1894, first Indian print 1977. Unless stated otherwise, all references to the *Buddhacarita* are from Cowell.
10 Although it is only right that the reader's attention throughout this work should be drawn to the Indian background of Buddhism, this in no way is to suggest that Buddhism is no more than a form of Hinduism, a point well made by Professor Gombrich; see *How Buddhism Began*, especially pp. 14–15.
11 M. Pye, *The Buddha*, p. 31.
12 E. Conze (trans.), *Buddhist Scriptures* (London: Penguin, 1959), p. 50.
13 W. Rahula, *What the Buddha Taught* (Oxford: Oneworld, 1998 reprint of 1st 1959 edn), p. 41.
14 E. Conze, *Buddhist Scriptures*, p. 51.
15 M. Carrithers, *The Buddha*, p. 74.
16 A. Powell, *Living Buddhism* (London: British Museum, 1989), p. 14.
17 E. Conze, *Buddhist Scriptures*, p. 57.
18 E. Conze, *Buddhist Scriptures*, p. 53.
19 See, *inter alia*, R. H. Robinson, W. L. Johnson, *The Buddhist Religion: A Historical Introduction* (Belmont, California: Wadsworth, 4th edn 1997, 1st edn 1970), p. 48.
20 M. Carrithers, *The Buddha*, p. 98.
21 *What the Buddha Taught*, p. 41.
22 See note 10 above.
23 R. H. Robinson, W. L. Johnson, *The Buddhist Religion: A Historical Introduction*, p. 10.
24 *Ibid.*

Chapter 2 *The Development of Community*

1 See W. Rahula, *What the Buddha Taught* (Oxford: Oneworld, 1998 reprint of 1st 1959 edn), p. 2. note 1, for definition of *sangha*.
2 M. Carrithers, *The Buddha* (Oxford: Oxford University Press, 1983), p. 87.
3 A. K. Warder, *Indian Buddhism* (Delhi: Motilal Banarsidass, 2nd revised edn 1980; 1st edn 1970), pp. 56–7.
4 E. Lamotte, "The Buddha, His Teachings and his Sangha", in H. Bechert and R. F. Gombrich (eds), *The World of Buddhism* (London: Thames and Hudson, 1984), p. 55. J. M. Koller, *The Indian Way* (New York: Macmillan, 1984), p. 134, notes that following his Enlightenment Siddartha requested that his companions no longer call him "friend", but "Tathagata" ("one gone thus") i.e. to Enlightenment.
5 R. F. Gombrich *et al.*, "Buddhism in Ancient India: The Evolution of the Sangha", in *The World of Buddhism*, p. 77.

6 R. F. Gombrich, *How Buddhism Began: The Conditioned Genesis of the Early Teachings* (London: Athlone, 1996), p. 13.

7 J. Snelling, *The Buddhist Handbook* (London: Century, 1987), p. 90.

8 Sangharakshita, *The Eternal Legacy* (London: Tharpa, 1985), p. 3.

9 J. Snelling, *The Buddhist Handbook*, p. 90.

10 J. D. Fowler, "Buddhism", in J. D. Fowler *et al.*, *World Religions: An introduction for students* (Brighton: Sussex Academic Press, 2nd revised edn 1999), p. 271.

11 J. Snelling, *The Buddhist Handbook*, p. 90.

12 R. F. Gombrich *et al.*, "Buddhism in Ancient India: The Evolution of the Sangha", p. 78.

13 See A. T. Embree (ed.), *Sources of Indian Tradition* (New York: Columbia University Press, 2nd edn 1988, 1st edn 1958), vol. 1, pp. 105–9.

14 R. F. Gombrich, "Buddhism in Ancient India: The Evolution of the Sangha", p. 15.

15 R. Gombrich, *Theravada Buddhism: A Social History from Ancient Benares to Modern Colombo* (London: Routledge and Kegan Paul, 1988), p. 56.

16 T. R. V. Murti, *The Central Philosophy of Buddhism* (London: Unwin, 1987 rp), p. 19.

17 *What the Buddha Taught*, p. 17.

18 J. M. Koller, *The Indian Way* (London: Macmillan, 1982), p. 137.

19 The observation is not mine but Sangharakshita's.

20 M. Pye, *The Buddha* (London: Duckworth,1979), p. 48.

21 E. Conze, *Buddhism: its essence and development* (London: Harper and Row, 1975. 1st edn published by Bruno Cassirer, Oxford, 1951), pp. 18–19.

22 Conze, *ibid.*, p. 107.

23 J. M. Koller, *The Indian Way*, p. 158.

24 E. Conze, *Buddhism: its essence and development*, p. 29.

25 *Buddhism: A Very Short Introduction* (Oxford: Oxford University Press, 1996), p. 53. The problem that the Buddhist has with desire is discussed admirably by Michael Carrithers in *The Buddha*, p. 77.

26 E, Conze, *Buddhist Scriptures* (London: Penguin, 1959), p. 72.

Chapter 3   *The Theravadin Doctrine*

1 J. D. Fowler, "Buddhism", in J. D. Fowler *et al.*, *World Religions: An introduction for students* (Brighton: Sussex Academic Press, 2nd edn 1999), p. 267.

2 Y. S. Chindoo-Roy, *Aspects of Theravada Buddhism* (Unpublished BA dissertation submitted to the University of Wales, 1990), p. 29.

3 H. von Glasenapp, *Buddhism: A Non-Theistic Religion* (New York: George Brazillier, 1966), p. 135.

4 L. S. Dewaraja, *The Position of Women in Buddhism* (Sri Lanka: Buddhist Publication Society, 1981), p. 6.

5 Y. S. Chindoo-Roy, *Aspects of Theravada Buddhism*, p. 49.

6 Nevertheless, not all Theravadins think alike; the Spiritual Director of the Buddhist Vihara in Birmingham, England, recently made clear that it is not necessary for everyone to go through the stages of monkhood or manhood in order to achieve *nirvana*. See Y. S. Chindoo-Roy, *Aspects of Theravada Buddhism*, p. 38.

7 H. Bechert, "To be Burmese is to be a Buddhist: Buddhism in Burma", in H. Bechert, R. Gombrich (eds) *The World of Buddhism* (London: Thames and Hudson, 1984), p. 155.

8 C. S. Prebish, *Historical Dictionary of Buddhism* (London: Scarecrow, 1993), p. 275.

9 J. D. Fowler, "Buddhism", in J. D. Fowler *et al.*, *World Religions: An introduction for students*, p. 268.

10 J. D. Fowler, *ibid.*, p. 266.

11 *Majjhima Nikaya*, i, 142; cf. *DN* ii, 140 following.

12 A. L. Basham, *The Wonder that was India* (London: Sidgwick and Jackson, 1982 reprint of 3rd 1967 edn), p. 273.

13 Y. S. Chindoo-Roy, *Aspects of Theravada Buddhism*, p. 52.

14 J. D. Fowler "Buddhism", p. 270.

15 W. Rahula, *What the Buddha Taught* (Oxford: Oneworld, 1998), p. 67 especially note 2. The chapter on "Meditation or Mental Culture", pages 67–75, remains one of the best.

16 Great Master Dogen, *Shobogenzo* (The Eye and Treasury of the True Law), four vols. (Tokyo: Nakayama Shobo, 1983), vol. 3, p. 40. See Rev Kinrei Bassis, "Not Necessary, But Useful", *The Journal of Shasta Abbey* (Shasta, Calif.), vol. xv, no. 4, p. 2.

17 M. Carrithers, *The Forest Monks of Sri Lanka: An Anthropological and Historical Study* (Delhi: Oxford University Press, 1983). Carrithers describes the monks as "radiant", which is an interesting choice of words. In the *Samyutta Nikaya* the Buddha also described monks who live in the present as "radiant."

18 Y. S. Chindoo-Roy, *Aspects of Theravada Buddhism*, p. 49.

19 *Ibid.*, p. 54. We will do well to note the closing words of this quotation.

20 C. Erricker, *Teach Yourself World Faiths: Buddhism* (Chicago: NTC Publishing Group, 1995), p. 148.

21 *Ibid.*

Chapter 4 *The Mahayana Doctrine*

1 P. Williams, *Mahayana Buddhism: The Doctrinal Foundations* (London: Routledge,1989), p. 25.

2 H. Narain, *The Madhyamika Mind* (Delhi: Motilal Banarsidass, 1997), p. 45.

3 R. H. Robinson, W. L. Johnson, *The Buddhist Religion: A Historical Introduction* (Belmont, CA: Wadsworth, 4th edn 1997), p. 84.

4 *Mahayana Buddhism*, p. 101. On the previous page, Williams reminds us

that the founding of the Hindu *Advaita* school occurred later than the Buddhist Mahayana *Sutra* in question, so if there is any influence to be perceived then the influence is *upon* the Hindu school and not *from* it.

5 *Ibid.*, p. 99.

6 N. Dutt, *Early Monastic Buddhism* (Calcutta: Calcutta Oriental Book Agency, 1960), p. 288.

7 *The Madhyamika Mind*, p. 98.

8 D. J. Kalupahana, *Buddhist Philosophy: A Historical Analysis* (Honolulu: University of Hawaii Press, 1976), p. 123.

9 Since nothing can usefully be said about the Absolute, a point made by Conze; see E, Conze, *Buddhist Thought in India: Three Phases of Buddhist Philosophy* (London: Allen and Unwin, 1983), p. 202.

10 *Buddhist Philosophy*, p. 129.

11 *Ibid.*, p. 134.

12 T. R. V. Murti, *The Central Philosophy of Buddhism A Study of the Madhyamika System* (London: Unwin, 1987 reprint of 1st 1955 edn), p. 231.

13 E. Conze, *Buddhist Thought in India: Three Phases of Buddhist Philosophy* (London: Allen and Unwin, 1983) p. 202.

14 B. P. Harvey, *An Introduction to Buddhism: Teachings, history and practices* (Cambridge: Cambridge University Press, 1990), p. 118.

15 Robinson and Johnson, *The Buddhist Religion*, p. 85.

16 H. Narain, *The Madhyamika Mind*, p. 33.

17 *Anguttara-nikaya* 2.38. See D. J. Kalupahana, *Buddhist Philosophy*, p. 112.

18 R. F. Gombrich, *Theravada Buddhism: A social history from ancient Benares to modern Colombo* (London: Routledge and Kegan Paul, 1988) p. 120.

19 Kalupahana, *Buddhist Philosophy*, p. 113.

20 T. R. V. Murti, *The Central Philosophy of Buddhism: A Study of the Madhyamika System* (London: Unwin, 1987rp), *passim*.

21 *Ibid.*, pp. 87 and 98.

22 Robinson and Johnson, *The Buddhist Religion*, p. 87.

23 *Buddhist Thought in India*, p. 203.

24 *The Diamond Sutra* (Leicester: Buddhist Publishing Group, no date), pp. 21–2.

25 J. D. Fowler, "Buddhism", in J. D. Fowler *et al.*, *World Religions: An introduction for students* (Brighton: Sussex Academic Press, 2nd edn 1999), p. 275.

26 *Buddhist Thought in India*, p. 202.

27 Robinson and Johnson, *The Buddhist Religion*, p. 90.

28 Robinson and Johnson, *The Buddhist Religion*, p. 92.

29 A. T. Embree (ed. and trans.), *Sources of Indian Tradition. Volume One. From the Beginning to 1800* (New York: Columbia University Press, 2nd edn 1988), p. 156.

30 Robinson and Johnson, *The Buddhist Religion*, p. 95.

31 B. P. Harvey, *An Introduction to Buddhism*, p. 140.
32 *Ibid.*, p. 141.
33 A. A. Powell, *Living Buddhism*, (London: British Museum Publications, 1989), p. 32.

Chapter 5   Nichiren

1 Y. Kirimura, *The Life of Nichiren Daishonin* (Tokyo: Nichiren Shoshu International Center, 1980), p. 6. The revised 1993 second edn curiously omits the name of the author.
2 *Nembutsu* is both a term meaning to meditate on a Buddha or invoke his name (in later useage it came to mean the recitation of Amida's name), and a generic term for those sects which seek to attain rebirth in the Pure Land by worshipping Amida Buddha. See *A Dictionary of Buddhist Terms and Concepts* (Tokyo: NSIC, 1983), pp. 287–8.
3 J. S. Strong, *The Experience of Buddhism: Sources and Interpretations* (Belmont, CA: Wadsworth, 1995), p. 336.
4 W. Hoyo, "Nichiren", in *ER*, vol.10, p. 426.
5 *The Major Writings of Nichiren Daishonin*, vol. 1 (Tokyo: NSIC, 1979), p. 236.
6 Y. Kirimura, *The Life of Nichiren Daishonin*, p. 25, footnote.
7 *Gosho Zenshu*, pp. 441–2.
8 *Daishonin* literally means "great sage", an honorific title given to Nichiren by the School of Nikko to imply that Nichiren is the original Buddha and not a great *bodhisattva*.
9 *The Major Writings of Nichiren Daishonin*, vol. 1 (Tokyo: NSIC, 1979), p. 180.
10 *Major Writings*, vol. 1, p. 181.
11 For a list of Nichiren's writings on Sado, see W. Hoyo, "Nichiren", p. 426. See also P. B. Yampolsky (ed.), *Letters of Nichiren* (New York: Columbia University Press, 1996).
12 *Major Writings*, vol. 1, p. 120.
13 H. Byron Earhart, *Japanese Religion: unity and diversity* (Belmont, CA : Wadsworth, 3rd edn 1982), p. 95.
14 W. E. Soothill, *The Lotus of the Wonderful Law* (London: Curzon Press, 1987), pp. 3–4.
15 B. Watson (trans.) *The Lotus Sutra* (New York: Columbia University Press, 1993), p. xvi.
16 D. Ikeda, (B. Watson, trans.), *Buddhism, the First Millennium* (London: Kodansha International, 1977), p. 126.
17 Libraries of books and articles have been written expounding the meaning of the invocation. The late Richard Causton's exposition remains one of the best. See R. Causton, *Nichiren Shoshu Buddhism* (London: Rider, 1988), chapter two. Following the schism between the Soka Gakkai and the priesthood, this work was republished recently under the title *The Buddha in*

Daily Life.

18 A point made by the Daishonin in his writing, *The One Essential Phrase*, see *The Art of Living: An Introduction to Nichiren Shoshu Buddhism* (Richmond, Surrey: NSUK, 1986), p. 17.

19 *Gosho Zenshu*, p. 513.

20 B. Wilson and K. Dobbelaere, *A Time to Chant: The Soka Gakkai Buddhists in Britain* (Oxford: Oxford University Press, 1994), p. 195. See chapter 10, "What Chanting Achieved".

21 S. Pritchard, "The True Object of Worship", *UK Express*, no. 317, November 1997 (Maidenhead: SGI-UK, 1997), p. 22. See also, "Map of the Gohonzon", *UK Express*, no. 322, April 1998, pp. 18–19.

22 *The Art of Living: An Introduction to Nichiren Shoshu Buddhism, UK Express* no. 180, June 1986 (Richmond: NSUK, 1986), p. 24.

23 *The Art of Living*, p. 24. See recently, D. Bloomfield, "Ichinen", *UK Express*, no. 319, January 1998, p. 6.

24 See *A Dictionary of Buddhist Terms and Concepts* (Tokyo: NSIC, 1983), pp. 303–7; also M. Senchu, "Nichirenshu" in *ER*, vol. 10, pp. 427–30.

25 See R. S. Ellwood, "New Religions in Japan" in *ER*, vol. 10, p. 413.

26 *Soka Gakkai International* (SGI: Tokyo, 1996), p. 2. An objective account of the Soka Gakkai is given in H. Byron Earhart, *Japanese Religion*, chapter 17, pp. 172–83.

27 R. S. Ellwood, "New Religions in Japan" in *ER*, vol. 10, p. 413.

28 *Soka Gakkai International*, p. 5.

29 See B. Wilson and K. Dobbelaere, *A Time to Chant* (Oxford: Oxford University Press, 1994), Appendix A, "The 1990–1991 Schism", pp. 232–45. The details of this bitter schism are also to be found in a series of monthly articles written by City and Westminster HQ leader Tony Loynes. See *SGI-UK Bulletin*, no. 213 (12 December 1997), pp. 4–5. The final article on the development of the SGI and the Priesthood Issue was written by Kasuo Fujii in *SGI-UK Bulletin*, no. 231 (2 October 1998), p. 4.

30 *UK Express*, no. 332, February 1999, p. 2.

Chapter 6 *Tibet: The Land of Snow*

1 G. Samuel, *Civilized Shamans: Buddhism in Tibetan Societies* (London: Smithsonian, 1993), p. 576.

2 J. Powers, *Introduction to Tibetan Buddhism* (New York: Snow Lion, 1995), p. 314, lists these as the Great Exposition School, the Sutra School, the Mind Only School, and the Middle Way School, though other authorities use titles various.

3 D. Snellgrove, "Tibetan Buddhism", in *ER*, vol. 2, p. 493.

4 *Ibid.*

5 J. S. Strong, *The Experience of Buddhism: Sources and Interpretations* (Belmont: Wadsworth, 1995), p. 261.

6 For an excellent discussion of the four Tibetan schools, see J. Powers,

Introduction to Tibetan Buddhism, chapters 11–15.

7   J. S. Strong, *The Experience of Buddhism: Sources and Interpretations*, p. 264.

8   J. Powers, *Introduction to Tibetan Buddhism*, p. 313.

9   T. R. V. Murti, *The Central Philosophy of Buddhism: A Study of the Madhyamika System* (London: Unwin, 1987 reprint of 1st 1955 edn), p. 87.

10 J. Powers, *Introduction to Tibetan Buddhism*, p. 314.

11 *Ibid.*, p. 317, note 2.

12 The Gelukpa tradition was not the first reform movement in Tibet. See J. S. Strong, *The Experience of Buddhism*, p. 265.

13 P. Kvaerne, "Tibetan Religions: An Overview", in *ER*, vol. 14, p. 500.

14 *Ibid.*

15 The subsequent events, including the consultation of the oracle and the eventual meeting with the Dalai Lama, are recorded in the excellent 1991 Everyman film, *Khensur Rinpoche*, produced and directed by Ritu Sarin Tenzing Sonam for White Crane Productions in association with Meridian films.

16 J. Powers, *Introduction to Tibetan Buddhism*, p. 90.

17 See L. S. Kawamura, "Tara", in *ER*, vol. 14, p. 338.

18 Robinson and Johnson, *The Buddhist Religion: A Historical Introduction* (Belmont: Wadsworth, 4th edn 1997, 1st edn 1970), p. 294.

19 C. H. Buchanan, "Women's Studies", in *ER*, vol. 15, p. 439.

20 P. Kvaerne, "Tibetan Religions: An Overview", in *ER*, vol. 14, p. 501.

21 J. Powers, *Introduction to Tibetan Buddhism*, p. 200.

22 A. Wayman, "Esoteric Buddhism", in *ER*, vol. 2, p. 474.

23 J. Powers, *Introduction to Tibetan Buddhism*, p. 219.

24 D. Snellgrove, *Indo-Tibetan Buddhism* (London: Serindia, 1987), p. 148.

25 John Grimes, *A Concise Dictionary of Indian Philosophy: Sanskrit Terms Defined in English* (New York: State University of New York, 1989), p. 357, lists "rule; ritual, scripture; religious treatise; loom; warp".

26 H. Guenther, "Buddhism in Tibet", in *ER*, vol. 2, p. 406.

27 Lama Thubten Yeshe, *Introduction to Tantra* (London: Wisdom, 1987), p. 29.

28 *Ibid.*, p. 21.

29 M. Brauen, "The Mandala, Sacred Circle in Tibetan Buddhism", in *The Middle Way*, vol. 72, no. 3 (London: The Buddhist Society, November 1997), p. 159.

30 E. Conze, *Buddhism: Its essence and development* (Oxford: Cassirer, 1951), p. 178.

31 J. Powers, *Introduction to Tibetan Buddhism*, p. 233.

32 *Ibid.*, p. 239.

33 H. H. the Dalai Lama, in *Tantra in Tibet* (London: George Allen and Unwin, 1977), pp. 29–30.

34 J. Powers, *Introduction to Tibetan Buddhism*, p. 260.

35 *Ibid.*, p. 274.

36 J. D. Fowler, "Buddhism", in J. D. Fowler *et al.*, *World Religions: An intro-duction for students* (Brighton: Sussex Academic Press, 2nd edn 1999), p. 298.

Chapter 7   Zen

 1 A verse of unknown composition, generally assigned to the Tang dynasty in China. See Sangharakshita, *The Essence of Zen* (Glasgow: Windhorse, 1992), p. 25. A slightly different translation is given by Venerable Myoko-ni, "Zen – Tradition and History", in *The Middle Way,* vol. 73, no. 1(London: The Buddhist Society, May 1998), p. 16, where, as is common today, the verse is attributed to the Indian monk, Bodhidharma.

 2 These words are in no way meant to deride the influence Zen Buddhism has had upon Japanese culture, an influence which is, of course, considerable; see, for example, A. W. Watts, "Zen in the Arts", in *The Way of Zen* (London: Arkana, 1957), pp. 193–220, E. Herrigel, *Zen in the Art of Archery* (London: Routledge and Kegan Paul, 1972), and especially D. T. Suzuki, *Zen and Japanese Culture* (Princeton: Princeton University Press, 1970).

 3 R. H. Sharf, "The Zen of Japanese Nationalism," in *History of Religions*, vol. 33, no. 1 (Chicago: University of Chicago Press, 1993), p. 2.

 4 H. Dumoulin, *A History of Zen Buddhism* (London: Faber and Faber, 1963), p. 269.

 5 *Soto Zen Buddhism*, video produced by Wessex Consortium (1990).

 6 H. Benoit, *The Supreme Doctrine* (2nd edn Brighton: Sussex Academic Press, 1995), p. 3. Heinrich Dumoulin, *A History of Zen Buddhism*, p. 281, warns that psychology cannot speak the last word on Zen.

 7 Benoit, *ibid.*, p. 15.

 8 C. Humphreys, in D. T. Suzuki, *An Introduction to Zen Buddhism* (London: Rider, 1991), p. 6.

 9 *Ibid.*, p. 38.

10 *Ibid.*

11 R. H. Sharf, "The Zen of Japanese Nationalism", p. 21.

12 D. T. Suzuki, *The Zen Doctrine of No Mind* (London: Rider, 1991), p. 14.

13 M. Goodson, "Introduction to Zen Practice: Some Points to Remember", *The Middle Way*, vol. 71, no. 4 (London: The Buddhist Society, February 1997), p. 212.

14 Venerable Myoko-ni, "Zen – Tradition and History", *The Middle Way*, vol. 73, no 1 (May 1998), p. 16.

15 D. T. Suzuki, "An Interpretation of Zen Experience," in *The Japanese Mind: Essentials of Japanese Philosophy and Culture*, ed. Charles A. Moore (Honolulu: University of Hawaii Press, 1967), p. 123.

16 Venerable Myokyo-ni, "Zen – Tradition and History", *The Middle Way*, vol. 73, no. 1 (May 1998), p. 14.

17 Sangharakshita, *The Essence of Zen*, p. 58.

18 D. T. Suzuki, *An Introduction to Zen Buddhism*, p. 34.

19 See H. Dumoulin, *A History of Zen Buddhism*, p. 161 for Dogen's description of sitting meditation, also J. Clark, "Introduction to Zen Practice", *The Middle Way*, vol. 71, no. 3 (November 1996), p. 158. See also J. Clark, "Everyday Practice", *The Middle Way* vol. 73, no. 1(May 1998), pp. 21–22, and "Everyday Practice, part three", *The Middle Way*, vol. 73, no. 3 (November 1998), pp. 134–36, by the same author.

20 D. T. Suzuki, *An Introduction to Zen Buddhism*, p. 41.

21 Venerable Myoko-ni, "Zen – Tradition and History", p. 15.

22 A point well made by Venerable Myoko-ni, *ibid*.

23 See "In Memoriam: Reverend Master Jiyu-Kennett", *The Middle Way*, vol. 72, no. 2 (August 1997), pp. 111–12. The nearby town of Shasta (not "Shaster" as it is misspelt in *The Middle Way*) is named after a North-American Indian tribe.

24 Venerable Myoko-ni, "Zen – Tradition and History", p. 17.

25 H. Dumoulin, "Zen", in *ER*, vol. 15, p. 565.

26 H. Dumoulin, *Zen Buddhism in the 20th Century* (New York: Weatherhill, 1992), p. 122.

27 D. T. Suzuki, *Essays in Zen Buddhism* II (London: Rider, 1970), pp. 90–91.

28 *A History of Zen Buddhism*, p. 290. Several fascinating examples of the *satori* experience are given on pp. 273–5.

Chapter 8 *Pure Land*

1 D. T. Suzuki, *Buddha of Infinite Light* (London: Shambala, 1997; completely revised edn of Suzuki's *Shin Buddhism*, first published by Harper and Row in 1970 from a talk given by the author in 1958 at the American Buddhist Academy in New York City), p. 61.

2 Sangharakshita, *A Survey of Buddhism* (London: Tharpa, 1987), p. 355.

3 C. S. Prebish, *Historical Dictionary of Buddhism* (London: Scarecrow, 1993), pp. 168 and 220.

4 E. Zurcher, "Amitabha", in *ER*, vol. 1, p. 235.

5 Sangharakshita, *A Survey of Buddhism*, p. 356.

6 H. Inagaki, *The Three Pure Land Sutras: A Study and Translation from Chinese* (Kyoto: Nagata Bunshodo, 2nd revised edn 1995, 1st edn 1994), Larger Sutra 7 (18), p. 243.

7 *The Smaller Sukhavati-vyuha Sutra* 10. Translated by F. Max Muller in *Sacred Books of the East*, vol. 49 (Oxford: Oxford University Press 1886, reprinted by Motilal Banarsidass: Delhi, 1981).

8 E. Zurcher, "Amitabha", p. 235.

9 See A. Bloom, *Strategies for Modern Living: A Commentary with the Text of the Tannisho* (Berkeley: Numata Center for Buddhist Translation and Research,1992). See also the entry "Tanni Sho" in *A Dictionary of Buddhist Terms and Concepts* (Tokyo: Nichiren Shoshu International Center, 1983), p. 417.

10 See H. Inagaki, *The Way of Nembutsu-Faith: A Commentary on Shinran's Shoshinge* (Kyoto: Nagata Bunshodo, 1996).

11 An observation made to me by Jim Pym, of the Pure Land Buddhist Fellowship. For a record of Ippen, see F. Jakai, "Jodoshu", in *ER*, vol. 8, p. 106. More particularly, see D. Hirota, *No Abode: The Record of Ippen* (Honolulu: The University of Hawai'i Press, revised edn 1997, first published 1986).

12 E. Zurcher, "Amitabha", p. 235.

13 F. Kotatsu, "Pure and Impure Lands", in *ER*, vol. 12, p. 90.

14 See D. T. Suzuki, *Buddha of Infinite Light*, pp. 55–67.

15 H. Shoto, "Jodo Shinshu", in *ER*, vol. 8, p. 102.

16 E. Zurcher, "Amitabha", p. 236.

17 F. Kotatsu, "Pure and Impure Lands", p. 90.

18 T. Unno, "Mappo", in *ER*, vol. 9, p. 182.

19 F. Jakai, "Jodoshu", in *ER*, vol. 8, p. 105.

20 H. Inagaki, *The Way of Nembutsu-Faith*, p. 37.

21 H. Shoto, "Jodo Shinshu", in *ER*, vol. 8, p. 102.

22 D. T. Suzuki, "Rennyo's Letters", in *Mysticism Christian and Buddhist* (London: Unwin, 1979, reprint of 1957 edn), pp. 119–24. See also, D. T. Suzuki, *Buddha of Infinite Life*, p. 39.

23 E. Zurcher, "Amitabha", p. 237.

24 F. Ryosetsu, "Nien-fo", in *ER*, vol. 10, p. 437.

25 G. Gatenby, J. Paraskevopoulos, *A Primer of Shin Buddhism* (Neutral Bay NSW: Hongwanji Buddhist Mission of Australia, 1995), p. 12.

26 S. A. Peel, *Jodo-Shinshu* (Antwerp: De Simple Weg, 1997), p. 15.

27 *Ibid.*

28 *A Primer of Shin Buddhism*, p. 14.

29 "Own-power", it should be noted, is not the same as "self-effort", which is a misunderstanding of Jodo Shinshu doctrine; see Rev. Joren MacDonald, "The Importance of Self Effort" in *Pure Land Notes*, New Series no. 10 (Oxford: PLBF, September 1997), pp. 2–3.

30 H. Byron Earhart, *Japanese Religion* (Belmont: Wadsworth, 3rd edn 1982), p. 94. More especially, see A Bloom, *Strategies for Modern Living*, pp. 4–5.

Chapter 9   *The State of the Art*

1 R. S. Ellwood, "Buddhism in the West", in *ER*, vol. 2, p. 436.

2 Sangharakshita, *The Three Jewels* (Glasgow: Windhorse, 1977), p. 98.

3 D. Keown, *Buddhism: A Very Short Introduction* (Oxford: Oxford University Press, 1996), p. 117. The author's chapter "Buddhism in the West" is informative and lucid.

4 G. H. Mullin, *Mystical Verses of a Mad Dalai Lama* (Wheaton, IL: Quest, 1994), p. 255, note 5; see also pp. 17 and 257, note 9.

5 I. Cotton, *The Hallelujah Revolution* (New York: Prometheus, 1996), p. 2.

6 R. S. Ellwood, "Buddhism in the West", p. 439.

7 *Pure Land Notes*, New Series no. 10, September 1997, p. 4.

Glossary

―――

Abhidamma	Pali (Skt. *Abhidharma*): one of the "Three Baskets" of Buddhist scriptures containing discussion and commentary on the teaching of the Buddha; literally "higher knowledge".
ahimsa	the doctrine of non-violence in relation to all living things.
Aksobhya	a *bodhisattva*.
Amida	known in Mahayana Buddhism as Amitabha (infinite light) or Amitayus (infinite lifespan), Amida is the Japanese form of the Sanskrit names for the supramundane ruler of Sukhavati, believed to be a paradisical Land of Bliss in the western part of the universe. Amida is regarded by devotees as Buddhahood itself, the embodiment of Wisdom and Compassion *par excellence*.
Amoghasiddhi	a buddha.
anatta	Pali (Skt. *anatman*): the Buddhist doctrine of no-self.
anicca	Pali (Skt. *anitya*): the Buddhist doctrine of impermanence – that nothing ever *is* but is always in a state of *becoming*.
arahant	Pali (Skt. *arhat*): an enlightened person.
Asalha Puja	Theravadin festival to celebrate the giving of the first sermon by the Buddha.
Avalokitesvara	(Chin. Kuan-yin; Jap. Kwannon; Tibetan Chen-re-zig); the *bodhisattva par excellence*, the *Bodhisattva* of Compassion, and the national *bodhisattva* of Tibet.
bhikkhu (male)	a Buddhist monk.
bhikkhuni (female)	a Buddhist nun.
Bodh Gaya	the place where the Buddha became enlightened and an important pilgrimage site.
Bodhidharma	the legendary founder of Ch'an Buddhism in China.
bodhisattva	semantically, the word means one whose essence or being *(sattva)* is perfect wisdom *(bodhi)*, but the term took on the meaning of one who has delayed his *parinirvana* (the destiny of the Enlightened) in order to help mankind.
bodhi tree	the name given to the tree under which the Buddha sat when he became Enlightened.

Brahmavihara	four sublime states: see *metta, karuna, mudita, upekkha.*
buddha	one who is enlightened or awakened.
Buddha-nature	the Buddhahood within all things.
butsudan	a Japanese shrine; in Nichiren Buddhism it is a cabinet where the *Gohonzon* is enshrined.
Ch'an	"meditation", the name given to a branch of Buddhism in China corresponding to, and being the foundation of, Japanese Zen.
Chokhor	see *Asalha Puja.*
dagoba	Sri Lankan monument housing relic(s) of the Buddha.
daimoku	the chanting of the title, *Nam-myoho-renge-kyo* by Nichiren Shoshu and Nichiren Daishonin Buddhists.
Dalai Lama	spiritual head of Tibetan Buddhism. *Dalai* means "ocean" (of knowledge).
Dhamma	Pali (Skt. *Dharma*): the teaching of the Buddha; Truth.
Dhammapada	Important and popular Buddhist scripture.
Dharmakaya	the "Truth body" of the Buddha; Ultimate Reality.
Dogen	the founder of Japanese Zen Buddhism.
dukkha	Pali (Skt. *duhkha*): pain, suffering, dis-ease, disharmony.
Eisei	Founder of Zen Buddhism in Japan.
Gohonzon	the embodiment of the Law of *Nam-myoho-renge-kyo* in the form of a *mandala*; a scroll with the title of the *Lotus Sutra* inscribed on it, the focus and object of worship for Nichiren Shoshu and Nichiren Daishonin Buddhists. *Honzon* means "object of fundamental respect"; *go* means "worthy of honour".
gojukai	ceremony at which a member of the Nichiren schools of Buddhism is presented with a *Gohonzon.*
gongyo	literally "assiduous (constant) practice"; the reciting of the *Hoben* (second) and the *Juryo* (sixteenth) chapters of the *Lotus Sutra* and the chanting of *Nam-myoho-renge-kyo* in front of the *Gohonzon* by Nichiren Shoshu and Nichiren Daishonin Buddhists.
gosho	literally "writing worthy of great respect"; the writings of Nichiren Daishonin.
Hana Matsuri	Japanese Mahayana Buddhist festival.
Higan	Japanese Mahayana Buddhist festivals held at the time of the equinoxes.
Hinayana	"Small vehicle" (to salvation), the pejorative term given by Mahayana Buddhists to the conservative Buddhist schools of thought. Modern scholars prefer the term "early Buddhism".
ichinen sanzen	the theory of Nichiren sects of Buddhism which accepts the interconnectedness of all life through three thousand

	operative factors in any one given moment.
Jatakas	stories relating the past lives of the Buddha.
jhana	Pali (Skt. *dhyana*): meditation.
jiriki	in Pure Land Buddhism the path to enlightenment by "own effort".
Jodo-e	a Japanese Mahayana Buddhist festival.
Joya no Kane	a Japanese Mahayana Buddhist festival.
kamma	Pali (Skt. *karma*): "action". The actions one makes throughout one's lifetime will determine one's future.
karuna	compassion, one of the four *Brahmavihara*.
Kathina	a Theravada Buddhist festival.
khandhas	Pali (Skt. *skandhas*) the five constituents which make up the self as we know it.
khwan	the Thai belief in a spirit believed to accompany an individual throughout his or her life.
koan	Zen paradoxical riddle.
kosen-rufu	literally "to widely declare and spread" (Buddhism); a fundamental principle of the Buddhism of Nichiren Daishonin.
Ksala perahera	a Theravada Buddhist festival.
Kusinara	the site of the Buddha's death and an important pilgrimage site.
lama	a standard Tibetan translation of *guru*, a spiritual teacher, a title given to the religious leaders of the monastic traditions in Tibetan Buddhism.
Losar	the Tibetan New Year festival.
Lotus Sutra	unquestionably one of the most influential of all Mahayana scriptures; of unknown origin and authorship.
Lumbini Garden	the place where the Buddha was born.
Magha Puja	a Theravada Buddhist festival.
mahakaruna	great compassion, one of the two pillars of Mahayana Buddhism.
Mahaparinibbana-sutta	"Account of the Great Final *nibbana*", the death of the Buddha.
Mahavairocana	a buddha and the central buddha of Shingon Buddhism.
Mahayana	"Great vehicle" (to salvation), the name given to the more progressive strands which emerged from early, conservative Buddhism.
Maitreya	"the Loving One", the future Buddha; the only *bodhisattva* worshipped today in Theravada countries. In both Theravada and Mahayana traditions, Maitreya's domain is the Tusita Heaven, where he is on the brink of achieving Supreme Enlightenment. In China he is known as Mi-lo-Fo, the "Laughing Buddha", a recognized Zen

	"holy fool".
mandalas	geometric, symbolic designs used as aids in meditation.
mantra	symbolic sounds and words.
mappo	"the final phase of the Doctrine", the present age that marks the impending end of the world; otherwise known as "the Latter days of the Law".
Mara	the Buddhist enemy of enlightenment.
metta	loving-kindness, one of the four *brahma-vihara*.
mondo	verbal interchange between Master and pupil in Rinzai Zen Buddhism.
Monlam Chenmo	Tibetan Buddhist festival at the time of the New Year.
mudita	sympathetic joy, one of the four *Brahmavihara*.
mudra	symbolic hand positions.
Nahan-e	Japanese Mahayana Buddhist festival.
Nam-myoho-renge-kyo	the title of the *Lotus Sutra* chanted by Nichiren sects of Buddhism.
nembutsu	a term meaning to meditate on a Buddha or invoke his name (in later useage it came to mean the recitation of Amida's name), and a generic term for those sects which seek to attain rebirth in the Pure Land by worshipping Amida Buddha.
nibbana	Pali (Skt. *nirvana*): enlightenment, total egolessness.
Nichiren Daishonin	the founder of Nichiren Buddhism who first declared *Nam-myoho-renge-kyo* on April 28, 1253.
Nirmanakaya	"transformation body", a manifestation of a buddha in earthly form.
Obon	a Japanese Mahayana Buddhist festival.
pagoda	Japanese monument housing relics of the Buddha.
Pancha Sila	the Five Moral Precepts basic to most schools of Buddhism.
panna	Pali (Skt. *prajna*): wisdom which brings enlightenment.
parinibbana	Pali (Skt. *parinirvana*): the final extinction of the Buddha and the end of his rebirths.
paticcasamuppada	the Buddhist doctrine of dependent origination.
Prajnaparamita	literally "Perfection of Wisdom"; the most important literature for Mahayana Buddhism.
puja	honour, respect, gratitude.
Pure Land	one of the main schools of Mahayana Buddhism centred upon the cult of Amitabha, the Buddha of Infinite Light.
Ratnasambhava	a *bodhisattva*.
rupa	image of a buddha or *bodhisattva*.
Sakyas	(pronounced Shakya): tribe of people in northern India into which the Buddha was born.
Sakyamuni	(pronounced Shakyamuni): "Wise one from the Sakyas",

	the name given to the first historically recorded Buddha, Siddhartha Gautama, by many Mahayana Buddhists.
samadhi	concentration, the advanced state of meditation.
samanna	Pali (Skt. *sramana*) one who rejected orthodox teachings and who searched for Truth independently.
samatha	meditation.
Sambhogakaya	"glorious body" of a buddha.
samsara	the "aimless wandering"; the round of death and rebirth into which beings driven by craving are repeatedly born.
Sangha	the assembly of monks in Theravada Buddhism; the community of Buddhists in Mahayana Buddhism.
Sarnath Deer Park	the place where the Buddha taught his First Sermon, and a place of pilgrimage.
satori	sudden, intuitive enlightenment in Rinzai Zen Buddhism.
Setsubon	a Japanese Mahayana Buddhist festival.
shinjin	literally "Entrusting Mind", though as a religious concept it defies translation; a term conspicuous in Pure Land Buddhism.
Soka Gakkai	literally, "Society for the Creation of Value"; Japanese Buddhist lay movement which accepts the teaching of the Buddha Nichiren Daishonin.
stupa	monument housing some relic(s) of the Buddha. See also *dagoba* and *pagoda*.
Sukhavati	the paradisical realm of the Buddha Amida/Amitabha.
Sukhavati Sutras	the principal scriptures of Devotional Buddhism.
sunya	(pronounced *shunya*): empty.
sunyata	(pronounced *shunyata*): Emptiness, a major doctrine of Mahayana Buddhism that all things are empty of permanent essence.
sutta	Pali (Skt. *sutra*) one of "Three Baskets"; a general term for a scripture.
svabhava	own-being.
tanha	craving, the cause of suffering and the second of the Buddha's *Four Noble Truths*.
Tantrism	literally "loom"; the esoteric, mystical aspects of Buddhism.
Tara	a fully enlightened female buddha in the Tibetan tradition.
tariki	in Pure Land Buddhism "relying on the strength of the Other One".
Ten Worlds	the theory of Nichiren sects of Buddhism that each individual at any moment has the potentiality for ten life conditions. They are hell, hunger, animality, anger, tranquillity, rapture, learning, realization (or absorption), *bodhisattva* and Buddhahood.

thera	an elder, a monk.
Theravada	"Way of the elders", the name given to the only surviving school of conservative Buddhism.
Three Jewels or *Three Refuges*	The Buddha, the *Dhamma* and the *Sangha*.
Tipitaka	Pali (Skt. *Tripitaka*): "Three Baskets", the scriptures of Theravada Buddhism and some Mahayana.
tulku	*bodhisattvas* in Tibetan Buddhism who are born on earth many times for the purpose of assisting humankind.
upekkha	equanimity, one of the four *Brahmavihara*.
urna	the third eye of the Buddha.
usnisa	the projection on the top of the Buddha's head which signifies his spirituality and great mind.
Vairocana	a *bodhisattva*.
Vajrayana	literally "diamond" or "adamantine vehicle"; Tantric Buddhism, particularly as it is evident in Tibet.
Vassa	the rainy season and a time for retreat to a monastery.
Vesak also *Wesak*	festival in Theravada Buddhism which celebrates the Birth, Enlightenment and Death of the Buddha.
Vinaya	monastic rules, one of the "Three Baskets" which comprise orthodox Buddhist scriptures.
vipassana	insight meditation.
wu-wei	inaction; going with the flow of things.
yogin	an adept at meditative practice.
zazen	meditation and the name it is given in Japanese Zen Buddhism.

Further Reading

The 16-volume *Encyclopedia of Religion* edited by Mircea Eliade (New York: Macmillan, 1987) is a mine of information on every aspect of Buddhism. Under the entry "Buddhism" in the general index of volume 16 is a comprehensive list of the articles to be found in the *Encyclopedia*. Each article is accompanied by an apposite bibliography.

For those who are completely new to the study of Buddhism, informed introductions to the religion are to be found in P. Harvey, *An Introduction to Buddhism: Teachings, History and Practices* (Cambridge: Cambridge University Press, 1992 reprint of 1990 edn) and the slim and readable volume by Damien Keown, *Buddhism: A Very Short Introduction* (Oxford: Oxford University Press, 1996).

Three excellent, yet quite different, approaches to the Buddha's biography are to be found in M. Carrithers, *The Buddha* (Oxford: Oxford University Press, 1983), M. Pye, *The Buddha* (London: Duckworth, 1979), and Bhikku Nanamoli *The Life of the Buddha* (Kandy, Sri Lanka: Buddhist Publication Society, 1972). For the Buddha's teaching, W. Rahula, *What the Buddha Taught* (Oxford: Oneworld, 1998 reprint of the 1st 1959 edn) remains the standard work; there is nothing better than this erudite, yet eminently readable, little book. Excellent primary sources include Maurice Walshe's *Thus Have I Heard: The Long Discourses of the Buddha* (London: Wisdom, 1987), *A Buddhist Bible*, edited by Dwight Goddard (Boston: Beacon Press, 1994, 1st edn 1938), and Edward Conze's *Buddhist Scriptures* (London: Penguin, 1959). *The Buddha—Karita or Life of Buddha by Asvaghosha* (New Delhi: Cosmo, 1977) is translated by Edward Cowell, as is *The Dhammapada* (Arkana, 1987) by Eknath Easwaran.

Richard Gombrich's work, *Theravada Buddhism: A Social History from Ancient Benares to Modern Colombo* (London and New York: Routledge and Kegan Paul, 1988), is a classic, as is Michael Carrither's *The Forest Monks of Sri Lanka: An Anthropological and Historical Study* (Oxford: Oxford University Press, 1983). More advanced students might also find useful Etienne Lamotte's *History of Indian Buddhism* (Louvain—la—neuve: Universite Catholique de Louvain, 1988), and A. K. Warder's *Indian Buddhism* (Delhi: Motilal Banarsidass, 1997 reprint of 2nd 1980 edn). More recently, see *How Buddhism Began: The Conditioned Genesis of the Early Teachings* (London: Athlone,

1996) by Richard Gombrich. An important book on the five *khandhas* is *Identity and Experience: The Constitution of the Human Being*, by Sue Hamilton (Luzac Oriental, 1996), a technical work based on the *Sutta Pitaka* of the Pali Canon. Paul Williams' *Mahayana Buddhism: The Doctrinal Foundations* (London: Routledge, 1989) remains a standard work, as does T. R. V. Murti's *The Central Philosophy of Buddhism: A Study of the Madhyamika System* (London: Unwin, 1987, 1st published 1955); now out of print, as I write (January 1999) Sussex Academic Press is hoping to republish this classic. An excellent comprehensive coverage of Buddhism is to be found in Heinz Bechert and Richard Gombrich's (eds), *The World of Buddhism* (London: Thames and Hudson, 1984) and in R. H. Robinson and W. L. Johnson, *The Buddhist Religion: A Historical Introduction* (Belmont, CA: Wadsworth, 4th edn 1997).

The *Buddhist Directory*, published by the Buddhist Society (58 Eccleston Square, London SW 1V 1PH), now in its 7th (1997) edn, is updated every few years; it gives information on Buddhist groups and centres in the UK and Ireland. For those interested in the spread of Buddhism in the West, *Big Sky Mind: Buddhism and the Beat Generation*, edited by Carole Tonkinson (Thorsons, 1996) is recommended, as is *Western Buddhism: New Insights into the West's fastest-growing Religion*, by Kulananda (HarperCollins, 1997), and Stephen Batchelor's *The Awakening of the West: The Encounter of Buddhism and Western Culture* (Berkeley CA: Parallax Press, 1994). Buddhism and Feminism are ably treated by Sandy Boucher, *Turning the Wheel: American Women Creating the New Buddhism* (Boston: Beacon Press, 1993), and Rita Gross, *Buddhism after Patriarchy: A Feminist History, Analysis, and Reconstruction of Buddhism* (Albany: SUNY Press, 1993). The consistency of contemporary ethical thinking and Buddhist morality are examined in *Buddhism and Human Rights*, edited by Damien Keown, Charles Prebish and Wayne Husted (London: Curzon Press, 1998).

A highly informed, well-documented, yet very readable and clear account of Tibetan Buddhism, written for an audience with little or no previous knowledge of the tradition, is John Powers' *Introduction to Tibetan Buddhism* (New York: Snow Lion, 1995). There is no finer single text on the Buddhist meditative path than B. A. Wallace's *The Bridge of Quiescence: Experiencing Tibetan Buddhist Meditation* (Open Court, 1998), though this is definitely not a book for the beginner. Still within the Tibetan Buddhist tradition is *The Healing Power of the Mind: Meditation for Well-Being and Enlightenment* by Tulku Thondup (Penguin Arkana, 1997). The more advanced student is also referred to David Snellgrove's eminent work *Indo-Tibetan Buddhism: Indian Buddhists and their Tibetan Successors* (London: Serindia Publications 1987). For the study of Tantric Buddhism, the reader is recommended G. Samuel's *Civilized Shamans: Buddhism in Tibetan Societies* (London: Smithsonian, 1993), and Ngakpa Chogyam's *Spectrum of Ecstasy: Embracing Emotions as the Path of Inner Tantra* (London: Aro, 1997).

The most useful books in Pure Land studies are *River of Fire: River of Water* by Taitetsu Unno (New York: Doubleday, 1998), *The Way of Nembutsu-Faith: A Commentary on Shinran's Shoshinge* (Kyoto, Japan: Horai, 1996), and *Plain Words on the Pure Land Way*, translated by Dennis Hirota (Kyoto, Japan, 1989). Dennis Hirota has also written *No Abode: The Record of Ippen* (Honolulu: University of Hawai'i Press, 1997 revision of the 1986 edn). Ippen was another tradition of the Pure Land in Japan, but it is a wonderful book. A handsomely produced work is D. T. Suzuki's *Buddha of Infinite Light: The Teachings of Shin Buddhism, The Japanese Way of Wisdom and Compassion* (Boston: Shambala, 1997); the work is a revision of Suzuki's *Shin Buddhism*, published in 1970. Primary sources for the study of Pure Land include *The Three Pure Land Sutras: A Study and Translation*, by Hisao Inagaki (Kyoto, Japan, 1995) and *Strategies for Modern Living: A Commentary with the Text of the Tannisho*, by Alfred Bloom (Berkeley, CA: Numata Center for Buddhist Translation and Research, 1992).

For Nichiren Shoshu and Nichiren Daishonin Buddhism, the late Richard Causton's work *The Buddha in Daily Life*, originally entitled *Nichiren Shoshu Buddhism: An Introduction* (London: Rider, 1988) is recommended. *Basics of Buddhism* by Pat Allbright (Taplow: Taplow Press, 1998) is an introduction written in plain language which gives a concise explanation of the basic principles of Buddhist thought; it also includes an overview of the history, aims and principles of Soka Gakkai International. *A Time to Chant: The Soka Gakkai Buddhists in Britain* by Bryan Wilson and Karel Dobbelaere (Oxford: Clarendon, 1994) is an independent study of SGI members in Britain; now available in paperback. For the life of Nichiren, see *The Life of Nichiren Daishonin* by Yasuji Kirimura (Tokyo: NSIC, 1980, 2nd edn 1993). Primary sources include W.E. Soothill, *The Lotus of the Wonderful Law or the Lotus Gospel: Sadharma Pundarika Sutra* (London: Curzon Press, 1987), *The Lotus Sutra*, translated by Burton Watson (New York: Columbia University Press, 1993), and the seven volume work, *The Major Writings of Nichiren Daishonin* (Tokyo: NSIC, 1979–94). See also, *Letters of Nichiren* (New York: Columbia University Press, 1996), translated by Burton Watson *et al.* and edited by Philip B. Yampolsky.

Excellent introductions to Zen Buddhism are *Zen Keys: A Guide to Zen Practice,* by Thich Nhat Hanh (Berkeley, CA: Parallax Press, 1995), and Shunryo Suzuki's *Zen Mind, Beginners Mind* (New York: John Weatherhill, 1970). The student interested in the psychology of Zen Buddhism is recommended to read Hubert Benoit's work *The Supreme Doctrine* (Brighton: Sussex Academic Press, 1995, first published in France in 1951 under the title of *La Doctrine Supreme*). The history of Rinzai Zen Buddhism is detailed in Martin Colcutt's *Five Mountains: the Rinzai Zen Monastic Institution in Medieval Japan* (Cambridge, MA: Harvard University Press, 1981). A full analysis of the place of the *koan* is given in *The Zen Koan: Its History and Use in Rinzai Zen,* by Miura Isshu and Ruth Fuller Sasaki (New York: Harcourt, Brace and World, 1965). *Zen Enlightenment: Origins and Meanings* by Heinrich Dumoulin (New

York: John Weatherhill, 1979) is a classic study of the understanding of enlightenment in the history of Zen Buddhism. Collections of the sayings of Zen masters include *Zen Comments on the Mumonkan*, by Zenki Shibayama (New York: New American Library, Mentor Books, 1975), *Moon in a Dewdrop: Writings of Zen Master Dogen*, edited by Kasuaki Tanahashi (San Francisco: North Point Press, 1985), and *Zen Flesh, Zen Bones: A Collection of Zen and Pre-Zen Writings* by Paul Reps (Garden City, New York: Anchor Press, 1961).

Finally, the reader is referred to a clearly written account of the use of symbols in Buddhism to be found in the chapter on Buddhism by Jeaneane Fowler in J. D. Fowler *et al.*, *World Religions: An introduction for students* (Brighton: Sussex Academic Press, 2nd revised edn 1999, 1st edn 1997), while a much more detailed exposition is Adrian Snodgrass' *The Symbolism of the Stupa* (Delhi: Motilal Banarsidass, 1992), as is Louise Frédéric's highly illustrative volume, *Buddhism: Flammarion Iconographic Guides* (Paris, New York: Flammarion, 1995).

Index

Abhidhamma (Pali)/*Abhidharma* (Skt.)
    30, 31, 62, 63, 78, 79, 94
Absolute   7, 19, 34, 48, 68, 79–82, 90, 91,
    92, 93, 95, 96–8
Advaitists   182
Aggregates, Five   17, **42–4,** 49, 51
Agni   5, 6, 187
akama   40
alms   21, 24, **25,** 64, 103
Amida   109, 110, 168, **171–84**
Amitabha   133, 168, **171–84**
Amitayurdhyana Sutra   175, 176
Amitayus   90
Amoghasiddhi Buddha   136
Ananda   21, 26, 30, 65, 115, 163, 175, 176
anatta/anatman   17, 31, 37, 45, 49, 73, 79,
    101, 182
anger   2, 18, 39, 52, 69, 71, 73, 107, 108,
    121, 122, 177
Anguttara Nikaya   31, 41, 65
anicca   49, 51, 73, 79
aptakama   40
arahant/arhat   17, 18, 21, 24–7, 30, 47, 58,
    59, 65, 68, 82, 84, 88, 97, 115
Aranyakas   7
Arya   4–6
Aryadeva   84
Asalha Puja festival   76
Asanga   93–4
ascetic   **14–19,** 20, 24, 36, 37, 48, 68
Asita   11
Asoka   28, 33, 34, 65, 76, 102
asrama   11, 14
asramadharma   11
Ashvaghosa   9, 20–2, 35, 161
atheistic   68
atmakama   40
atman   7, 37, 40, 43, 47, 50, 69, 80–2, 101
attachment   13, 43, 52, 58, 100, 130, 141,
    144, 150, 156, 162, 170 181
Avalokitesvara   129, 131, 135–8, 145–6,

172, 176–7
aversion   2, 16, 44–5, 52, 96, 101, 120, 144,
    166
avidya   40
awake   17, 27, 65, 93, 123, 129, 138, 156–7,
    162, 170, 180

Bangkok   76
bardo   137
Bardo T'odrol   137
Basham, A. L.   6, 69
basket of discipline   30
basket of higher teaching   30–1
basket of sermons   30
becoming   41, 44–5, 47, 58, 85, 122, 138,
    152, 156
bell   149
Benares   20, 76
Benoit, Hubert   156
Bhagavat   18
Bhakti   173
bhavana (meditation)   **70–4**
bhikkhu   30, 59, 61
bhikkhuni   30, 68
Bhutan   127
Bimbisara   20, 25
bodhi   12, 135, 172
bodhi citta   **89,** 138, 152
bodhi tree   20, 75
Bodhidharma   159, 161, 163, 167
bodhisattva   11, 12, 16, 28, 32, 36–7, 83,
    89–90, 91–4, 97, 99–100, 104, 106,
    109–11, 114–15, 121, 128–9, 131, 133,
    135–6, 137–40, 143, 145–6, 148, 152,
    172–3, 176–8, 180
Bon   129, 132, 133
Book of Discipline   30
Brahma   18, 61
Brahman   7, 34, 40, 80, 82, 98, 102, 136
Brahman: *atman* synthesis   7, 69, 81, 82
Brahmanas   7

Brahmavihara **59–62**, 64, 73
brahmin 6, 11, 19, 37, 38, 61
Brauen, Martin 145
buddhas and *bodhisattvas* **135–6**
Buddha, the life of **8–23**
buddha-field 90, 177
buddha land/country **99**, 107, 175, 176
Buddha-nature 28, 36–7, **100–2**, 104, 111, 118, 150, 152 153, 162–70, 179
buddha-world 145
Buddhacarita 9, **10–23**
Buddhahood 1, 81–4, 88, 89, 92, 97 98, **100–2**, 106, 108, 111, 114, 118–26, 132, 143, 154, 162, 163, **170**, 174, 175, 177
buddhaksetra (Skt.)/*buddhakkheta* (Pali) 177
Burma 9, 34, 65, 67, 75, 102
butsudan 1

cakra 151
Cambodia 9
canon 23, 28, 32, 33, 78, 143, 155, 168
Carrithers, Michael 10
causality 46
celebration 64
ceremony 36, 76, 104, **140–2**, 165, 178
Ch'an 129, 130, 161, 167, 179
chanda 47
Chandaka 15
chant 119, 121, 123, 124, 126, 138, 139, 164, 173, 178
Chenresig 135
China 1, 102, 104, 113, 114, 127, 130, 135, 161–3, 167, 169, 172, 173, 177–9
Chinese 117, 118, 120, 127–9, 134, 135, 142, 145, 158, 159, 161, 163, 164, 168, 172, 175, 177, 179
circumambulation 75, 138, 145, 149, 180
Cittamatra **93–102**
class and caste 11, 19, **37–8**, 67, 103
Commemorative days 186
compassion 24, 25, 28, 61, 64, 80, 88, 89, 94, 100, 121, 128, 130 131, 135, 138, 139, 143, 146–51, 166, 167, **172**, 174, 182, 183
conceptualization 138
conditioned genesis/conditioned arising **46–7**, 85, 87, 88
conduct 66
Confucianism 104
consciousness 7, 10, 39, 43, 45, 50, 53, 54, 57, 60, 91, 93, 95–7, 107, 108, 111, 114, 115, 120, 121, 124, 134, 137, 147, 151–3, 163, 168, 169, 181

Conze, Edward 43, 44, 81, 82, 90, 92, 146
cosmos 8, 9, 17, 36, 69, 83, 84, 98, 100, 102, 114, 115, 118, 122, 123, 145, 151, 152, 170, 172, 173, 175, 176, 179
council 3, 28–34
craving 47, 48, 52, 72, 86, 96
creation 46, 52
Creator God 40, 46, 68, 69, 82

Dai-bo 113
Dai-Gohonzon 74, 112–13, **117**, **119–20**, 186
daimoku 116, 117, 120
Daishonin 48, 74, 109–20, 125, 186
dakinis 148
Dalai Lama 127, 130–7, 147, 148, **193–4**
dana 64, 65
deity 5, 6, 19, 36, 68, 99, **131**, 133, 138–51, 173
deity yoga **147**
Delight (daughter of Mara) 16
delusion 25, 29, 39, 40, 45, 54, 60, 69, 95, 96, 118, 121, 131, 140, 156, 177, 182
dependent origination 44, **46–7**, 85, 87, 88, 91
desire 2, 14–16, 39, 43–8, 52, 55, 58, 59, 95, 96, 101, 120, 124, 143–5, 150, 155, 175, 182
Devadatta 20
deva-vision 16
Devotional Buddhism 79, 103, **171–84**
devotion 69, 74, 79, 89, 99, 117, 136, **171–84**
dhamma/dharma 6, 14, 16, 19, 20, 24–40, 46, 49, 52, 62–5, 68–70, 75–9, 83–4, 91–102, 106–9, 140, 160, 163, 175–6, 180, 183
dhamma (moral and intellectual subjects) 71
Dhammapada 31, 52–8, 94, 161
dharmas **87–8**
Dharmakaya 92, 93, **98–102**, 151, 153, 174, 175, 180
dhyana 16, 41, **59–60**, 62, 70, 83, 161, 167, 184
Diamond Mandala 152
Diamond Sutra 83, 89, 90
Digha Nikaya 31
Dipankara 9
disciple 20–5, 29, 37, 77, 78, 84, 108, 112–14, 132, 160, 161, 164, 169, 170
Discontent (daughter of Mara) 16
discourse 61
Discourse of the Great Decease 20

Discourse on Universal Love *(The Metta Sutta)* 60–1
doctrine 8, 26, 28, 30, 35, 37, 43, 46, 51, (Theravada **63–77**), (Mahayana **78–104**), 130, 133, 155, 158, 172, 176–9, **184**
Dogen 161–3, 167, 169
Dozen-bo 105
Dragon's Mouth 110, 111
Drepung monastery 134
duality 17, 71, 82, 85–7, 91, 95–8, 101, 144, 151, 152, 168, 170, 181
dukkha 13, 38–49, 79, 143
Dumoulin, Heinrich 155, 169, **170**
Durga 136

early Buddhism 25, 29, **33**, 37, 68, 79–84, 87, 97, 102, 104, 124, 128, 137, 164
ego 16, 17, 46, 54, 60–2, 72, 73, 90, 96, 101, 121, 124, 142, 153, 155, 162, 170, 181, 182
egoless 25
eight *dhyanas* **59–60**
emptiness 41, **80**, 82, 84, 85, **86–93**, 94–7, 131, 138, 146, 147, 151
empty 84, 85, 87, **86–93**, 94, 95, 98, 138, 149
E/enlightenment 1, 2, **4–23**, 24–9, 38, 48, 54, 65, 68, 70, 75, 80, 83, 84, 88–92, 97–108, 114–19, 123, 125, 128–62, 167, 168, **170**, 172, 175, 178–82
equanimity 16, 41, 61
Esala perahera festival 76
ethics 34, 57, 73

false pride 148, 149, 162, 181
fasting 74
festivals 2, 64, **74–7**, **140–2**
first cause 46, 47
First Council **30–2**
First Patriarch 63
Flurry (son of Mara) 16
four signs 12
Four Abodes of Mindfulness 172
Four Unlimited **59–62**
Four Noble Truths 2, 20, 38, **39–54**, 86, 124, 143, 159
Fourth Council **34–5**
Friends of the Western Buddhist Order **194–5**

Gaity (son of Mara) 16
Gambu tree 15
Ganges 10, 16, 20, 28, 99, 115, 177

Gaya 16
Ge-luk-pa 130–2, 141
geshe 141
god 5, 6, 12, 18, 19, 28, 68, 75, 83, 98, 110, 119, 133, 134, 137, 139, 140, 156, 175
Gohonzon 111–13, **117**, **119–20**, 126
Gombrich, Richard 9, 22, 35
gongyo 116, 120
Gorbachev, Michail 125
gradual enlightenment 2, 130
grasp 86, 95, 144
Great Physician 39, 44, 47, 49, 107
greed 2, 39, 44, 47, 54, 60, 69, 177, 182
Gridhrakuta, Mount 115
Ground of all Being 7, 68
Guenther, Herbert 142
guru 7, 104, 130, 133, 147–50
Guru yoga **150–1**
guthok *141*
Gutor festival 140

hagiographa 8–10, 20
Haichiman, *bodhisattva* 110
hatred 14, 39, 43, 54, 57, 60, 108, 150, 166
Heart Sutra 83
Hei no Saemon 110–11
Hevajra Tantra 131, 132, 139
Higher *Dharma* 31, 63, 78
Highest Yoga Tantra 131, 138, 143, 148
Himalayas 10, 34, 103, 118, 127, 137
Hinayana 33, 74, 78, 82, 104, 128
Hinduism **4–8**, 11, 14, 19–21, 34–9, 68, 69, 80, 81, 102, 103, 136, 138, 173, 182, 187
Hoben 115, 116
Honen 180, 181, 184
Honganji 184
honzon 117
Hoyo, Watanabe 107
Hsuan-tsang 104, 142
Hui-neng 158

ichinen sanzen **122–4**
Idealist 96
ignorance 14, 17, 20, 40, 43–7, 52, 54, 58, 70, 73, 82, 90, 103, 109, 124, 135, 146, 148, 150, 156
Ikeda, Daisaku 125, 126, 186
illusion 15, 156
image 75, 148
incense 70, 71, 75, 83, 139
India 1, 3, **4–8**, 10, 20, 28, 29, 33–9, 44, 49, 63–6, 78, 79, 99, 101–4, 113, 118, 127–35, 142, 159, 161, 167, 170–5

Indo Europeans 4
Indra 6, 18, 146
Indus Valley 4, 5
initiation 75, 104, 140, 145, 147
insight meditation 71
instantaneous enlightenment 2
intuitive knowledge 18, 168
invocation 116, 117, 179–81, 186
Ippen Shonin 177
Iran 62, 174
Isipatana, the Deer Park 20, 24, 39, 76
Islam 103, 140
Izu Peninsular 103, 140

Japan 1, 36, 102, 104–10, 113,114, 125,
    151, 161–8, 171–4, 179
Japanese 1, 9, 74, 104, 110–18, 130, 151,
    154, 158, 167, 168, 178–81
Japanese festivals **184–6**
Jatakas 9, **9 n 4**, 31
Ji 171
jiriki 178, 181–4
Jishu 177
Jodo 106, 171
Jodo Shinshu 181, 183, **184**
Jodoshu 171, 181, **184**
Jogyo 111
Juryo 116

Ka-gyu-pa 130–2
Kalupahana, David 81
Kamakura 106–9, 167
kamma/karma 9, 16–22, 37, 43, 44, 47,
    48, 52, 53, 56, 64–70, 74, 75, 88, 96, 99,
    118–24, 139–47, 173–8, 182
Kamthaka 14
Kandy 16
Kanishka 34, 102
Kanji 109
Kanjur 136
Kapilavasta 11
Kapilavatthu 38
kapse cakes 141
Karandavyuha 172
karuna 60–2, 64
Kasagamori 106, 107, 116
Kashi 20
Kashmir 34, 104
Kathina festival 76
Katmandu 135
Kegon 36
Kennett, Rev. Master Jiyu 164, 195–6
Keown, Damien **47–8**
Khensur Rinpoche 134

Khuddaka Nikaya 31
klu 139
koan 154, 155, **168–70**
Kokuzo, *bodhisattva* 106
Korea 102, 113, 173, 179
Kosala 29
kosen-rufu 120
ksatriya 10, 38
Kuan-yin 135, 172, 178
Kukai 151, 152
Kumarajiva 113, 117
Kusinagasa 21
Kvaerne, Per 140
Kwannon 172
Kyoto-Nara area 106

lama 127, **133–5**, 145, 147–9
Lankavatara Sutra 82, 159
Latter Day of the Law 106, 180
Laws of Manu 65
lay people/laity 21, 24, **25**, 26, 29–33, 56,
    64–70, 74–6, 100, 103, 109, 124, 126,
    133, 139–41, 165, **166–7**, 179
Lhasa 133, 134, 139, 145
liberation 14, 15, 21, 41, 47, 63, 68, 99,
    100, 131, 145, 156
light 75, 131, 137, 149
Lights, festival 75, 76
lineage 129–31, **150**, 151, 164
Losar festival 141
lotus 16, 18, 105, 108, 118, 146, 149, 175,
    176
Lotus Sutra 82, **83**, 105–112, **113–19**,
    120–6, 151, 172, 179

Madhyamika 81, **83–93**, 94–8, 130, 171
Madhyamikavada **171**
Magadha 20, 25, 28, 29, 33
magga 39, 48
Magha Puja festival 76
mahakaruna 80, 88, 89, 100, 101, 104, 128
Mahapadana Sutta 23
Mahaparinibbana Sutta 67
Mahaparinirvana Sutra (Mahayana) 21,
    80, 82, 101
Mahasanghika 32, 33, 63, 79
Mahakasyapa 160–1, 163
Mahavairocana **151–2**
Mahayana 2, 3, 12, 22, 27, 30–7, 60–4, 74,
    78–104, 106, 113–17, 128, 133–43, 147,
    154–8, 164, 167, 171–9, 182
Maitreya 94, **172**, 177
Majjhima Nikaya 31, 41, 69, 72
Makiguchi, Tsunesaburo 125

Malaya 34
mandala 2, 111, 117, 119, 138, **144–5**, 152, 153, 183
mandala offering **150**
Mandela, Nelson 125
manifest 7
Manjusri 131, 135
mantra 1, 74, 138, **146**, 147, 150–3
mappo 106, 108, 179, 180
Mara 16, 18, 19
Marpa 132
master 50, 70 131, 132, 155, **157**, 158, 161–9
master–pupil relationship 129, 146, **157**, **163–4**, **169**
maya 88
meditation 1, 14, 16, 21, 32, 50, 54, 68, **70–4**, 75, 80, 83, 89, 93, 94, 106, 128–32, 136–53, **154–70**, 173, 176, 179, 183, 184
meditational deity **147**, 151
Menander/Milinda **50–1**
merit 12, **25**, 50, 65, 66, 76, 88, 90, 138, 139, 147, 150, 173, 177
metta **60–2**, 64
Metta Sutta **60–1**
Mi-lo-Fo **172**
Middle Way 11, 20, 36, 37, **49–54**, 81–94, 100, 130
Milarepa 132
Milindapanha 34, **50–1**
Mitra 6
moksa 11, 19, 39, 46
monastery/monastic 30–6, **63–77**, 98, 105, 127–40, 145, 155, 160, **164–6**, 167–8, 179
mondo **170**
Mongolia 110, 112, 113, 127, 174
monism 6, 102
monks 20–4, **25**, 26–38, 50, 56, 57, 60, **63–77**, 79, 84, 87, 93, 100–5, 129, 132, **133–5**, 136–44, 151, 154, 159, 160, **164–6**, 167–72, 175
Monlam Chenmo festival 141
monotheism 6
moral 49, 52–9, 66, 71, 72, 80, 89
Morgan, Rev. Master Daishin 155, 159, 162, 164, 195
Mother Goddess 5
mu 168–9
mudita **60–2**, 64
mudra 138, 152, 153
Mukata 21
Mulasarvastavada school 130

Mulasarvastivadins 128
Mullin, Glenn 189
Murti, T. R. V. 81, 84, 130
Muslim 35, 103, 140
Myokyo-ni, Ven. 159

Nagarjuna 83–5, 130–1, 171
nagas 84
Nagasena 34, **50–1**
Nam-myoho-renge-kyo 107–26, **116–19**
Namu Amida-Butsu 106, **171**, 173, 181
Narain, Harsh 79, 81
Naropa 132
Nembutsu 106–13, **171–84**
Nepal 10, 35, 103, 104, 127, 135, 174
neti neti 40
New Year festival 75, 137, 140, 141
New Year's *Gongyo* 186
nibbana/nirvana 12, 17–39, 48–54, 59–62, 65–72, 80–90, **91–2**, 93–101, 123, 173–8, 182
Nichiren 1–3, 36, 74, 83, 90, **105–26**, 186
Nichiren Shoshu 124, 126
Nichiren Shu 124
nihilism 45, 93, 94, 98
Nikko school 108, 111, 119
Nikko Shonin 109, 112, 113, 124
Nine consciousnesses 120
Nirmanakaya 98, **99**, 151
nirodha 39, 48
Nirvana Sutra 82
no-self 37, 44, 80, 81, 101
noble paths 121
Noble Eightfold Path 20, **49–55**
non-duality 90, 91, 96, 100, 101
Northern Buddhism 3, 27, 31, 33, 36
nuns 26, 30, 38, **66–8**
Nying-ma-pa 130, 131

Obaku 168
object of worship/devotion 99, 111, 113, 117, **119–20**, 174, 176, 177
object 11, 13, 69, 89, **90**, 94–6, 150, 162
occult power 5, 9, **62**
Om mani padme hum 146
On Attaining Buddhahood 108
oracle 134–9
oral tradition/chanting 28–31, 65, 80, 142, 150
ordain/ordination 24–8, 50, 65–8, 75, 105, 107, 127, 140, 164
order 27, 50, 70, 76, 130, 133
Order of Buddhist Contemplatives 164
Original Vow 173, 178, 180

orthodox 27–35, 69, 70, 83, 84, 124, 143, 157
outcastes 38
own-being 85–90, 95, 138

Padmasambhava 129, 132
Pali Canon 8, 22, 28, 29, 33–5, 79, 84, 139, 173
Pali 9, **9 n 5**, 21, 24, 27–41, 48, 58, 62, 69, 81, 177
Pancha Sila 53, **54–7**
panentheism 34, 152
panna/prajna 49, **62**, 64, **80**, 83, 86–9, 94, 100, 101, 184
parable of the burning house 115
parable of the good physician 116
paramitas **80**, 89
parinibbana/parinirvana 8, 18–21, 69, 88, 89, 97, 172
parinibbuto 21
path and fruit 131, 132
paticca-samuppada **46–7**
Patimokkha 30
patriarch 159, 163, 164
Perfection of Wisdom **80–93**, 146
permanence 41, 42
pilgrimage 139, 145
pillars 61, **80**
pipal tree 16, 20
Potala Palace 133, 139, 145
Powers, John 130
practitioner **148–51**, 152–3, 161, 174
Prajnaparamita **80–93**, 114, 135, 158
precepts 2, 25, 30, 53, **54–7**, 67, 74, 75, 157, 164, 167
Primal Vow 175
prostrate 71, 137
prostration 69, 70, 138, 145, **148–9**
Pu-tai **172**
puja **69–70**, 136–9
pure consciousness 70, 97, 98, 120, 121
Pure Land 2, 3, 36, 90, 99, 107–10, **171–84**, **194**
Pye, Michael 10, 17, 43
Pym, Jim 187, 194

Rahula, Walpola 17, 21, 41
raja 10–12
Rajagaha (Pali)/Rajagriha (Skt.) 30, 31, 38, 115, 175
reality 11–16, 40–5, 60, 87, **90**, **94–7**, 98–101, 138, 142–7, 160–3, 176, 183
realization 7, 14, 17–21, 27, 32, 38–43, 48, 53, 55, 60, 71–2, **80**, 82, 87, 91, 95, 100–1, 106, 111, 117, 121–5, 129, 132, 142 – 8, 152–70, 182–3
rebirth 37, 38, 43, 47–8, 52, 65–70, 74, 123, 134–7, 173–84
refuge 70, **148**, 150, 173, 178–9
reincarnation 31, 37, 104, **133–5**
Reiyukai 124
relic 21, 29, 76
Rencho **105–8**
retreat 127, 160
Rg Veda 56
Rhys Davids, T. W. 190
Rinpoche 134, 191
Rinzai 167–70
Rissho Koseikai 124
Rissho Ankoku Ron **109**, 110
ritual 2, 36, 71, 74, 107, 116, 129, 133–6, **137–40**, 141–4, **147**, 152–5, 168
roshi 164
rupas 36

Sa-kya-pa 130–2
sacred 80, 149, 157, 161, 174, 178, 181
sacrifice 5, 39, 55, 56, 66, 139
Saddhatissa 55–6
Sado Island 106, 110–12, 119
Sakkaya Niruttiya 29
sakti 136
Sakya 9–11, 26, 37, 132
Sakyamuni 9, 18, 46, 75–83, 110–24, 141–3, 151, 156, 160–4, 168–70, 175–9
salvation 27, 33, 37, 59, 64–9, 79, 88–9, 115, 128, 135, 156–7, 173–84
Sam-ye 129–30
samadhi 49, 54, **58–62**, 70–1, 94, **170**
Samannaphala **58–9**
samatha 70–1
Sambhogakaya 89, 98, **99**, 174
samgiti 28
samkhara-dukkha 42
samsara 9, 11, 16, 19, 38–40, 47, 52, 68, 69, 83–92, 96–100, 123, 128, 131, 137, 139, 178
samudaya 39, 44
Samyutta Nikaya 31, 59
sangha 20, **24–7**, 30–38, **63–70**, 103, 160
sannyasin 20
Sanskrit (Skt.) 9, 24, 27–33, 37–8, 42, 49, 59, 62, 64, 70, 85, 113, 117, 120, 135, 143, 145, 151, 168, 173, 177–81
Santaraksita 129
Sariputra 27
Sarvastivadins 34
sastras 158

Satipatthana Sutta **71–2**
satori 156, 162, 168, **170**, 180
sattva 135, 172
scripture 21, 28–36, 54, 58, 65, 69, 76, 93, 104, 113–16, 135, **136–7**, 140, 154–9, 164, **174–8**, 181
Second Council **31–3**
seed/store consciousness **96–7**, 102
Seicho-ji **105–6**, 107, 116, 119
S/self 7, 8, 17, 36–51, 69–73, 80–2, 85–8, 95, 96, 101, 102, 124, 134, 142, 161, 162, 182, 183
Serene Reflection Meditation 165
sermon 29, 60
Sermon, First 20, 24, 39, 76, 93
shaman 79, 137
Sharf, Robert 155
Shasta Abbey 164
Shingon 36, 106, 107, 112, **151–3**
shinjin 180, **181–3**
Shinran 171, 180, 181, 184
Shinto 113
Shoshinge 177
siddhas 132
shrines 69–70
Siddhartha Gautama/Siddhatta Gotama 9–23, 97–9
Sikhism 103
sila 49, **58–9**, 184
Simili of the Raft 72
Siva/Saivites 103
Sixth Patriarch 159
skandhas/khandhas 42–5, 49, 51, 101
skilful means/skill-in-means 80, 89, **92–3**, 97, 99, 107, 114–16, 124, 143, 175
Snellgrove, David 128, 129, 142
Soka Gakkai International **124**, 186, **192–3**
Soka Kyoiku Gakkai 125
Song-tsen-gam-po 129
Soto Zen 1, 157, 159, 161, 164–9, **195–6**
soul 2, 12, 14, 42, 43, 49 51, 59, 60, 69, 88, 92, 98, 176
Southern Buddhism 3, 27, 31, 33
spirit 49, 69, 137, 140, 159
spiritual 43, 63–9, 73–80, 92, 98, 124–8, 133–4, 139, 144–50, 155, 158, 161–6, 171, 174
Splendid Sun 105
Sri Lanka 9, 29, 34, 67, 72, 75, 76, 102, 103
Srimala-devi Simhanada Sutra 82
State Oracle 134
statue 70, 75, 101, 113, 141, 183
Sthaviras 32–4

Strong, John 130
stupas 21, 34
subject and object 90, **91**, **95–6**, 97, 100, 101, 168, 170, 181
suchness 20, 91, 97, 101
sudden enlightenment 129
sudra 38, 66
suffering 2, 11–14, 38–47, 52–61, 81, 86, 94, 143–4, 148, 155–6, 166–7, 183
sukha 40
Sukhavati Sutras 175–7
Sukhavati 173–9
Sullen Pride (son of Mara) 16
Sumatra 34
Sun Lotus 108
sunya 81, **87–93**
sunyata 80, **86–93**, 98, 146, 158
Sunyata-vada 86
sutta/sutra 21, 30, 35, 58, 71, 78–85, 90, 93, 94, 100, 101, 106–9, 114–18, 130, 135, 143, 151, 155, 158–61, 167, 168, 175–7, 183
Sutta Pitaka 30, 31, 54, 78, 159
Suzuki, D. T. 154, **157–9**, 160–9, 190
svabhava 85, **86–93**, 101, 138
symbol 20, 38, 49, 70, 75, 118, 135–7, 141, 142, **144–53**

T'ien-tai 108, 113, 114, 118, 122, 123
Taiseki-ji 113, 119, 124
tanha 47, 48, 121, 143
Tannisho 177
Tantra 1, 23, 62, 103, 104, 127–41, **142–53**, 179
Tao Te Ching 16
Taoism 104, 140, 167, 179
Tara, *bohisattva*/buddha 129–36
tariki 178–84
tathagata 18, 20, 26, **100–2**, 156, 176
tathagatagarbha 82, **99–100**
tathata 91, 98, **100–2**
temple 21, 69, 70, 75–7, 105, 106, 113, 116, 119, 124, 145, 146, 162
ten life conditions/worlds 2, 119, **121**
Ten Perfections 171
Tendai 36, 107, 113, 114
Tendai Hokke 106
Tenjur 136
Tensho Daijin 110
Thailand 9, 75, 76, 102
The Opening of the Eyes 111
The True Object of Worship 111
theism 19, 36, 37, 68, 69, 79, 99
thera 68

Theravada   3, 9, 12, 27, 29, 32–7, 47, 54–62, **63–77**, 79, 80, 84, 88, 89, 106, 128, 139, 172, 182, **196**
Third Council   **33–5**
Therigatha (Psalms of the Sisters)   65
thirst   47, 48
Thirst (daughter of Mara)   16
thread   30, 118
three defilements   2, 39, 54, 69, 147, 150, 177
Three Jewels   69, 70 148
three monks   79
Three Mysteries   153
Three Refuges   25, 75, 137
Three Baskets   29
Throssel Hole Priory   155, 159, 164, 166
thusness   20, 60, 91, 95, 98, 101
Tibet   1, 36, 84, 102, 104, **127–51**, 173
Tibetan   1, 2, 3, 9, 28, 74, 76, 84, 89, 113, **127–51**, **193–4**
Tibetan Book of the Dead   137
Tipitaka/Tripitaka   29, 30, 34, 54, 78, 79
Toda, Josai   125
trance   62, 71, 136, 137
tranquillity   16, 17
transcend   19, 40, 68, 81, 83, 86, 97, 98, 138, 154, 168, 174, 175, 176, 178
transmission   154, 158, 160, 161, 163, 164
Trikaya   89, **97–102**, 176
Triple Treasure   181
T/truth   7, 17, 31, 48, 52, 54, 65, 71, 83, 86, 87, 106, 109, 111, 135, 136, 142, 147, 151, 154, 160, 161, 172
Tsongkhapa   132, 189
Tsurugaoka   110
um-no   132
Tusita Heaven   172, 177
two/twin pillars   **80**, 88, 89, 138

Udana   60, 81, 87, 92
ultimate   39, 82
Ultimate Reality   4, 7, 8, 17, 40, 48, 71, 80, 81, 86, 91, 92, **95**, 96–8, 152, 153, **170**
Ultimate Truth   8, 17, 48, 54, 71, 86, 93, 114, 117, 122, **170**
Unmanifest   7, 98, 101
unreality   40
Upaka   24
Upali   30
Upanisads   6–8, 36–40, 50, 69, 80, 82, 98, 102
upaya   89, **92–3**, 107, 116, 143, 175
upekkha   **60–2**, 64
upesaka   33
uposatta   74

Vaisali   21
vaisya   38
Vajra   **146**, 149
Vajrasattva meditation   **149–50**
Vajrayana   104, 128, 142, 143
varna   38
Varuna   6
Vasettha   61
Vassa/Asala festival   75, 76
Vasubandhu   93, 94
Vedanta   7
Veda/Vedic   5–7, 29, 65–8, 103, 146, 187
Vesali   26, 38
vihara   68
Vijnavada   93
Vimalakirti-nirdesa   82
Vinaya   27, 30–2, 66, 67, 74, 77, 78, 104 107, 130 136, 152
Vinaya Pitaka   30, 68
vipassana   70, 71
Vipassi   23
Visistacarita   111
Visnu   6, 79, 103
visualization   138, 142, 145–51, 176–80, 183
volition   43
vow   16, 67, 68, 75, 88–91, 175, 180, 182

Wesak festival   75, 159
wheel   20, 35, 38, 40, 44, 49, 52, 93, 100
Wheel of Becoming (*bhavacakra*)   44–6
Williams, Paul   78, 80
wisdom   27, 34, 40–4, 49, 52, 58, 61–4, 71, 80, 82–9, 94, 98, 106, 121, 124 125, 130 135, 138, 139, 146–52, 156–60, 171–4, 182–4
Womb Mandala   152
women   12, 14, 19, 24, 26, 32, 43, 56, **65–6**, 133, 139, 159
worship   56, 65, 69, 83, 89, 113, 140, 173, 176, 181

yajna   6
yanas   128, 136
Yellow Hats   132
yin and *yang*   140
yoga   15, 54, 93–5, **97**, 132, 138, 151, 153
Yogacarin   59, 82–4, **93–102**
Yuzu Nembutsu   171

zazen   **161–5**, 168
Zen   2, 3, 36, 72, 74, 107, 130, **154–70**, 172
zendo   166
Zennichimaro   **105–6**
Zesho-bo Rencho   105